An Island Called Home

AN ISLAND
CALLED HOME

Returning to Jewish Cuba

Ruth Behar

Photographs by Humberto Mayol

Rutgers University Press | NEW BRUNSWICK, NEW JERSEY, AND LONDON

Second printing, 2007

Library of Congress Cataloging-in-Publication Data
Behar, Ruth
An island called home : returning to Jewish Cuba / Ruth Behar.
p. cm.
Includes bibliographical references.
ISBN 978-0-8135-4189-1 (hardcover : alk. paper)
1. Behar, Ruth 2. Jews—Cuba—Biography. 3. Cuban Americans—Biography.
4. Jews, Cuban—United States—Biography. 5. Cuba—Biography. I. Title.
F1789.J4B43 2007
920.'0092407291—dc22
2007008409

A British Cataloging-in-Publication record for this book
is available from the British Library.

Visit our Web site: http://rutgerspress.rutgers.edu
Manufactured in the United States of America
BOOK DESIGN AND COMPOSITION BY JENNY DOSSIN

My people, of a solitary star,

who wander, searching for a home someplace . . .

RAFAEL CAMPO

For my son Gabriel,

with gratitude for sharing this journey with me

and with the hope that Cuba will be a part of you too

CONTENTS

Contents

Contents

CUBA

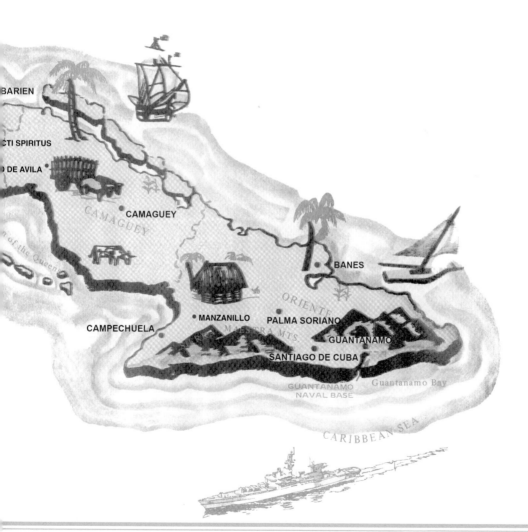

BARIEN

CTI SPIRITUS

O DE AVILA

CAMAGUEY

· CAMAGUEY

n of the Queen

BANES

ORIENTE

· MANZANILLO   PALMA SORIANO

CAMPECHUELA

MAESTRA MTS.

GUANTANAMO

SANTIAGO DE CUBA

GUANTANAMO
NAVAL BASE

Guantanamo Bay

CARIBBEAN SEA

An Island Called Home

RUNNING AWAY FROM HOME
TO RUN TOWARD HOME

"You're going to Cuba again? What did you lose in Cuba?"

That's what my grandmother Esther, my Baba, said every time I'd see her in Miami Beach on my way to yet another return visit to the island I had left as a child. Actually, she'd say it in Spanish: "*Otra vez a Cuba? Qué se te perdió en Cuba?*" Baba's mother tongue was Yiddish, but we spoke to each other in Spanish. She was from the Polish town of Goworowo and immigrated to Cuba in 1927 at the age of nineteen, hoping to become a cabaret singer, but instead she'd married my grandfather Máximo, my Zayde, and worked with him selling fabric to get the rest of her family to safety in Cuba before the dark night of the Holocaust. Then after Fidel Castro came to power, she'd left Cuba for the United States.

The whole decade of the 1990s, I would land at Gate G9 and just after midnight I'd tiptoe into her apartment with the big *gusano* bag—the duffel bag, which I think only Cubans call a "worm," a curious use of language, because *gusanos* was the word Fidel Castro used to refer to all of us who left Cuba after the Revolution. That wasn't the only bag I brought with me. I also had the rolling bag and the carry-on bag. I'd hear Baba snoring and think to myself, "Good, I haven't woken her up." And suddenly Baba would be standing in the doorway of her bedroom, as ethereal as an apparition. Without her false teeth, her hair covered in netting, no make-up, and her petite figure nestled in a long cotton night-gown, she looked older than old.

"Baba! Babita!" I exclaimed and gave her a hug and kiss.

"At last you got here," she'd say. "I thought you'd never arrive." I'd apologize for waking her, but she'd look at me quizzically and say she wasn't asleep. "But you were snoring," I would say to her, and she would deny it. Then the reprimands would begin.

"That's even more bags than the last time. You're just one person. How much can you carry? You're going to get a *kile*." That was Yiddish for hernia.

My bags were stuffed with books for writer-friends, paper and paint for artist-friends, and things for Caro, my old nanny, and her family—clothes, aspirin, slippers, shoes, soap. In the course of my trips, I learned of a last relative in Cuba, a second cousin of my father's named José Maya, who lived in abject poverty and begged in the streets, and soon I was bringing things for him too, though not for long because he died wretchedly, maggots in his wounds. Acquaintances in Miami gave me yet more things to take to their relatives. More clothes, more aspirin, more slippers, more shoes, more soap. I was the mule, bringing the packages to Cuba. I was Santa Claus. I was Robin Hood, taking from the rich to give to the poor.

"How many times can you keep going back? I don't think you need to go back anymore. Can you tell me the *real* reason you're going this time?"

Does my own beloved Baba think I'm a spy? An agent of the Cuban government? What strange things does she imagine I do in Cuba?

"Baba, I can't explain. I just need to go to Cuba."

She shakes her head and the worried look in her misty eyes melts my heart. "But *mamale*," she says. "*Shayne maydele*, tell me, how can you carry all of that by yourself?"

And then a few days later it was time to say goodbye to Baba. I'd already said goodbye to my husband, David, and my son, Gabriel, back in the quiet university town of Ann Arbor, Michigan, where I worked as a professor of anthropology. David knew he had no choice but to accept my burning need to return to Cuba. At first Gabriel would cry and cling to me, but as the years passed, he got used to me leaving for Cuba for a week or two at a time, and he no longer cried. "Bye, Mommy, see you soon," he'd say casually, and it was I who wept as soon as I was on the plane and out of sight. There was the good-bye to my mother in New York, who'd call me at Baba's and say "We love you" in English, careful to say "we," so as to include my father, who never said good-bye before I left for Cuba because he was opposed to my trips. Out of respect for my father, my mother would never go to Cuba, but every time I went she took pleasure in going shopping for the things people requested. She said she did it to help me—"You're so busy, you work so hard"—but I knew it was her way of accompanying me to Cuba.

Saying goodbye to Baba was the hardest of all. Baba would stand at the door of her apartment, number 401, and try not to cry. Why was I leaving her, for God's sake? She needed me, she was alone and lonely, she suffered from cataracts, migraines, insomnia, she wouldn't be around forever. Shaking her head, Baba would watch me struggle to fit all my bags into the tiny elevator. Before the door shut, I'd say goodbye for the last time. She lived in one of those Miami Beach-style garden apartments that opened onto an outdoor hallway, and when I looked back at her, if I breathed deeply, I could smell the ocean. It was sixteen long blocks away, but I could smell the ocean. Unmistakable. The smell of journeys without end.

All those years in the 1990s, and then during the first six years of the new century, after Baba had died, I kept thinking I was running away from home in order to run toward home. I was running toward the home that I and my family and thousands of other Jews had left on the island. I wanted to reclaim that lost home—the home in Cuba I believed was my true home.

.   .   .

Baba was right about the fact that for years I went to Cuba without a clear idea of what I was seeking. She died in 2000 and losing her was the impetus for the journey that became this book. What began as a vague desire to find my lost home in Cuba gradually became a more concrete search for the Jews who make their homes in Cuba today.

Are there Jews in Cuba? To speak of the existence of Jews in Cuba always produces a shock effect. And yet Jews have been a part of Cuban history since the earliest days of the Spanish conquest.

Maybe it's not too far-fetched to say that since 1492, Jews have sought to make a home for themselves in Cuba. The first Jews to set foot in Cuba weren't practicing Jews but *conversos*, Spanish Jewish converts to Catholicism. Given the choice of converting to Catholicism or being banished from Spain—the land that Spanish Jews called *Sepharad,* which means Spain in Hebrew—many left for the Muslim lands of North Africa and Turkey, becoming the Sephardic Jews, while many others chose to remain in Spain and convert. But there were *conversos* who felt so torn between their Jewish ancestry and their Spanish identity that they became hidden Jews, secretly holding on to Jewish beliefs and customs. The Spanish Inquisition was created to root out these "Judaizers," whose refusal to eat pork and donning of clean white clothes on the eve of the Jewish sabbath seemed threatening to an empire built on the unity of the Catholic Church and the Crown. Jews and "Judaizers" were prohibited from settling in the New World, as were Spanish Muslims, who had also been expelled from Spain.

Luis de Torres, a translator, is credited with being the first *converso* to settle in Cuba. He traveled with Columbus, who had deemed Cuba "the pearl of the Antilles," expecting that his fluency in the languages of Spanish, Hebrew, Aramaic, and Arabic would be of use in communicating with the natives. But while exploring the interior of the island, he met an unhappy end; he was slaughtered along with the rest of his garrison.

Other *conversos* must have tried their luck in Cuba in the succeeding centuries, because Inquisition records involving "Judaizers" suggest that several more did find their way to the island. But little is known about them and their Jewish ancestry. Under the surveillance of the Inquisition, only subterfuge was possible. Jewish traditions couldn't be passed on openly and so they largely fell away. In contrast, African religions were also persecuted by Spanish colonizers, but African slaves succeeded in passing on the heart of their ancestral Yoruba religion through the creation of a clandestine parallel cosmology. African deities were syncretized with Catholic saints, so that Ochún, for example, was meshed with Cuba's patron saint, La Virgen de la Caridad del Cobre. Believers pretended to worship the Virgin when they were actually worshipping Ochún.

Until after the end of slavery in Cuba, until after the end of the Spanish empire, it was impossible to build a Jewish community on the island. The first practicing Jews to arrive in Cuba were American Jewish expatriates, who settled in Cuba after the War of 1898. Spanish colonial rule had ended and American postcolonial domination had begun. These American Jews saw economic opportunities to invest in a Cuba that was free, but under close American supervision. They were followed by Sephardic Jews, who arrived from Turkey as early as 1904 and continued coming in greater numbers following the dissolution of the Ottoman Empire and the Balkan Wars. Many were men fleeing service in the Turkish army.

The next group to arrive was the most numerous—Ashkenazic Jews, largely from Poland, escaping pogroms, dismal economic conditions, and rising anti-Semitism. They came starting in 1921, when the United States imposed a quota on their immigration to the United States, and their numbers increased after the passage of the Immigration and Nationality Act in 1924, which further sealed the border. Hungarians, Belgians, and large numbers of Jews escaping Nazi Germany followed. But the presence of numerous Polish Jews made such an impact that non-Jewish Cubans assumed all Jews in Cuba came from Poland. Not only did Cubans adopt the term *polaco*, or Pole, to refer to Jews in general, they referred to Yiddish as *el idioma polaco*, the Polish language. The irony of this identity switch was not lost upon the Jews who came to Cuba from Poland, where their Jewishness had made them unworthy of being viewed as Polish. The term *polaco* has stuck to this day, even with so few Jews left in Cuba.

At the moment when Jews were choosing Cuba as a destination, the island was being transformed into a modern, ethnically diverse, pluralistic society. Although some of the indigenous Taino population had survived the Spanish conquest, until the middle of the nineteenth century the population of Cuba consisted mostly of Spaniards and Africans and their descendents. During the middle of the nineteenth century, Chinese migrant laborers were brought to Cuba to work alongside African and creole slaves. But it was in the first decades of the twentieth century that Cuba underwent an explosion of immigrant arrivals as Cuban elites sought to "whiten" a country they feared had become "too black" after independence. Arab immigrants came from Syria, Palestine, and Lebanon, Hindu immigrants from Delhi, Japanese immigrants from the province of Fukuoka. Swedes and Finns came, and numerous Spaniards, mainly from the province of Galicia and the Canary Islands.[1] Black workers from Jamaica and Haiti also tried to immigrate to Cuba as agricultural laborers, but most were turned away.[2]

As the ethnic mosaic of the island became more complex, the Jews didn't create a single community that brought them together as one people. They were divided into a variety of cultural and linguistic groups. They may have all appeared to be *polacos* to outsiders, but among themselves they were distinct. Often, they looked down upon each other, questioning whether their brethren were real Jews. American Jews viewed themselves as Americans living in Cuba; they maintained American schools and hired English-speaking rabbis for their synagogue, which was known as *el templo americano*. Sephardic Jews, who spoke Ladino, an old form of Spanish which they kept throughout their migrations after the expulsion from Spain, felt at home in the Spanish language and quickly assimilated to life in Cuba. Ashkenazic immigrants, who spoke Yiddish and whose way of life was rooted in Yiddish culture, had to learn a new language and adjust to a way of life that was much more foreign to them. They brought intense ideological commitments, and were divided between those who favored Zionism and those who thought the Jewish future depended on international ideals of socialism, communism, and atheism. The sheer energy of some of the Polish Jewish activists was astounding. Barely had they removed their woolen coats and they were helping to found the Cuban Communist Party in 1925, with an interpreter present to translate the Spanish proceedings into Yiddish.[3]

But the main characteristic that distinguished Yiddish-speaking Jews was that many traveled to Cuba with the hope that the island would be a stepping stone to the United States. In Yiddish they called the island *Akhsanie Kuba*, or "Hotel Cuba," a temporary lodging, not a real home.[4] Cuba was a substitute America. The real America, the one to which they aspired, was on the other side of the ocean, ninety miles away. But the quota system in the United States had made it impossible for them to enter. Lured by ads in the European Yiddish-language press proclaiming Cuba's open door policy, they knew that anyone landing in the port of Havana could stay, and after a year in Cuba, a person in transit could immigrate easily to the United States.[5] While some succeeded in crossing over, the United States soon closed that door too. And an island that had been called a hotel now had to be called a home.

For my Zayde, a penniless Russian immigrant who stepped off the boat thinking he'd arrived in Buenos Aires—where his sister awaited him—finding a home in Cuba began with hard work on the railroad.[6]

Later, like most male immigrants to Cuba, he worked as a peddler. The Jewish peddlers were visible far and wide in the Cuban landscape, taking their wares not only to cities, but to towns and villages and sugar mills in the countryside. On their backs they carried shirts, ties, shoes, sandals, blankets. Sometimes they peddled statues and images of Jesus and the Virgin Mary, and if a Yiddish tale is true, they did so with great fear of revealing their Jewish identity and with shame for handling idols.[7] They were willing to take payment on the installment plan and thereby introduced a credit system that allowed poor workers to purchase goods they would otherwise have been unable to afford.

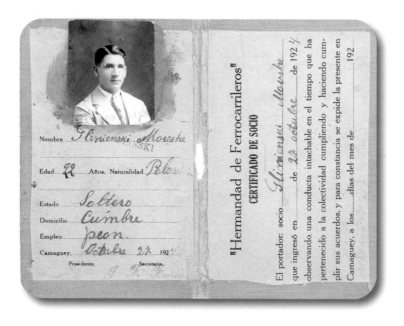

Jews weren't allowed to become Cuban citizens in the 1920s. By the 1930s, when citizenship became attainable, it was too costly for most of the immigrants. The majority were struggling non-citizens, and as the war neared, anti-Semitic propaganda from Nazi and Falangist sources made their situation more precarious. Assistance from American Jewish organizations, especially the Hebrew Immigrant Aid Society (HIAS) and the Joint Distribution Committee (JDC), became crucially important. Eventually the immigrants prospered, but only once they came to see themselves as Jewish Robinson Crusoes who had to "make their America in Cuba."[8]

By 1950 a handful were wealthy merchants who owned large stores and wholesale enterprises. But the majority, like my Baba and Zayde, ran mom-and-pop shops in La Habana Vieja, as well as in provincial cities scattered around the island.

Jewish-Communist ideals were abandoned as the immigrants put down roots and became solid members of the Cuban middle class.[9] Their Cuban sons were able to pursue professional careers, becoming lawyers, engineers, architects, physicians, accountants. Their daughters married young and mainly stayed home, occasionally becoming involved in philanthropy or helping out in their parents' stores, in an era when the conservative values of 1950s America prevailed among Cuba's middle class.

Marriage within the Jewish subcommunity to which a person belonged was the norm for the first-generation children of European immigrants. When my parents married in 1956, their union was looked upon as an "intermarriage," because my mother was Ashkenazic and my father was Sephardic. My Baba and Zayde couldn't believe there were Jews who didn't speak Yiddish, while on my father's side, my Abuela and Abuelo viewed Spanish as a *Jewish* language. If a union among culturally different Jews could produce such intense conflicts, marrying outside the Jewish tribe was simply taboo. And racism among Jews in pre-revolutionary Cuba made it unthinkable for black Cubans to be potential marriage partners.

The immigrants created an island within an island. In a few short decades they built a wide range of educational, social, and cultural institutions. These included Jewish schools, Jewish newspapers, and Jewish mutual aid associations. The *polacos* had Yiddish radio, the *Vida Habanera* newspaper in Yiddish and Spanish, and the Centro Israelita. The *turcos* in Havana had their daily gatherings to play dominos and their Colegio Teodoro Hertzl, as well as their Sephardic associations in the Oriente region. There were women's associations and a Jewish business association. Jewish restaurants included Moishe Pipik, which was kosher, Café Lily, and Cafeteria Boris.

Five synagogues existed in Havana. The oldest was the Union Hebrea Chevet Ahim, built by Sephardic Jews in 1914. Three synagogues were built in the mid- to late 1950s, on the eve of the Cuban Revolution: Adath Israel; the Patronato de la Casa de la Comunidad Hebrea de Cuba; and the Centro Hebreo Sefaradí. So determined were the Jews to remain in Cuba that they also built synagogues in the provincial cities of Santa Clara, Camagüey, and Santiago de Cuba, and founded Jewish associations across the island, from Matanzas to Ciego de Ávila and Guantánamo.

After the creation of the State of Israel in 1948, a few socialist-leaning Jews left Cuba to build Kibbutz Gaash (among them my great-uncle Jaime Levin), but the majority stayed. They faced the challenge of their divided loyalties to the Jewish homeland and the Cuban island by thinking of both nations as interwoven. The Cuban and Israeli flags were displayed together in the synagogues. In an artistic rendering of this symbiosis, a special chair made in honor of a bar mitzvah celebrated at the Centro Sefaradí had the two flags etched side by side into the wood frame.

By 1959 there were at least 15,000 Jews in

Cuba and possibly as many as 16,500 in a population of six million people.[10] These are inexact numbers because Jews who didn't affiliate with Jewish organizations or who married outside the tribe disappeared from the record. But the close-knit communities of American, Ashkenazi, and Sephardic Jews were secure and established on every level—economic, cultural, religious, and social. With only a few exceptions, Jews chose to stay out of Cuban politics. They had created an enchanted world and didn't want to awaken to the discord brewing on the island. The Jews of Cuba were convinced they had found a safe haven—and expected to stay forever.

Then suddenly it was all over, the tropical paradise was no more. Everything had to be abandoned, the dead left in their graves, the Torahs left in their synagogues, the schools, and the stores, and the homes, and everything in them, forsaken.

Accounts vary, but at least 90 percent and maybe up to 96 percent of the Jewish community fled soon after Castro came to power. Yet the majority supported the Revolution in 1959. Listening to Castro's early speeches, they felt as optimistic as other Cubans about the idea of building a democratic society. The Jews no longer thought of their island as "Hotel Cuba." They had created a home, and they wanted a new country to arise, unfettered by the rampant corruption that had turned Cuba into a backyard colony of the Americans.

They welcomed the reforms that sought to create greater equality.

My mother said that she and my father, who married when she was twenty and he twenty-two, were thrilled to receive a reduction on their rent. Her first revolutionary act was to buy a lamp she'd wanted and not been able to afford.

But my mother recalled that her uncle Moisés, who owned real estate in Havana as well as a thriving cash register store, wasn't so happy with the revolutionary reforms. Like other Jews with a stake in capitalist ventures, he kept a nervous eye on the transformations being carried out by Castro. By 1961, as more and more businesses were seized by government militia, their Jewish owners didn't hesitate any longer—they took the first plane out, many on the very day they lost their stores. In turn, people who owned nothing in Cuba had no choice but to follow, for they depended for their livelihood on the Jewish businesses that had been confiscated.

My father, for example, had been an employee of my mother's uncle Moisés, working as an accountant in his store, La Casa de los Molinos. Even those much less well off, like my Abuelo, who had remained a peddler, felt they had to leave, because they couldn't imagine an existence where they were no longer free to sell their wares from door to door. *Vida Habanera*, in the last *almanaque hebreo* published in Cuba in 1960, vouched for Fidel Castro's declaration that the Revolution rejected "discrimination against the Hebrews and other forms of hatred and racial prejudice as fascist," but these words were not enough to keep the vast majority of Jews, including the editors of the Jewish magazine where the declaration appeared, from leaving Cuba.[11] Ashkenazic Jews who had experienced the effects of the Russian Revolution knew that Castro's embrace of communism would bring forth such inevitable consequences as the nationalization of schools, the control of the family by the state, and the imposition of atheism, all of which signaled an end to Jewish religious life on the island.

When the Jews left Cuba, it was truly an exodus, for they fled quickly and en masse—nearly everyone gone by 1965. They departed with the urgency of a people who believed the sea had parted only long enough to let them go. The dissolution of the community was swift, intense, like a lit candle snuffed by the wind.

.   .   .

Although I was only a child, I was part of the exodus of the Jews who left Cuba after the 1959 Revolution and settled in the United States. When we left, you could only take one suitcase with you. All Cubans who "abandoned the

country" were viewed as traitors to the cause of national liberation. What to take on a trip that, at the time, no one knew if it would last a few weeks or an entire lifetime? Homes, including everything inside them—furniture, clothes, linens, pots, plates—had to be surrendered to the state. Jewelry and precious valuables could not be taken out of the country for they had been redefined as national wealth that was needed to build the Revolution.

During the dramatic departure of middle-class Cubans in the early 1960s, among whom were most of Cuba's Jews, as many as 2,000 Cubans arrived in Miami each week. Material possessions became as evanescent as the sea breeze. Uncertain travelers clung to the one thing even the cruelest of immigration officers wouldn't take away: old family photographs. Nothing was as cherished as those pictures tucked into sad suitcases. Losing everything was unbearable, but looking at the pictures it was possible to recall the light and shadow of an existence in Cuba that grew phantomlike as the years passed.

Our family moved from Poland and Russia and Turkey to Cuba in the 1920s, and from Cuba to Israel to New York to Miami in the 1960s and 1970s. And the photographs traveled with us. In those days, photographs were made to last and they withstood our uprootings with hardly a rip or a tear. I marveled at how beautiful we had been in Cuba—we were beautiful then, because all of us, including my great-grandparents, Abraham and Hannah, were young and our faces shone with hope. In the afterlife, our post-Cuba life, we were traumatized and scarred, but the photographs remained as pristine as the day they were taken. Stashed in disorderly piles in cardboard boxes, except for my parents' wedding photographs that remained immaculate in a sturdy album, these pictures were a substitute for the Cuba I longed to see with my own eyes but couldn't.

The laws of both my home country and my adopted country forbade me to see Cuba again. The passports of those who left the island were stamped *salida definitiva*. Literally that meant "definitive departure," or "no return." Jews who left for Israel, as we did before heading for the United States, had their passports stamped *repatriados*, or "repatriated," which implied that Jewish Cubans were trading their Cuban *patria* for the Jewish homeland that corresponded to them. To compensate Cubans for losing their *patria*, the United States granted Cubans political asylum, giving them extraordinary privileges as refugees from communism, privileges that no other Latino community received. But the trade embargo against Cuba also made it virtually impossible for Cubans to return to the island.

Growing up in New York, I was grateful for the little archive of black-and-white photographs my parents and grandparents were able to salvage in the midst of our hurried departure. Even though I was almost five years old when we left, I had no memories of Cuba. Looking at the photographs of my family in Cuba was how I first saw Cuba again, the Cuba I wanted to remember. Maybe if I stared at them long enough, I'd remember something of my lost childhood on the island.

As the years passed and it became obvious that we wouldn't be returning to live in Cuba, and as we realized, even more hopelessly, that perhaps we would never more set eyes on the beloved island, the photographs became a strange kind of evidence of our former existence in a place where all of us were once beautiful and young. Until I returned and saw it with my own eyes, I wondered if the time my family spent in Cuba was a dream. But the photographs of me playing on our old balcony, walking on the Malecón with my mother, dressed in a school uniform in front of the bus that took me to my pre-school at the Centro Israelita, all offered proof that I once had a home on the island.

Looking at the old photographs, I wondered what had become of our lost Jewish home in Cuba. What traces were left of the Jewish presence,

of the cemeteries, synagogues, and Torahs? Who was taking care of this legacy? What Jewish memories had managed to survive the years of revolutionary atheism? What had become of the handful of Jews who stayed on the island? Who were they? Why had they chosen to stay? But whenever I expressed my interest, my mother would say, "If they stayed in Cuba, it's because they're *comunistas*. Why would you want to go and meet *comunistas*?" She uttered that word, *comunistas*, with anger and venom, but also a touch of fear. "Be careful, they're very smart," she was always quick to add. "They'll brainwash you with all their pretty words!"

.   .   .

I was a disobedient daughter and I returned to Cuba. My first visit was in 1979, during the brief thaw in U.S.-Cuba relations under Jimmy Carter. I went to Cuba for a week, together with students and professors from Princeton University, where I'd begun graduate study in anthropology. I hoped to gain permission to do my dissertation research in Cuba—but I was too suspect as a Cuban American of undecided political sympathies. I wanted to understand both sides, to be a bridge between Cubans who left and Cubans who stayed.[12] The polarization of the time didn't allow for such a position.

So I ended up taking a detour and doing research in Spain and Mexico, working in small communities where people were observant Catholics and went regularly to church. Naturally, I too was expected to go to church—in anthropology one must do as the natives do. I learned to recite the rosary in Spanish and soon became expert at falling to my knees when the priest raised the Host at the culmination of the Mass. Everyone assumed I was Catholic; after all, I was from Cuba and spoke Spanish fluently. Being accepted made me afraid to call attention to my Jewish difference. It was cowardly of me, but I chose to keep quiet about my identity. I told myself I wasn't a religious Jew, that it didn't matter if now and then, for the sake of anthropology, I cross-dressed as a *conversa*, a hidden Jew, a secret Jew. But I wasn't at peace. And whenever I was back in Michigan, I had to continually explain my identity to Midwestern American Jews, who found it hard to comprehend how I could be both

Cuban and Jewish. I worried that I no longer knew how to be a Jew anywhere in the world, at home or away from home.

When I finally returned again to Cuba in the 1990s, my aim wasn't to study the Jews. I wanted simply to be a Jew in Cuba. I found that the combination of Cuban pluralistic tolerance, lax Catholicism, African-derived Santería beliefs, and revolutionary secularism made it easy to be Jewish in Cuba. I could say I was Jewish to any and every Cuban. People responded with curiosity and even admiration, rather than with apprehension. This was liberating after years of acting like a *conversa* and hiding my Jewish identity in Spain and Mexico. Among Jews in Cuba I also felt comfortable, because when I first knew them, they were often as uncertain about their Jewishness as I was about mine. Not that Judaism was foreign to me. I'd gone to Hebrew school, I could read liturgical Hebrew, and in my family we had observed the major Jewish holidays. But I was no longer sure how to go on being a Jew. I found it reassuring to be among Jews in Cuba who didn't know what exactly to say or do at Jewish services, to be among Jews who were learning how to be Jews. If there was hope for them, there was hope for me.

.   .   .

Throughout the 1990s I hung out in the synagogues, I rubbed shoulders with the Jews in Cuba, but I never took notes, never took photographs, never filmed. Maybe some were *comunistas*, as my mother had warned, but I didn't ask and they didn't tell.

What tormented me was that I had no memories of the island.

So I went looking for memories.

In La Habana Vieja, I returned to the apartment on Calle Aguacate, where my mother had lived, which was located above my grandfather's lace store, Casa Máximo.

I returned to the tenement facing the Port of Havana on Calle Oficios, where my father had lived, and stood on the balcony from where my Abuela had tossed a package of unkosher meat, infuriating my Abuelo, who'd brought it home victoriously in a time of hunger and misery.

I walked in and out of the rooms of the apartment in the tree-lined neighborhood of Vedado where I'd lived as a little girl. "Everything is exactly as your parents left it," the current occupant assured me. The sofa, the dining table and chairs, the vanity, the matrimonial bed my parents had left behind—it was all still there.

That's how it was for years. I returned to the same places over and over, until I no longer knew what I was returning for.

Panic attacks overwhelmed me when I walked on the Malecón and looked out at the wide sea. I learned that Olokkún, a Santería deity, watched over the spirits of African slaves who had perished on the journey to Cuba. Their graves were at the bottom of the ocean.

Rarely did I venture beyond what had been our old homes in Cuba. I was terrified of getting lost in Havana and never being heard from again.

My Fidel-phobia was huge. I feared I'd be forced to meet Him in person and that I'd be struck dumb.

I was a professor of anthropology, but all I could do was write poem after poem about my reencounter with Cuba.

I was accustomed to going to other places to do fieldwork. But could Cuba be a fieldsite? Cuba was my native land. How could I be an anthropologist there?

·   ·   ·

In the early 1990s you couldn't even find a map of Cuba for sale in the United States. On the rare occasions when I flew to Havana from Toronto, I would encounter planeloads of Canadians going on $500-a-week, all-inclusive trips to beach resorts in Varadero. I found their carefree attitude toward Cuba shocking and their swaggering about getting such a cheap tropical vacation more than a little repulsive. Flying from Miami, on the other hand, was a totally different kind of voyage, inundated with mostly working-class Cuban Americans employed in factories in Hialeah who had saved money for years to be able to bring suitcases full of clothing, shoes, and medicines to their families. Luggage weight was strictly limited to forty-four pounds, including carry-on luggage and handbags, as it still is today. Cuban Americans used their imagination to get around the limitations. Women made crazy, wildly beautiful hats, reminiscent of Carmen Miranda's fruit-laden creations, brimming with scrunchies and barrettes, costume jewelry, bottles of aspirin, and tampons. Security was intense and you were asked to arrive at the airport five hours before takeoff, usually in the middle of the night. During those interminable hours waiting at the airport, people would tearfully tell me their stories of going to visit a sister or son or mother they hadn't seen in decades. But what always broke my heart the most was encountering on the way back to Miami the same people with whom I'd flown to Havana. On the way south, they'd been loaded down with huge *gusanos* and rolling bags and clear plastic zip-up bags, filled to bursting with enough aspirin to last for a century of headaches. My fellow Cuban travelers paid exorbitant overweight fees in Miami. Then in Havana they had to pay duty on all the goods they were importing. On the way back from their trip, they had nothing. Everything stayed in Cuba. Everything. Even their suitcases.

.   .   .

The more I went to Cuba, the more I needed to go. I had become a Cuba addict. And like any addict, I needed my fix. My Cuba fix. Not even my grandmother's admonitions, my mother's paranoia, my father's disapproval, my husband's quiet relinquishing of time we might have spent together, my son's tears, or even my own heartbreak every time I said goodbye was enough to stop me. After a few months of being away from the island, I started to feel an intense desire to return. Despite all my fears and anxieties and phobias, I wanted to be in Havana, where I was born. I missed Cuban voices, Cuban streets, Cuban sunlight. I missed the sense of life lived on the edge. I missed how my pulse raced.

Not that it was easy to go to Cuba. Every couple of months I put myself through a grueling amount of paperwork just to be able to be back on the island for fourteen days. Since I was born in Cuba, each time I returned I had to request special permission from Cuban immigration to revisit the island. I may be an American citizen, but the Cuban government still considers me a Cuban. Each time, I had to fill out the same exact forms, noting the names of my parents, the address where we last lived in Cuba, the year we left, the reason I wished to return. Each time, I was put through the same security check, for all Cubans who have left are counterrevolutionaries. Each time, I received my "reentry permit" a day or two before my flight, never knowing if the permission to travel would come through until the very last minute. Sometimes I asked myself why I kept going back. I only knew I couldn't stay away. It was as if I felt I would never know Cuba, no matter how many times I returned. I could go dozens of times and I still wouldn't know it. If I ever thought that I knew how things worked, I would realize I didn't understand anything. And so each return was to see if I got it the next time.

Under both Cuban and American laws, it wasn't possible to keep traveling to Cuba on sentimental journeys to search for a lost home. But there was no problem with my going back as an anthropologist—an anthropologist who was studying the Jews of Cuba. Even though I didn't want to turn my native land into a fieldsite, anthropology became my passport; anthropology became my magic carpet. Only as an anthropologist could I return to Cuba two and three times a year to do ongoing research. Anthropology also became my shield. Nobody could criticize me for breaking with the Cuban exile position which held that no Cuban should set foot again in Cuba until Fidel Castro was gone. The key rite of passage for anthropologists is fieldwork. We must see the places and people we write about with our own eyes. I had to see Cuba, be in Cuba.

.　　.　　.

The early 1990s in Cuba, "the special period in a time of peace," was a time of uncertainty, of constant blackouts, of hunger. The collapse of the former Soviet Union left Cuba stranded. Soviet subsidies had supported a social welfare system that gave Cubans access to inexpensive rationed food, education, and health care that allowed them to live in dignity, but with a quixotic view of the workings of their own economy. Bereft of this support, which absurdly had come from halfway around the world after the United States broke off relations with Cuba, the Cuban government scrambled to amass hard currency to purchase oil and other necessities in the newly capitalist world system.

The government's solution to their economic crisis was to increase foreign tourism, including from the United States, an ironic measure given the existence of the embargo. Just as ironically, the money of the *gusanos*, "the worms of the Revolution," was allowed back into the island by making it easier for Cubans who had left to return and to send money to their families. Cubans living in a variety of locations in the diaspora would now be viewed as part of greater Cuba, as *la comunidad en el exterior*, "the community in the exterior." Even wishy-washy liberal Cuban Americans (like me) who hadn't made up their minds about Cuba would be welcome, so long as we refrained from making public statements against Castro. These measures worked: by the end of the century, tourism and remittances had become Cuba's main sources of revenue.

To facilitate the flow of hard currency, in the summer of 1993 the U.S. dollar, the money of the "imperialist enemy," was declared a legal currency in Cuba, to exist side by side with the Cuban peso. New hotels sprung up, especially in tourist resorts like Varadero, and the historian Eusebio Leal began the project of restoring Havana, a city so fascinatingly in ruin that it was continually likened by outside observers to Pompeii. The dollar shops expanded, offering tempting products that the majority of Cubans couldn't afford with their salaries in devalued *pesos*. Cubans felt forced to engage in *la lucha*, the struggle to "invent dollars." They sold siphoned goods from government factories, hotels, and stores where they worked. And they hustled tourists. Prostitutes, female and male, became a common sight in Havana. Controversy spun around them—were they the best-educated sex workers in the world or ungrateful people who dishonored the Revolution?

Riots broke out in Havana in 1994. Fidel Castro opened the ports and thousands of *balseros* flung themselves into the sea in hopes of reaching the United States. It will never be known how many ended up buried in ocean graves. But while the *balseros* took to the sea, a reverse migration took place, from the United States to Cuba. The year 1994 was also the moment of the historic Art Biennial in Havana, which attracted scores of American curators looking for new Cuban art. And they came away so enthralled with what they saw that Cuban art soon found its way to American galleries and museums, including the Museum of Modern Art in New York. Then, in 1996, the guitarist and world music producer Ry Cooder went to Havana, recording the music that became the Grammy award-winning compilation *Buena Vista Social Club*.

Art and music are exempt from the U.S. embargo because they are placed under the category of educational resources. They quickly became the key venues through which Americans again saw Cuba after decades of minimal information. A flood of Cuban photographic images came pouring into the United States that made hypervisible the island's ruined beauty.[13] The circulation of Cuban art and music, together with a growing nostalgia industry for everything Cuban, from cigars to *mojitos* to the Tropicana Club, aroused American consumer desires to repossess Cuba.[14]

As economic changes opened Cuba up to the gaze of the capitalist world, Cubans were also looking inward. For three decades, Cubans had lived under a constitution that declared it "illegal and punishable to oppose the Revolution with religious faith or belief." Throughout the 1960s, 1970s, and 1980s, all mention of God, spirits, and saints disappeared from everyday speech. But in 1991, the Cuban Communist Party decided to reverse its adherence to the Marxist dogma that religion was the opiate of the people. The stigma attached to religion was removed and it was decreed that even Party members could have religious affiliations. By 1992, it was written into the Cuban constitution that the state was now secular rather than atheist.

This reversal came as a shock to most Cubans. Out of fear of being labeled reactionary, Cubans had destroyed images of Catholic saints, bibles, and sacred objects of Santería. Among Jews it was common to hide away a *tallit*, an old prayer shawl that belonged to a grandfather. Jews stopped wearing Stars of David and many took down the mezuzahs, traditional talismans, from their doors. The few Jews left in Santiago de Cuba sent away their Torah to the Adath Israel synagogue in Havana because their synagogue had closed and it was thought that no one who knew how to read Hebrew from the ancient scroll would ever again live there.

And then suddenly Cubans were at liberty to pray, to speak of God, to assemble openly in churches, temples, and synagogues. Seeking spiritual solace at a time when revolutionary ideals were unraveling, Cubans began to practice a range of religions—Catholicism, Protestantism, Pentecostal faiths, Buddhism, Hinduism, Islam, Masonic ritual, Judaism, and Santería and palo monte, religions of African origin that had survived the brutality of slavery. Religion offered fresh possibilities for self-expression, and a language of power that asked human beings to put their faith in the divine rather than in an earthly leader. Embracing their newfound spiritual freedom, Cubans were soon flaunting Christian crosses and Jewish stars around their necks. After the Pope's visit in 1998, there were Christmas trees again. The streets of Havana became filled with Santería initiates, dressed in white from head to toe, as required during the first year after being reborn into the path of the *orishas*, the African deities.

With the return of both the U.S. dollar and God to Cuba, the island became safe again for Americans. For the U.S. government, it was not the presence of the dollar but the presence of God again on the island that offered the most hope that capitalism and democracy would soon follow. Religious licenses became the easiest travel licenses for Americans to obtain, and Catholic, Protestant, and Jewish "missions" promptly appeared in Cuba. Bibles and the message of God's bounty arrived together with donations of powdered milk and aspirin.

Other American travelers also found reason to go to Cuba. Undergraduate students thought it was "cool" to study Spanish in Cuba, while graduate students in anthropology flocked to do fieldwork on the "hot" topics of prostitution and Santería. Journalists from mainstream and minor newspapers were soon covering Cuba more consistently and addressing not only the island's troubles but its cultural and carnal charms.

On one end of the spectrum was Andre Codrescu's *Ay Cuba! A Socio-Erotic Journey*, which originally aired on National Public Radio in 1998. Codrescu, evoking Gauguin in Tahiti, highlighted the "swarms of young women in Lycra miniskirts, short shorts, and high platforms," who stalked even the most indifferent of male tourists and whose sexual services were a bargain for the American sex shopper.[15] At the other end of the spectrum, in June 1999 *National Geographic,* the magazine that has long served as a weather vane indicating which exotic countries are farflung enough and yet also safe enough for Americans to visit, ran a cover story about Cuba.[16] Somewhere between these two poles was the writer Pico Iyer, who swooned over the pure bliss of being in Cuba: "Sometimes, when I go out at night and sit on the seawall alone, feeling the spray of salt, the faint strumming of guitars carried on the wind, and the broad empty boulevards sweeping along the lovely curve of Havana Bay, I feel that I could never know a greater happiness."[17]

By the dawn of the new century there were a lot more Cuba addicts out there, as I discovered when I was included in a local journalist's article about "Ann Arbor's Cuba Craze." The article noted that interest in Cuba was growing among Americans, "like a rampant tropical vine, nourished in part by the Internet, a spate of new books and media exposure during the past five to seven years," as well as by reports "that in Cuba a warm, gracious people appear to get along fine without shopping malls, cell phones and SUVs."[18] In my own conversations with several neighbors in Ann Arbor who traveled to the island, what stood out as the allure of Cuba was that the United States wasn't there, McDonald's wasn't there, other Americans weren't there. Only one place remained in the world where Americans could take short vacations from themselves and learn that it was possible to be happy with less—that place was Cuba.

You'd think I would have felt pleased that other Americans were becoming Cuba addicts. But addicts must like privacy, because the truth was that, as a *Cuban* American, I felt unnerved by American desires for Cuba. The more Americans I met who waxed romantic about Cuba, the more I felt that I was losing Cuba all over again.

. . .

My mother and other Cuban Jews who left the island in the 1960s were convinced that no semblance of Jewish life could have survived the onslaught of revolutionary atheism. But I discovered that Jewish life had waned in the first decades after the Revolution, but it hadn't completely disappeared.

Throughout the 1960s and 1970s, the synagogues in Havana and the synagogue in Santiago de Cuba functioned with the participation of Jewish elders. The synagogues were kept afloat by monthly membership dues, rental money the government paid for use of their auditoriums, and the yearly sale of Passover products. After diplomatic relations were broken between Cuba and the United States, it was the Canadian Jewish Congress (CJC) that provided the Jewish community in Cuba with a yearly shipment of Passover foods—which included matzah, matzah meal, tuna, oil, tea, horseradish, wine, and sometimes also kosher soup and powdered milk. People registered to receive these foods, and as the practice of religion declined throughout the island, "the matzah package" became the last link that Jews in Cuba maintained to their heritage. The package also supplemented a monotonous diet of rice and beans, and made up for a shortage of bread. Most of those who went to the trouble to get the package no longer celebrated the seder and didn't pass on to their children the story of why Jews ate matzah for a week each year to commemorate their flight from slavery in Egypt. But the taste of the Jewish bread of affliction stayed on their tongues and reminded them of their secret history.

By the 1980s, Jews had mainly chosen, like other Cubans, to pull away from religion. They sought to underplay what made them different in order to integrate themselves into the revolutionary process and its ideology of national unity. Most of the Jews who still lived in Cuba then were children of Jewish men or women who had married non-Jewish Cubans, and they in turn went on to marry yet another generation of non-Jews. Families that had a Jewish heritage were dispersed throughout Havana and the provinces. They didn't know each other or couldn't meet with one another because of difficulties with transportation. Jewish education wasn't available. Elders who might have passed on cultural traditions grew old and died, and there were no young people to take their place.

With only a handful of Jews keeping up religious practices, they developed what became known as "the Cuban minyan." In normal circumstances, the minyan consists of a quorum of ten Jewish adults. In the Orthodox tradition it is ten Jewish men. The minyan is the minimum number of Jews needed to carry out a complete religious service.

But in Cuba, for a very long time, the minyan consisted of however many

Jews were present, however many Torahs were needed to fill in for people, and God.

· · ·

Under these circumstances, how could the Jews of Cuba be led back to their history and to the synagogues? The prospects looked dim, except to Dr. José Miller, a dental surgeon born and raised in the country town of Yaguajay, who had taken over the presidency of the withering Jewish community of the island in the late 1970s.

Miller believed that a Jewish revival could happen in Cuba with the assistance of the American Jewish Joint Distribution Committee (JDC). In 1992, in the midst of the religious opening in Cuba and the U.S. government's encouragement of humanitarian and religious missions to the island, he requested the assistance of the JDC and received it.[19] But even a charismatic leader like Miller didn't foresee the full impact that the presence of "el Joint"—as Cubans call the JDC—would have in Cuba. By the time of Miller's death in 2006, the Jewish community would completely reinvent itself. From a withering community, it would be transformed into a showcase for the "miracle" of Jewish survival in Castro's Cuba. And the Jews of Cuba would move to center stage in the imagination of American Jews, occupying the role of a lost tribe that needed to be saved and brought back into the fold of the world Jewish community.

Once "el Joint" found its way to Cuba, many other Jewish organizations followed. B'nai Brith, ORT, Hadassah, the Lubavitch of Canada and

Argentina, and the Jewish Conservative movement all wanted a place at the table in Jewish Cuba. American synagogues adopted Jewish communities on the island as sister temples, while campus Hillel organizations promoted Cuba as the new hip place to go on social justice missions. Synagogues all over the United States organized trips based on the idea of helping the Jews of Cuba to survive through donations of food, medicine, clothes, and books, as well as through Jewish education.

Flyers and brochures and web sites advertising Jewish Cuban outreach programs made two pitches—to aid the Jewish "rebirth" and allow American Jews to "experience" Cuba while being "more than a tourist." As the anthropologist Edward Bruner has noted, "Tourism is deprecated by almost everyone. Even tourists themselves belittle tourism as it connotes something commercial, tacky, and superficial."[20] By organizing themselves as missions, American Jewish groups avoided thinking of themselves as merely tourists, and gave meaning to their journeys to Cuba.

These missions to Cuba have played an important unifying role for American Jews, who in the last thirty years have become divided among themselves.[21] Conflicts have arisen over the meaning of Jewishness and the relationship between Jews in the diaspora and the State of Israel. For nearly two millennia Jews were a diasporic people, living in many lands, until 1900 when more than 80 percent of world Jewry lived in Europe. After the Holocaust, that 80 percent became split between the United States and Israel, which have become divergent centers of Jewish life.[22] Where Israel was once seen as "the center of the Jewish solar system with diaspora communities orbiting as distant planets," now American Jews have started to call for a relationship among equals.[23] More radical voices are challenging the split between Jewish homeland and Jewish diaspora and calling for a vision of global Jews, "new Jews," who feel that their sense of identity isn't based in "a nationalistic claim to land," but "a claim to culture, history, and heritage, whether that happens to be in New York, Moscow, Buenos Aires, Berlin, or Jerusalem."[24] A longing for Jewish multiculturalism has led to a fascination with the "fragile branches" of the Jewish diaspora, and a desire among American Jews to reclaim obscure Jewish communities that have endured in Africa, Asia, and Latin America.[25]

Cuba enters into this changing panorama of American Jewish identity just at the moment when philanthropy becomes one of the most important means of anchoring that identity in the goal of rescue and salvage of Jewish cultures around the world.[26] In Cuba, American Jews can simultaneously hold on to the idea that Jews are "one people" and the opposite idea that Jews are a multicultural people making their home in many parts of the world. Uncertain though they may be about their own Jewishness, Cuba proves to be a fulfilling destination, where it is possible to witness and aid the "rebirth," "renaissance," and "renewal" of a needy Jewish community in a country that is so close but may as well be at the end of the world because of the U.S. embargo.

The American Jewish givers derive tremendous emotional satisfaction from their giving, as can be seen in numerous testimonials. Stanley Falkenstein, who has traveled to Cuba more than thirty times, bringing wheelchairs and eyeglasses, was able to articulate feelings shared by many other American Jews. As Falkenstein states in a 2005 open letter to the Jewish community of Cuba: "You have given me the best gift I have ever received in my life. I have found in you the meaning and purpose of my life."[27]

American Jews who travel to Cuba are willing to put aside any doubts they might have about communism in Cuba and the continuing restrictions on freedom of speech. Jaime Suchlicki, a Cuban Jewish historian based in Miami, thinks American Jews are either naïve or engaging in a game of self-deception. "The American Jewish community uses a visit to Cuba as an excuse to do a junket," he declares. After a visit to a Havana synagogue, "they can say, 'I have helped Cuban Jews.'"[28]

·   ·   ·

The tiny Jewish community of a thousand that now exists in Cuba has often been called a "remnant" of the community of fifteen to twenty thousand that reached its peak as Fidel Castro was coming into power in 1959 and that fled the island soon after. Born from the ashes of the old community, the Jews who live in Cuba today share a common history with the Cuban Jews who left. Yet it is inaccurate to call them a "remnant." The new community bears no resemblance to the old, even if the Jews still in Cuba are the ones who guard over the cemeteries, synagogues, and Torahs that were once the patrimony of those who left. Between the wealthy Cuban Jews who now live in Miami— among them the CEO of Perry Ellis—and the financially strapped Cuban Jews who reside in Cuba, the only remaining tie is an island they all, at one time or another, have called home.

In the early 1990s, before there was much contact between the two communities and aid was only starting to trickle in for the Jews in Cuba, I experienced the surrealistic disjuncture of crossing from one Jewish Cuban location to another. One week I was in Havana, at Shabbat services at the dilapidated Patronato, where people looked tired and worn, and the sweat poured from their bodies as it did from mine; afterward, I shared with them a chicken lunch funded by "el Joint" that for many was their most substantial meal of the week. The next week I was with Baba at the Cuban Hebrew synagogue in Miami Beach, or "El Círculo," as members refer to their community, for a Selichot service marking the coming of the Jewish New Year. At the lavish four-course meal preceding the service, people glittered in suits and ties, sequined dresses, and diamonds, and they shivered from the overly active air conditioner.

But it is not just economic differences that make these two communities so unlike one another. Among Cuban Jews in Miami, intermarriage is almost unheard of, except with American Jews, who are considered the next best thing to another Cuban Jew. Theirs is a clannish world made up of those who kept the faith and survived as Jews in Cuba by excluding any Jews who ventured out from the tribe.

In contrast, the Jewish community in Cuba today looks a lot like the rest of Cuba: a mix of white, black, and everything in between. Most members of the community are descendents of the uncounted Jews who married non-Jewish Cubans and were lost to the Jewish community in the period before the Revolution; they are the Jews who were exiled before the exiles became exiles. Only about twenty-five Jews in Cuba today are "pure Jews," people born of a Jewish mother and a Jewish father, though relative to their size they have played an important role in maintaining Jewish history and memory.[29] Jewish tradition only accepts as Jews those born to a Jewish mother, and since most

Jews in Cuba are children or grandchildren of Jewish men, the majority are converts.

Many in the community are seeking to leave the country for Israel, which welcomes Cuban Jewish immigrants. Without realizing it, they are reenacting the "Hotel Cuba" scenario of an earlier generation by living physically in Cuba, but dreaming of being elsewhere, in a land of milk and honey. Finally, as my mother warned me, there are Jewish *comunistas* in the community, who identify as ethnically Jewish, but have nothing to do with synagogue or religious life. They are devoted to the ideal of the Revolution and have no intention of ever living anywhere but in Cuba.

The Cuban Jews who left in the 1960s received a cold reception from American Jews when they arrived as refugees in Miami, and this compelled them to work hard to achieve wealth and independence. They built Ashkenazic and Sephardic synagogues of their own in the heart of Miami Beach, and rose up the ranks of the Jewish Federation in Miami. They became givers, not to have to depend on anyone's charity.[30] This, too, is a striking contrast with the Jewish community still in Cuba, which exists under a communist system and would not be able to survive without the charitable assistance of the Joint Distribution Committee and the various American Jewish missions.

Thanks to "el Joint" and other American Jewish assistance, Cuba now has an organized Jewish community. Curiously, even with the continuing U.S. embargo, Jewish synagogue life in Cuba has come to resemble standard American Jewish practice. Although most Jews who stayed in Cuba are Sephardic, Jewish ritual life is dominated by Ashkenazic prayer books and traditions, because financial support comes from Ashkenazic institutions and communities. Reform, Reconstructionist, and secular humanist forms of Jewish practice are mostly unknown in Cuba.[31] Despite the recent self-questioning trends in American Jewish thought, Jewish history is taught with a focus on the Holocaust and the creation of the State of Israel as the redemptive closure to the Jewish diaspora.

An entire program of education and community building has been set in place that is supervised by American Jews, as well as Latin American Jews employed by the Joint Distribution Committee.[32] Not only have Jews in

Havana been able to benefit from this program, but so too have Jews in the provinces. A network exists of clubs for children, youth, middle-aged adults, and the elderly, bringing together Jews from all over the island so they can know one another and occasionally enjoy a vacation in a Cuban resort that would otherwise be beyond their means. Vans and buses funded by the JDC pick up and return people to their homes, so that they can go to synagogue and attend Jewish celebrations. The matzah continues to arrive, now in greater amounts and varieties.

There is no rabbi living permanently in Cuba, but Rabbi Shmuel Szteinhendler, an Argentine rabbi, has been a JDC representative since the early 1990s. He periodically visits the different regions of Cuba to perform weddings and conversions, and bless young men and women celebrating their coming of age in bar mitzvah and bat mitzvah ceremonies. The JDC also sponsors *mohels*, who are trained to perform circumcisions in the ritually prescribed way that has set Jewish males apart since the days of Abraham. Beginning in the early 1990s and continuing to the present, the JDC has sent young Argentine teachers to Cuba for periods of two or three years to teach Hebrew and Jewish history, and to lead religious services. These teachers share with Jewish Cubans not only the Spanish language, but their own experience of Latin American underdevelopment. Over the course of their stay, they become enmeshed with the fate of the Jewish Cuban community and protective of the dignity of the community, making sure that the constant presence of onlookers and charity givers doesn't turn the community into a circus show.

While Jews in Cuba aren't well off financially, there are many highly educated professionals, with doctors, engineers, and lawyers predominating. Members of this small elite have become the leaders of the Jewish community. After fifteen years of foreign support and instruction, they know as much, or more, about Jewish history and religion as do the American Jews who come on "missions" to help them become born-again Jews.

The community has its own resident historian, Maritza Corrales Capestany, who is married to a Sephardic Jew.

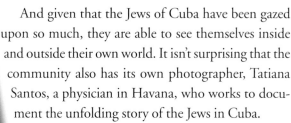

And given that the Jews of Cuba have been gazed upon so much, they are able to see themselves inside and outside their own world. It isn't surprising that the community also has its own photographer, Tatiana Santos, a physician in Havana, who works to document the unfolding story of the Jews in Cuba.

Jews in Cuba are well aware of their economic dependence. Yet Isaac Roussó Lilo, the president of the B'nai Brith Maimonides Lodge in Cuba, rejects the idea that Jews in Cuba receive "charity." He is proud to oversee a program that distributes small grants to needy people in the Jewish community on a regular basis and that also offers an emergency fund to help people deal with unexpected problems, such as the repair of a leaking roof or a medical crisis.

Isaac says he detests the word "charity," which doesn't exist in the Hebrew language. The only word he feels should be used to describe the material help Jews receive in Cuba from their brethren is "tzedaka," which means justice.

· · ·

As a student of anthropology, I read many books about exotic people, but I never thought that "my people," the Jews of Cuba, would come to be considered exotic.

Initially, when I started spending time with Jews in Cuba in the early 1990s, there were no books or films about them, no photographs of them on web sites. The movie *Hotel Cuba*, the work of two historians, was available, but it focused on pre-revolutionary Cuba.[33] A few studies, again by historians, looked at Jews generally in Latin America, but they too were concerned with the past rather than the present.[34]

By the mid-1990s, books, articles, and films began to appear, and in the last five years there has been an explosion of information about Jews in Cuba.[35] The presentations range from scholarly to popular, and include the Travel section of the *New York Times*.[36] Several web sites now exist with up-to-the-minute accounts of Jewish life in Cuba and lists of what American Jews should bring to help Jews on the island. The fascination with the idea of a Jewish-Cuban fusion has even influenced a Cuban American musician who came of age in Miami performing in the Yiddish theater; he calls his music "Cuban Klezphardic," and gives titles like "El Polaco" and "Shalom a Shango" to his compositions.[37]

This avalanche of attention has turned the Jews of Cuba into an over-studied, over-observed, and over-photographed tribe. They are undergoing an experience very similar to that which so-called primitive people, like the Kung of the Kalahari desert, have been through, of being observed by a never-ending stream of curious anthropologists, tourists, missionaries, and well-wishers.

I understand the nature of the American fascination with Cuba's Jews. Where else but in Cuba do you find Jews whose backs are being watched by Che Guevara? Where else but in Cuba does Che, the icon of revolution, act as guardian angel of the Jews and seem so thoroughly at home in the synagogue?

The idea that Jewish life has been possible at all under Fidel Castro contributes to the exotic appeal of Cuba's Jews, who maintain their identity in a web of contradictions and paradoxes. Since Israel votes with the United States to maintain the U.S. embargo, Cuba is officially pro-Palestinian and doesn't have diplomatic relations with Israel. Yet Israel, together with Spain, is a major investor in the Cuban economy. Jews in Cuba suffer no discrimination. Quite the opposite is the case: the Cuban government goes out of its way to accommodate Jewish needs, neither interfering with the functioning of the kosher butcher shop in Havana nor the distribution of matzah, neither interfering with the activities that go on in the synagogues nor the numerous departures of community members to Israel. Although the Cuban press frequently expresses anti-Zionist views, there is wide admiration and respect for the Jewish people. *Schindler's List* was shown on Cuban television and was the subject of much sympathetic discussion. It has not escaped the notice of the Cuban government that American Jews have fueled the revitalization of the Jewish community and that they have also been among the most active grassroots diplomats, engaging with Cubans through cultural exchanges and volunteer medical assistance programs.

Fidel Castro, some say, has a soft spot for the Jews, possibly for personal reasons. Might Castro be a hidden Jew? His daughter claims that one of Castro's grandfathers was a Jew from Istanbul. But all that Castro has ever told reporters is that his Jewish identity harks back to the days of the Inquisition, when Spanish Jews took on names like Castro and became *conversos* to escape being burned at the stake.[38] Irrespective of Castro's family tree, it is well known that Cubans as a whole like to think of themselves as the "Jews of the Caribbean." On the island, Cubans see Cuba and Israel as similarly fierce and independent nations, small in size but huge in ambitions, surrounded by historical enemies who seek to topple their efforts to build paradise on earth.[39] Cuban exiles and immigrants, in contrast, see themselves as diasporic in the classical Jewish sense; in the words of poet Rafael Campo, as "people, of a solitary star/ who wander, searching for a home someplace."[40]

Such shared Jewish and Cuban sensibilities make the actual Jews still living in Cuba a potent symbol of what it means to search for a home in the world. Jews in Cuba have come to represent something larger than themselves—they are Jews in extremis, Jews in an outpost of civilization, Jews still forging a life in the last of the communist lands, Jews close and yet far from the United States, Jews who breathe the revolutionary air of Che Guevara, Jews shockingly poor in material things, lacking such accoutrements of modern life as credit cards and frequent flyer numbers, but who are rich in spirituality. Their aura is such that hundreds upon hundreds of people continue to travel to Cuba to show their support and feel the joy of communing with them.

The fact that so many celebrity visitors are drawn to the Jews in Cuba has turned them into celebrities as well. Steven Spielberg, the Hollywood filmmaker, felt compelled to visit with the Jews while in Havana for a festival of his films in 2002. Before leaving, he wrote the Jews of Cuba a note—"When I see how much cultural restoration has been performed by you and others, it reminds me again about why I am so proud to be a Jew." He added the words "Thank you" before signing his name, as if to express his gratitude to the Jews in Cuba for simply existing.

.   .   .

And yet even with many eyes gazing at them, the Jews of Cuba remain mysterious. I have spent fifteen years catching glimpses of their lives and still can't claim I fully know them. But to speak of "the Jews of Cuba" is ostentatious, for the community is miniature and in continual flux. No matter how many people die or leave the island, somehow there are always a thousand Jews in Cuba (or some like to say fifteen hundred). The number seems to have been arrived at kabbalistically and neither death nor diaspora changes anything.

To gain an understanding of Jewish life in Cuba today, a life I always realized might have been mine had my own Jewish family stayed on the island, I had to be an anthropologist in my native land. I had to put myself in the position of the person who is always in between, an insider and an outsider at the same time. I identified with the Jews still in Cuba, but wasn't one of them because I didn't live in Cuba. I identified with the American Jews, but wasn't one of them because I was Cuban. I identified with the Cuban Jews in the United States, but wasn't one of them because I went to Cuba too often.

Who was I, then? I was an anthropologist with an aching heart. It was after my Baba died, after years of saying goodbye to her, that I went on the journey that took me from the core of Jewish life in Havana to anthropology at the end of the world with the last Jew in Palma Soriano. How I wish I could have shared these stories with my Baba! Surely had she known it was these stories I would eventually bring back in my suitcases from Cuba, she would not have worried so much about me.

I might have made the focus of this book the religious revitalization that has taken place in the Jewish community in Cuba, which is very visible and impressive. I had spent a lot of time in the synagogues attending religious services and celebrations and had many photographs of Jews in Cuba performing their Jewishness. But there was a subtle, intimate layer of Jewish belonging I wanted to explore. What I found compelling was the intrahistory—the relationship people had with the Jewish past and the fierce ways they were holding on to this past, which they had made their own through conversion or the belated recuperation of their heritage.

Since I always went to Cuba on short lightning trips, I appeared and disappeared from the island like a ghost. At times, especially when I spoke to people waiting to leave for Israel, I felt I was interacting with ghosts. On my short stays in Havana and even briefer trips to the provinces, my interviews with the people I sought out often turned into intense, emotional, once-in-a-lifetime encounters. I thought of these encounters as tangos—improvised conversations that led to surprising revelations and exchanges. I arrived in people's apartments, houses, and offices, prayed with them in the temples, intruded upon them in the street, asking them to tell me what it meant to be Jewish in Cuba. And because I was afraid of forgetting, I brought along a photographer on my journey—to make sure that the Cuba I was seeing would still be with me when I said goodbye again.

I knew that I returned to Cuba with a longing for memory and I worried about imposing that nostalgia on Jews in Cuba, until I discovered that they too longed for memory. Like my two Jewish grandfathers who worked as peddlers when they arrived in Cuba, I felt I had a bundle on my shoulders—in that bundle were the memories kept by the Jews who left Cuba and those who stayed, and it became my role to carry these memories back and forth.

Even after so many return trips, I still don't remember anything of my Jewish childhood in Cuba. But I am grateful to have the stories of the people who continue to hold on to a solitary Jewish star on the island that Columbus was right to call a pearl—and thanks to them, I believe there will always be a home for Jews in Cuba.

Buenos Aires, Passover, April 5, 2007

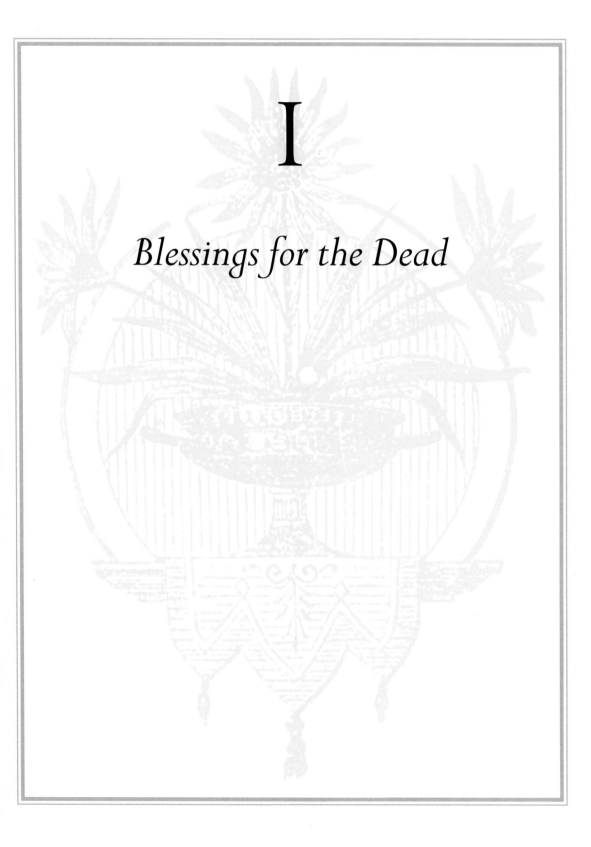

I

Blessings for the Dead

I

LOOKING FOR HENRY

The first Jew I went looking for in Cuba was a ghost named Henry Levin. He was gone before he could celebrate his bar mitzvah and claim his Jewish heritage. The son of my great-uncle Moisés and great-aunt Zoila, my second cousin Henry died an untimely death on the eve of his twelfth birthday in 1954.

Even though Henry died before I was born, I had heard so much about him I felt as if I'd known him. My mother spoke to me of how smart Henry was—he was too smart for his age, she'd say. At his funeral, attended by hundreds in the Jewish Cuban community of that era, everyone became drenched in the unceasing rain that fell as his casket was lowered into the earth. His bones stayed behind in Cuba, but for our family the loss of Henry became a trauma of such dimensions that we all carried his memory

with us into our second diaspora in the United States. The family that had fled Poland in the 1920s and 1930s, barely escaping the Holocaust, questioned how God had protected them from destruction on such a grand scale only to take this innocent boy from them in a time of peace. Reuniting at first in the small town of Agramonte, in a sugar-growing region where they were the only Jews, the family found its way to Havana and the city of Matanzas by the 1950s. They led quiet and comfortable lives, blessed to have settled on an island Eden where kindness and mangos were abundant, and even the snakes weren't poisonous.

In my mother's family, it was Moisés and Zoila who had achieved the greatest success. They lived in a two-story house facing the royal palms of the Quinta Avenida in the exclusive Havana neighborhood of Miramar. Tere, a devoted nanny, took care of Henry and his older sister Alma. A cook and a cleaning woman worried about all the menial tasks. Their office supply store, La Casa de los Molinos, in the heart of Havana, was a thriving business, and they could afford vacations in Miami.

Everything fell apart when Henry turned eleven. First he complained of pains while walking. Then he said he didn't want to go to school. Finally, when the family assembled for meals at the dinner table, Henry was so tired he would fall asleep.

Moisés and Zoila took Henry to the best doctors in Havana, but they could find nothing wrong with him. In the summer of 1954, they got on a plane and went to the Mayo Clinic in Minnesota. There they discovered Henry was suffering from leukemia and his death was imminent.

On the plane ride back, Zoila prayed for a crash, so as not to have to return to Cuba to face the extinction of her son from this earth.

"What good is money if I can't save my son?" Moisés said, his voice breaking. But he didn't weep. He was one of those who came into the world with tearless eyes.

Moisés and Zoila bought Henry incredible gifts in his sunset days—a red English bicycle, an electric train that circled around their marble-tiled living room, and, most spectacular of all, a man-sized accordion, from which Henry coaxed sounds sweet as the aroma of frangipanis.

The doctors in Minnesota had predicted that in the final, and worst, stage of the illness Henry would be in pain, day and night. This pain, for which there were neither words nor medicines, was so cruel he cried in exasperation, "Even the hair on my head hurts." His parents tried to make him feel hopeful. They told him he would be well again and celebrate his bar mitzvah on his thirteenth birthday.

When he died, Henry was buried in the oldest Jewish cemetery on the island, located across the bay from Havana in Guanabacoa. It rained hard that twenty-second of October in 1954 and the gravediggers struggled with their shovels to keep the earth from collapsing around the casket. Henry became, for all eternity, part of the soil of Cuba. He would be of the island, always of the island. He would never know what it felt like to be uprooted. Death had made him irrevocably Cuban.

All this I knew about Henry from listening to the family stories. He was so much a part of my life that I would have gone looking for him on my own, even if Moisés and Zoila hadn't asked me to go to the Jewish cemetery in Guanabacoa and take a photograph of Henry's tomb. But once they asked me to search for Henry, I felt that I was on a sacred mission. Moisés and Zoila had left Cuba in 1960 with their daughter, Alma, and they were heartbroken that Henry had to be left behind in his island grave. They wanted to see his tomb again—in a photograph at least—to make sure that the letters of his name had remained intact and were still honoring his memory.

Jews are a people who won't let go of the dead. The dead are honored through the recitation of the Kaddish at religious services. When Jews build temples, they cover the walls with the names of the dead. But before they build temples of worship, Jews build cemeteries. They want to be buried amid Stars of David. They want to be with members of the tribe when they return to dust.

But it wasn't until I went to the old Jewish cemetery in Guanabacoa for the first time, looking for Henry's tomb, that I learned the issue isn't simply that Jews won't let go of the dead; it's the dead who also won't let go of us, the Jews.

It was in December of 1991 that I took a taxi out to Guanabacoa. I knew that Guanabacoa was renowned for the strength of its Afrocuban religions—both for Santería, or Regla de Ocha, which follows the ways of the orishas, or

the saints, and for palo monte, which follows the ways of nature and the ancestors—and I wondered how a Jewish cemetery had come to be planted in this
territory. I'd been told the cemetery was huge—for the Jews had expected to
stay in Cuba for a long time and thought they'd need a lot of space to bury their
dead for generation upon generation.

The driver, being from Havana and not knowing his way around Guanabacoa, drove around in circles, asking for directions at every turn. "Where is
the cemetery of the Jews?" he asked, and people shrugged or stared in disbelief,
as if to say, "You mean there are Jews buried around here?" One man finally
knew how to lead us there, but only after he'd rephrased our question. "Oh,
you mean the cemetery of the *polacos*, don't you?" he said. "To get to the cemetery of the Poles, take that road over there. It's at the edge of town, by the railroad tracks."

When we finally arrived at the cemetery, I had my camera ready. I imagined the rest would be easy: I'd find the tomb, snap the picture, and leave. But
from the moment I got there I could feel myself becoming tense—what if I
didn't find Henry? Or what if I found him and he didn't let me go? According
to Tere, the Afrocuban nanny who cared for Henry until his death and continued to visit his grave after my family left, you had to be careful with dead
spirits; they could attach themselves to your shadow and haunt you, try to take
you with them into the other world.

At the gate of the cemetery a sign reads, in English, "Founded in 1906."
The cemetery was built by the United Hebrew Congregation, the community
of expatriate American Jews who settled in Cuba at the turn of the twentieth
century, after the Spanish-American War.

I enter through a tall iron gate and find myself in a city of ghosts who
respond to many languages. Inscriptions on the headstones are written in English, Hebrew, Yiddish, and Spanish. Tombs from the 1950s include photographs of the departed that could have been taken yesterday. I stop to marvel
at how they have withstood tropical rainstorms and the blazing sun.

But I despair. I've promised a picture to Moisés and Zoila in Miami, but I
cannot find Henry. I see a rabbi's grave, apart from the rest. I see a monument
in Yiddish to the Jewish socialists killed fighting against the dictatorship of

Machado. I see a Holocaust memorial, where the plaque declares that soap made out of Jewish flesh lies buried there.

And then I find it—the tomb of my second cousin Henry. A simple, stark tomb, adorned only with his name and the dates of his short life. I reach for my camera, but the shutter won't click. I try again. And again. Again. My camera freezes, is transfixed, dies.

I have to return the next day for Henry Levin's tomb with a friend's camera. It's as if Henry, after being apart from the family for so long, wants me to visit him not once but twice.

The second time I know how to find him. I'm no longer lost among the dead. I feel suddenly at home among these Jewish ghosts and I allow myself to wonder—Is this where I want to be buried when my time comes? But I chase away that thought. I turn right, count the rows, walk up a dusty trail, and find Henry.

I snap the picture, and as Jews do, I place a stone on his grave.

I tell myself that all is well—I will be able to report to Moisés and Zoila that their son's tomb is intact, that the letters of his name have not budged, that the tomb is exactly as they left it. I will have a photograph to prove everything I have told them is true.

But I'll refrain from telling them about the tombs that are in a state of neglect, the tombs forgotten by the world, the tombs which make you shiver in the marrow of your bones, the tombs announcing what it means to vanish and be nothing.

A few years later, Moisés and Zoila will themselves return to Cuba, together with Alma, for a weekend visit, long enough to catch a glimpse of their house (now turned into a school) and their store (now in ruins), long enough to shake hands with the *viejos* in Agramonte, the old folks who remember them still, and give them ten-dollar bills as souvenirs, long enough to stand at the cemetery saying goodbye again to Henry.

After a few more years, the cemetery will become a required stop for the American Jewish tour groups who go to the island looking for the Jews of Cuba. Havanatur buses will pull up to the very door of the cemetery. Steven Spielberg will also visit Henry and the other Jewish ghosts in Guanabacoa. The dead will no longer be as lonely.

Slowly, I will be able to let Henry go—slowly, I will come to forget that my tie to Cuba is through this dead boy, and I will go looking for the Jews who live today on the island.

2

A KADDISH FOR THE JEWS WHO REST IN JEWISH CEMETERIES IN CUBA AND FOR RAQUEL'S MOTHER WHO DOES NOT

It is only after many visits to Henry's grave that I learn there is another Jewish cemetery, across the train tracks in Guanabacoa—the Sephardic cemetery. Built in 1942, it is watched over by an Afrocuban family who live next door to the train tracks. Despite the family's vigilance, they tell me that Jewish bones are often looted from the cemetery for use in palo monte rituals, which derive from a mixture of the Bantu culture of Central Africa and Spanish Catholicism. Paleros believe that magical power can be drawn from these Jewish bones because they belonged to unbaptized souls.

No one visits the Sephardic cemetery unless you have family buried there. No tour buses stop at the gate. But for me, it is in this patch of uneven ground, where weeds sprout too fast and Stars of David lie broken at every turn, that I will find the other part of my Jewish heritage—the Sephardic heritage of my father's family, stemming from my grandfather, Isaac Behar, who took to the sea and fled to Cuba to escape serving in the Turkish army, and my grandmother, Rebeca Maya, who was sent to the island, like a mail-order bride, to be married to the husband her Turkish parents had chosen (but he, alas, was impatient and had already married another woman when she arrived, and so she married my grandfather).

Here I will find the Behar last name etched on tombstone after tombstone, as if no other name existed in the world. At first I will think we all have common origins in the Spanish town of Béjar, but later I will hear another explanation, that our ancestors took the name Behar because of the Hebrew words for "firstborn" *(beḥor)* and "chose" *(baḥar)*, as in "chosen people."

Whatever the origins of our name, among so many Behars buried in the Sephardic cemetery of Guanabacoa, I will ask myself again—Is this where I want to be buried when my time comes? The question will frighten me less when I pose it later. I will even be able to imagine, without worrying, one of my unbaptized bones being stolen on a humid night to help an ailing soul.

Over the years, I will keep returning to this Sephardic cemetery, photographing and filming, getting to know every tombstone. But one ghost will haunt me the most: the ghost of Elisa Behar, who died in childbirth. Who was Elisa Behar? A long-lost relative? No one can tell me. All I will know, for years, is that she was so loved by her husband, Salomón, that on her tombstone he memorialized her story with a poem and a picture.

A MI ELISA

Cuando a tu lecho se acercó la muerte,
Tú soñabas, mi bien y en tus delirios
Contemplabas entre ángeles y lirios
Tus caras hijas que la adversa suerte
Negó al calor de tu amoroso pecho.

Y embriagada de amor y de ternuras
En coloquio ideal con tus criaturas
Me dijiste "Adiós" y al fin partiste
A la región magnífica del cielo.

Mas yo mi amor que por tu ausencia sufro
El alma presa de fatal quebranto
Cabe esta losa inconmovible y fría
Mi vida anego en doloroso llanto . . .

¡Quiera el Señor iluminar mi suerte,
Y nos una otra vez allá en la muerte!
Tu Salomón

TO MY ELISA

When death came calling at your bed, my love,
You were asleep, and in your fevered dreams,
Surrounded by angels and lilies, you gazed upon
Your dear daughters, those whom hostile fate
Denied the warmth of your sweet loving breast.

And then, entranced with tender strains of love,
In ideal dialogue with your lost babes,

You said "Adiós" to me, and soon departed
For heaven's most magnificent climes.

But I, my love, who grieve to miss you so,
My soul beset with deadly sorrow
Here by this cold, unmoving stone,
I am weeping out my life in sobs of woe . . .

May the Lord see fit to shine upon my fate,
And join us once again, beyond, in death!
        Your Salomón [Salomón Barlía]

Such an elaborate tombstone, I assumed, was the handiwork of a Jew who had left Cuba. Little did I know that the story behind it was waiting for me inside Cuba . . . several years into the future, several return trips later.

.   .   .

Once I feel at home with the Jewish ghosts who float over Havana, I will travel across the island, looking for more Jewish cemeteries, looking for all the dead Jews that can be found in Cuba.

When I enter Jewish cemeteries in the towns of central and eastern Cuba, where Jews settled in the 1920s and 1930s, tears come to my eyes at the sight of all the tombs inscribed with Hebrew letters and decorated with a simple Star of David. Although I am not religious, I too want a solitary star on my tombstone when I die, even if I do not know yet on which soil I want my tombstone to rest.

Turning Cuban soil into Jewish soil, I come to realize, was the first step that Jews took to secure their place in the landscape of Cuba, especially in the remote areas of the island. Jewish settlers from Eastern Europe and Turkey found their way to these areas because they weren't so crowded with new immigrants and it was less expensive to acquire and maintain family businesses there than in Havana. Many Jewish families—like my mother's family—spent their initial years in out-of-the way places, where there was less competition for cus-

tomers, building up capital by selling their
wares to country folk. Eventually, if all went
well, they moved to Havana, where they
could live among Jews and make sure their
children married within the tribe. But if the
misfortune of sudden death struck, they could
take consolation in the thought that there was
Jewish earth consecrated and waiting for them in
Cuba's hinterland.

How else to explain the existence of a tiny
Jewish cemetery in Camajuaní, dating from
1925, that was only used for seven years? The
tombstones are cracked and split in pieces,
but I want to think that the dead aren't
unhappy there, for they are surrounded by
palm trees and quaint bohíos—the
thatched-roof huts of the countryside.

After the cemetery in Camajuaní ceased to be used because it had grown too
small for the expanding Jewish population, a new Jewish cemetery was built in
nearby Santa Clara in 1932. It is much bigger—the Jews will never run out of
room there. But the dead in Santa Clara struggle to be left in peace.
The goats think the land belongs to them and they
are always trying to clamber over the walls and leap
between the tombs.

Farther east, in Camagüey, where the first grave
dates back to 1924, the Jews called their city of the
dead the "Israelite cemetery" and built a tall cement
wall to protect themselves, leaving only a narrow door
through which to enter. Inside, the air tastes sour, and
the stones you need to place on the graves are buried in
the milky mud and you have no choice but to get dirt
under your fingernails when you dig them out.

This, too, isn't a cemetery visited by foreigners, or

even very much by the Jews who still live in Camagüey. Located on the out-skirts of the city, it is a long bike ride to get to the cemetery. But the road is flat and the sky calm as the sea, even if the sea is only a memory in Camagüey.

On the eastern edge of the island, when you finally can glimpse the sea again, there is the Jewish cemetery of Santiago de Cuba, founded in 1926 by Sephardic immigrants. Eugenia Farín Levy, the president of Santiago's Jewish community, tells me she often visits the tomb of her mother, Victoria Levy. She'd made a promise to her mother, a promise she couldn't keep—that she'd marry a Jewish man. Eugenia made the promise before the Revolution, before the exodus of the Jews out of Cuba. Afterward, there weren't enough Jews left to find a marriage partner. So Eugenia did the next best thing—she married a good man. He wasn't Jewish, but he didn't stand in the way of her raising their two daughters as Jews. When she visits her mother's grave, Eugenia thinks about the effort it takes to remain Jewish in Cuba—and how much easier it would be to give it all up. Not that she would do so. She dons a *kippah* as con-

fidently as any man—for her mother
had no sons—and recites a Kaddish,
leaving her mother a stone she has
pulled from the sandy earth.

There is only one Jewish cemetery
on the island that I will not get to
visit—in the small town of Banes—
but Julio César Alomar Gómez in
Santiago de Cuba will be kind enough to show it to
me on a videotape, so that I will not worry about failing to call upon those Jewish ghosts, so that I will be able to leave the island satisfied that my quest was complete and thorough.

.   .   .

After visiting (virtually) every Jewish cemetery in Cuba, I thought I had accomplished my mission: I had found all the dead Jews there were to find.

But then I learned that not all Jews in Cuba are buried in Jewish cemeteries. I have to admit that for me this is a shocking discovery.

I grew up among Jews who weren't religious, Jews who ate kosher meat at home, but indulged in the sin of consuming Cuban pork sandwiches at the Rincón Criollo Restaurant on Junction Boulevard, Jews who observed the major Jewish holidays and went now and then to Shabbat services, but who couldn't let a Saturday pass without going shopping. But they were superstitious Jews and it was their superstitiousness they passed on—they were afraid that unspeakable punishments would strike us if we defied the two fundamental Jewish taboos. It was prohibited to marry outside the tribe, an act that brought upon the family, so cursed, unbearable suffering, grief. It was prohibited to be buried anywhere but in a Jewish cemetery—or risk the sorrow of eternal solitude.

But in Cuba, I learned that Jews disobeyed both these prohibitions: many had married outside the tribe and had also chosen to be buried in Catholic cemeteries.

In the case of Raquel Marichal Maya's mother, she made her choice because of love. Her mother's Sephardic Jewish family was from Turkey and her father's Catholic family was from Spain. Raquel says her parents were passionate about one another. Although Raquel's mother raised Raquel as a Jew, when she was dying she asked to be buried with her husband in the historic Colón cemetery in Havana, a Catholic cemetery. "Maybe she believed in reincarnation," Raquel told me, because her mother didn't want to be separated from her husband after death.

Raquel respected her wishes and put her Jewish mother to rest in the same crypt with her Catholic father. There isn't even a Jewish star to mark her Jewish difference in the sea of crucifixes.

After learning the story of Raquel's mother, I think about the story of my Aunt Ida, my father's older sister. In the early 1950s, the family was living in a tenement on Calle Oficios in La Habana Vieja. Ida ran away at the age of fifteen with a sailor, married him, later divorced, and then married another man,

both times choosing Cuban husbands who weren't Jewish. My grandmother was devastated by Ida's rebellious ways. She tore her clothes as if her daughter had died. But as the years passed, she came to accept the two children and four grandchildren born of Ida's marriages, came to accept that Ida had abandoned her Jewish ways. The one thing she couldn't accept was that at her death Ida would rest for all eternity among non-Jews.

An entire diaspora later, my grandmother died in Canarsie, where she'd ended up living next door to the best friend from Turkey who'd been her neighbor in Cuba too. It was my mother who found the envelope in my grandmother's robe labeled with the words *para el entierro de Ida*—"for Ida's burial." The envelope was stuffed with four hundred dollars in five and ten dollar bills that my grandmother had saved, month upon month, from her grocery money—all so that Ida might be buried in a Jewish cemetery.

But my Aunt Ida—thank God—hasn't died yet. I've never dared to ask her what she thinks about the four hundred dollars her mother left in preparation for her demise.

Maybe I shouldn't have been so shocked to find Jews in Cuba who'd become utterly relaxed about our basic Jewish prohibitions—my Aunt Ida had chosen that path long ago. Perhaps my grandmother's stubborn effort to bring Aunt Ida back to the tribe, by trying to guarantee that at least she'd be with her people at death, had led me to think that Jews only ended up buried among non-Jews as a last resort. I guess that's why I was amazed by the fearlessness of Raquel's mother. She dared to imagine love could be stronger than our tribal obligation, stronger than the punishment of exile.

Among Jews there is only one prayer for the dead and that is the Mourner's Kaddish. It is a prayer one is obligated to recite for one's parents, and that one can also recite for one's closest relatives—a spouse, a child, a sibling. The Kaddish is a portable prayer. It is brief, easy to remember, hypnotic. It doesn't speak of the afterlife, it speaks of the desire for peace. When Jews invented their prayer for the dead, they knew they were a wandering people, a people always searching for a home someplace, a people who might not always find a final resting place in a Jewish cemetery.

I have never recited the Kaddish. My parents are fortunately still alive, and

I was taught that until your parents have died, you must not recite the Kaddish for anyone. It is bad luck to do so. This fear is a deeply ingrained part of the Jewish superstitiousness that has been passed on to me. I can't overcome the fear, even though I've learned that many Jews now believe the Kaddish can be recited at any time for people you wish to honor.

It's with fear that I am offering this chapter as a Kaddish.

I want it to be a Kaddish for all the Jews in Cuba who rest in Jewish cemeteries.

And I want it to also be a Kaddish for all those Jews in Cuba who, like Raquel's mother, chose to end their lives in exile from the tribe—they too are a part of us and must not be given up for lost.

II

Havana

3

A TOUR OF

HAVANA'S SYNAGOGUES

Of all the old photographs my family brought out of Cuba, one always caught my attention: I am a small child, standing in front of a synagogue in Havana.

When I saw this photograph for the first time, I remember asking my mother where the synagogue was located.

She looked at me wistfully and said, "A block from our apartment. Not even a block. We could see it from our two bedrooms and from the terrace. It was called the Patronato. It was the prettiest synagogue in Cuba. It was new when we moved next door. We lived so close, we saw it every day. I never thought a day would come when I wouldn't see it again."

How could I have imagined that I would eventually return dozens of times to the Patronato? That I would see the synagogue my mother thought was so pretty from our abandoned apartment? I would visually reclaim the world my mother stopped seeing almost half a

century ago—as if by seeing it with my eyes I'd somehow be able to give it back to her.

On my first return trips to Cuba in the 1990s, it wasn't hard for me to find my way to the Patronato. The neighbors who'd lived down the hall from us before we left Cuba were still living in the same apartment in our old building. Every time I went to the Patronato, I had to pass by the building, so I made it a habit to visit our former neighbors on my way to or from the synagogue. Consuelito, a green-eyed blond of my mother's generation, welcomed the opportunity to reminisce about the old days whenever she saw me. She was an "insile," who lived with as much nostalgia for the 1950s as a Cuban "exile" in the United States. She had even kept the swizzle sticks from the last New Year's Eve party in 1958 before the Revolution swept into Havana.

All this somehow seemed *beshert*—meant to be—as if the girl in the childhood photograph would not let me turn my back on the Patronato and the rented apartment down the street that had once been my Cuban home.

The Patronato

On a Saturday morning in 1991 I had wandered in for Shabbat services at the Patronato and found a handful of other congregants trying their best to follow along as Jewish elders intoned chants and prayers at the dilapidated *bimah* in the front of the room. The elders knew enough Hebrew to read from the prayer books, but when it came time to read the Torah portion for the week, they didn't know how to read from the scroll. They read in Hebrew from the printed text, the *chumash*, which they placed on top of the open scroll. Sweat lined their brows, for the dusty fans were no match for the hot, stuffy air that clouded the cavernous sanctuary, which had been built for a large congregation that had been gone for decades. Pigeons flew in and out through the torn roof.

The Jews of Cuba had not yet been "discovered" by American Jews and Hollywood filmmaker Steven Spielberg. As the 1990s unfolded, I watched as the Patronato was transformed before my eyes, this synagogue that I associated with my lost childhood. By the year 2000 it had been restored to its former

grandeur with support from the Joint Distribution Committee as well as the Greater Miami Jewish Federation. Despite their opposition to the Castro regime, several wealthy Cuban Jews in the Miami Federation had decided to participate in the restoration of the Patronato because they couldn't bear to see their beloved Cuban synagogue fall to ruins. Even though it was unlikely they would return to live in Cuba, they wanted to leave a monument to their presence on the island and allow other Jews to build a new community in the synagogue they had left behind.

When the Patronato reopened, there were plush seats again in the main sanctuary, central air conditioning had been installed, a computer center was provided by ORT, and a video screening room made it possible for the youth to form a film club.

On the second floor of the Patronato, a pharmacy was created to provide medications and vitamins to the Jewish community and any others who requested it. To promote goodwill, the Joint Distribution Committee also arranged for American Jewish doctors to period-

ically volunteer their time in Cuban hospitals.

With its many programs and facilities, the Patronato has become the headquarters for the revived Jewish community of Cuba. It was a Jewish center built on a huge scale by Cuba's richest Jews before the Revolution—the "patrons" of the community, thus the word "Patronato"—and the patina of power and wealth has stuck, as has the sense that the Patronato is the core of Jewish life in Cuba. The location of the synagogue, near La Rampa and hotels in Vedado, makes it easy for foreigners to find, and they often assume it's the only synagogue that exists on the island. Just about every Jewish visitor makes a pilgrimage to the Patronato; it is a required stop on Jewish Cuba missions and tours.

Almost all the donations from abroad land in the Patronato, which occupies a building that takes up almost an entire block off Linea, a major street in Havana that leads to the Malecón and the sea. Imposing as the building is today, the Patronato was much larger in the past. Half of the original structure was sold to the Ministry of Culture during a moment of low religious participation and turned into the Bertolt Brecht Theater. But the Patronato is still impressive. Its distinctive modernist architecture has a rainbow-like arch that rises over the sanctuary, expressing a hopeful vision of the Jewish future. Sculptured bronze symbols of the twelve tribes of Israel line the façade.

When Fidel Castro came to meet with the Jews for the first and only time in 1998, the same year Pope John Paul II visited Cuba, the encounter was held at the Patronato. It was the last day of Hanukkah, or Janucá, as it is written in Spanish. The eighth candle of the menorah would be lit to commemorate the miracle of the oil that was only supposed to last one day and lasted eight days. According to Jewish tradition, that oil was found by a handful of Maccabean rebels when they reclaimed the destroyed Temple of Jerusalem after resisting Hellenic rule. One doesn't have to strain the metaphor to see the parallel between the Cuban revolutionary struggle to gain freedom from U.S. domination and the Jewish story of a small group of warriors winning their religious autonomy against a great imperial power. On the day of the Janucá party, which fell on Sunday, December 20, word came that Fidel Castro would be present. By nightfall, blue-uniformed police were posted all along the block of the Patronato.

Fidel strode into the room in green fatigues and soldier's boots. I saw the myth come so close I could have reached out my hand and stroked his beard. It is well known that, in his presence, people are transformed. Men yearn for his charisma. And even intelligent women become air-headed coquettes, offering praise, blowing kisses. I promised myself I would stay calm. I stationed myself near the door in case I had a panic attack. But then I saw two bodyguards guarding the exit. I couldn't leave. The festivities began: a speech by Dr. Miller, another speech by the young Argentine Jewish leader sent to Cuba to educate the community, the singing of "Oseh Shalom," the song of peace, a children's skit, Israeli dancing, and the lighting of the candles. And then, Fidel Castro.

With the menorah behind him, dreidel decorations hanging above his head, and children sitting on the floor munching their candies and chocolates, Fidel Castro stood and spoke for nearly an hour. In his trademark style, he talked without notes and about a wide range of subjects, but he was hoarse and his voice barely managed to travel to the back of the room. He spoke of Abraham's near sacrifice of his son Isaac, comparing it to Aztec sacrifice. He spoke of the human sacrifice of the Holocaust and the importance of ending racism. He spoke of the gifts that the Jews had given to the world: not only their own religion, but Christianity, Islam, and Marxism. Of course, he said, chuckling, everyone knows that his religion is Marxism.

He spoke of much else that I can't remember, because as the speech progressed, I found myself suddenly "shooting" pictures of him. From the back of the room, I moved to the front and every few minutes I pressed the shutter, sending out flashes of light. A hawk-eyed bodyguard watched me intently. If I were an assassin, I thought . . . and dared not think any further, for fear my thoughts might be heard. So many attempts had been made on Fidel Castro's life; he'd survived poisoned milkshakes and exploding cigars. In Cuba, there are people who believe he has spiritual protection from the heart of Africa; they say he received potent magical power directly from the Yoruba priests.

At the end of his speech children and adults ran to greet him. I attempted to step forward to take more pictures, but the bodyguard shoved me back with a flick of his wrist, enough to let me feel the might of those who surround Fidel Castro. Maybe the bodyguard *had heard* my thoughts . . . I tried as an anthropologist to marvel at what had taken place—a communist leader buoyantly embracing the Jewish people, something unheard of in modern times—but as the daughter of Cuban exiles I couldn't join the others who were having their pictures taken with the Comandante. I quietly disappeared out into the street like a ghost.

It was Adela Dworin, previously the librarian and vice president of the Patronato and now the president of the Jewish community of Cuba, who had invited Fidel Castro to meet with the Jewish community, winning him over with her relaxed manner and cooing lullaby voice, behind which is a determined woman. Adela has been associated with the Patronato and the Jewish library's collection of 15,000 books since her youth, when she gave up her budding law career to dedicate herself to preserving Jewish memory in Cuba. There is nothing Adela doesn't know about the history of the Jewish community. When we met, the first thing she told me was that she'd never forgotten the funeral of my cousin Henry, how hard it rained, how my Aunt Zoila cried bitterly.

Since the boom in American interest in the Jews of Cuba, hardly a day goes by when Adela doesn't give a tour of the Patronato. She is fluent in English and Yiddish and for the last decade and a half she has greeted every Jewish group and every Jewish celebrity who has traipsed through Cuba looking for the Jews.

When Adela isn't giving tours of the Patronato, she can be found serenely sitting at her desk under the Star of David bookshelf that was carved into the wall by the founders of the temple who left in the early 1960s.

And on any given day, when it's not tourists coming by looking for Jews,

it's regular Cubans stopping in to inquire about how to join the Jewish community.

"What do we need to do to become Jews?" these Cubans will ask. They act as if there's a checklist of activities they need to carry out and then the matter will be settled.

Adela always tells them the same thing: that conversions are only available for descendents of Jews or those who are married to Jews.

The disappointed people take their leave and Adela sighs. "What can we do?" she says. "It would be madness to allow everybody who comes in off the street to convert."

A constant stream of individuals stop by to inquire if by any chance they might happen to be Jewish. Word has gotten around that being Jewish in Cuba brings benefits—besides the chicken dinners on Friday night and Saturday midday, there is access to alternative information, a well-stocked pharmacy, a lively set of social events, and the possibility of leaving Cuba via Israel. For practical and sentimental reasons, Cubans want to learn whether a strange family surname, or the memory of a grandmother who didn't eat pork, might be sufficient evidence of their Jewish heritage. These would-be Jews wander into the Patronato and it is Adela who must turn them away. With the assistance of the Joint Distribution Committee, the island has been scoured from end to end, and Adela knows there aren't very many hidden Jews left to find in Cuba.

For members of the Jewish community, the Patronato is a crossroads where locals and foreigners intersect, and it is also an educational center and a travel agency of sorts, for permission to leave for Israel must come from Adela and other Jewish leaders, who authorize departures and control the flow of information. On weekdays people come for the Hebrew classes—which are a necessity for those emigrating to Israel—or to use the computers upstairs in the ORT-funded computing room, or simply to relax in one of the wicker chairs in the lobby. They also come when a child has a sudden fever and they need an aspirin. Medicines are distributed at the Patronato on Tuesday afternoons by Dr. Rosa Behar, but in cases of emergency people go directly to Adela. She has a stash of medicines, vitamins, powdered milk, candies, and chocolates, all kept under lock and key in a large closet at the entrance to the library. If you're a Jew in Cuba, it's wise to be on good terms with Adela.

Chevet Ahim and Centro Hebreo Sefaradí

While the Patronato has flourished, the oldest synagogue in Cuba, the Chevet Ahim in Old Havana, has languished. This Sephardic synagogue, which once had a sanctuary, a school, a library, and a restaurant in its second-floor location, was forced to close in 1995 because of the tumbledown state of the building. But the Star of David lamp remains tethered to the ceiling that is on the verge of collapsing. Rumors have been circulating for some time that Eusebio Leal, the historian of the city, has plans to turn the building into a Jewish Museum—but there are no signs yet of any restorations.

With the loss of the Chevet Ahim synagogue, the Centro Hebreo Sefaradí has become the only remaining institutional legacy of the Sephardic presence in Cuba. When it was first conceived before the Revolution, the Centro Sefaradí had been intended to be the Sephardic equivalent to the Patronato. It is located just a few blocks away in Vedado, up the block from the Avenida de los Presidentes. Construction of the temple began in 1957, and though initial prayers were recited in 1958 for Rosh Hashanah, it was not completed until after the Revolution in 1960. There was enough time to engrave the names of the temple founders on a plaque by the entrance before they all fled.

The Centro Sefaradí hasn't received anywhere near the attention of the Patronato, and certainly nothing close to the same level of funding, but it survives because of the dedication of its president, José Levy Tur. Its main sanctuary, a huge auditorium with an Orthodox-style balcony for the women to sit separately from the men, is no longer in use for Jewish prayer and ritual. The Afrocuban band Síntesis rents the space from the Centro Sefaradí for their rehearsals. Weekly religious services take place in a small room next door, which was built to be used for the women's club meetings. A *bimah*, or ark, has been set up in the room and the Torahs have been brought over from the Chevet Ahim synagogue. In the afternoons, if you happen to be in the little sanctuary, you can hear Síntesis singing to the Afrocuban deities, the *orishas*, from the other side of the wall.

On Friday nights and Saturday mornings, it is older Jews of Sephardic heritage, and their families, who come to the Centro Sefaradí.

After prayers, they come to chat and to pass the time.

I have always appreciated the homey feeling of the Centro Sefaradí. The

meals after religious services are more creole in style at the Sefaradí than at the other Havana synagogues, where the food tends to be very bland without being any more kosher. At the Centro Sefaradí they will serve you a generous portion of rice, black beans, and savory chopped-meat picadillo. Bread is often lacking, but there is all the matzah you can eat. And there's always Cuban coffee, sweetened with just the right amount of sugar.

The warm-hearted Cuban spirit of the Centro Sefaradí has much to do with José Levy's leadership. For Levy, his Sephardic legacy is tied to the memory of his father. Like many other Sephardic Jewish men who came alone to Cuba from Turkey, his father had married out of the Jewish faith. But his father felt anguished at the thought that the Jewish bond would be broken in the next generation. He managed to pass on to José an abiding passion for their heritage. After retiring from the merchant marine, José taught himself Hebrew and Jewish history. Each week at Saturday morning services at the Centro Sefaradí, he offers his own commentary on the Torah. Even though José also

married out of the faith—in fact, he has outmarried three times—he made it a point to bring his younger daughter Danayda, born from his second marriage to an Afrocuban woman, into the Jewish fold. Gradually he passed on everything he knew about Judaism to her, and Danayda accepted her father's legacy with the same love with which it had been given. At the same time, she learned tolerance for other religions, growing into adulthood living with a mother who is a Jehovah's Witness and an older sister who believes in Santería.

At a time when few black faces were visible in the Jewish community in Cuba, it took pride and perseverance for Levy to claim a Jewish birthright for his daughter. He brought Danayda with him to every Jewish ritual from the time she was a little girl. She learned to stand tall among the men who held the Torah and wrapped themselves in the blue-striped prayer shawls, and that was how she learned to be a Jew.

Adath Israel

The Patronato and the Centro Sefaradí have affiliated with the Conservative Jewish movement in the United States and both men and women participate equally in leading religious services. In contrast, the Adath Israel synagogue in Old Havana, at the intersection of Acosta and Picota, has affiliated with the Lubavitch of Argentina and Canada and follows Orthodox norms and ritual observance. The synagogue houses the only *mikvah* (ritual bath) in Cuba, which was restored in 2005. Among Orthodox women, the *mikvah* is used monthly for purification following menstruation, but in Cuba its main use will be for women and men undergoing conversion to Judaism, which requires immersion in water after the convert has passed an examination on Jewish history and law with a court of three rabbis. Before the *mikvah* was restored, Jewish converts immersed themselves in the sea, which is all around them on the island of Cuba, as the rabbis watched; now the converts will forget the sea when they become Jews.

Adath Israel, completed in 1959, is located in the working-class neighborhood near the Port of Havana where the majority of the Jews lived when they

first arrived. The streets are dirty, crooked, and narrow. People live in crowded apartments and they can be seen carrying plastic buckets filled with water from a corner hydrant when there is no running water in their homes, which is often. The sight of well-showered American Jews decked out in shorts, sneakers, and cameras, not to mention the occasional bearded and black-robed Lubavitch rabbi, still attracts some attention in the neighborhood, but people have mostly gotten used to these foreigners, and with typical Cuban humor they joke about how the *polacos* have suddenly become very popular.

Under the influence of the Lubavitch, who visit periodically but have not yet established a permanent presence in Cuba, religious services are held daily, morning and afternoon, at Adath Israel. Since it is an Orthodox temple, it is only the men who read from the Torah and lead services. The women sit on the other side of the divider, some of them praying, some of them chatting with each other, some of them daydreaming.

Roberto Behar, who leads services and chants Torah at Adath Israel, is not

my relative, but he was a close friend of my father in their youth. They were both children of poor Turkish immigrants living in La Habana Vieja. They played dominoes together, and when my father was dating my mother, Roberto briefly dated my Aunt Sylvia. But since those years he and my father haven't spoken.

I see Roberto resting during a break in the services, bent as if by the weight of the *tefillin* strapped to his head—the leather box filled with biblical verses that Jewish men must wear every morning when they pray in the Orthodox tradition. And I think about the message he sent to my father, which I recorded with my video camera: "Alberto, your daughter wants to know how we know each other. Well, we studied together at the Teodoro Hertzl school. We were young then. Now we're old. But we're still alive. We're still alive! So what's the problem?"

4

THE KOSHER BUTCHER SHOP

The most photographed kosher butcher shop in the world has to be the kosher butcher shop around the corner from the Adath Israel synagogue on Calle Cuba, between Acosta and Jesús María. Foreign observers are continually amazed to learn the shop is open for business in Castro's Cuba.

Rationed kosher beef has been provided in the shop to registered members of the Jewish community since the earliest years of the Revolution. Such generosity toward the Jews is based on a curious cultural interpretation. In Cuba, the most common form of meat is pork, and since Jews are forbidden by their religion to eat pork, this deprivation needs to be compensated by allowing them a ration of beef. And that ration of beef makes the Jews uniquely privileged. While the Revolution brought health and education to the masses, it turned beef into a luxury food. Beef has been in short supply for decades, which is why Cubans who can remember the old days will often fantasize about eating a big plate of pounded palomilla steak and onions (always a favorite at Miami Cuban restaurants). Cattle are so tightly controlled that it is a federal crime to slaughter a cow without official permission. You hear Cubans joking frequently about how killing a cow will land you in jail for a longer sentence than killing your mother!

Samuel Zagavalov Montero, son of a Russian immigrant, has been working in the shop since 1980. I ask him to explain how the meat is distributed to members of the Jewish community.

"We give three-quarters of a pound of meat per person three or four times

a month. We give two chickens every month to those who are on special diets. Ours is the only butcher shop in Cuba that sells beef. It costs one Cuban peso for three-quarters of a pound. We also give people soup bones if they want them."

I ask Samuel if Humberto and I might accompany him some time when he slaughters a cow, so we can take pictures.

Samuel looks at me as if I'm a raving lunatic.

"It's bloody and it's dangerous," he says.

He doesn't know if he could get permission for us to be there. Maybe Humberto could go, but he doubts I could.

And just to be sure I understand how impossible my request is, he explains, "The slaughterhouse is in Nueva Paz. When we go sacrifice a cow we leave Havana at four in the morning. It take us two to three hours to select our cattle. Then we have to perform the sacrifice. After we behead the animal, we have to drain the blood, weigh the carcass, and load up the car. We get back to

Havana at four in the afternoon. Then we have to remove the bones and be ready the next day at six in the morning to distribute the meat."

Samuel and his partner at the shop, Mario Parra Grinberg, look exhausted. All the meat has been given out. They have scrubbed the marble counter clean. The last chunks of beef are wrapped in tightly knotted plastic bags. There is a smell of ammonia.

Samuel, being Cuban, after all, wants to make sure that our conversation ends on a friendly note. He knows he's let me down by declaring the slaughterhouse off limits to me as a woman and a foreigner. He doesn't want me to go away upset with him.

He says, with a lopsided smile, "In this neighborhood everyone knows me. When a person gets sick, we help him or her out with a bit of beef. People here respect us. They call this the butcher shop of the *polacos*—the Poles. People are always asking me, 'What do I have to do to become Jewish?' They'll say, 'Find me a *polaco*! Find me a *polaca*! So I can get married and eat beef for the rest of my life.'"

5

THE SHIRT THAT
HOLDS SADNESS

When I arrive at the Patronato, I walk past the bronze José Martí bust at the entrance, past the framed picture of the great medieval Sephardic doctor and philosopher Maimonides, past the framed picture of Einstein, and go directly inside to the library. There are an assortment of books in Spanish, Yiddish, Hebrew, and English, but most people go to the library not to read but to find out the latest gossip.

Adela Dworin is sitting at her usual place under the Star of David bookshelf.

"What's new?" Adela asks, looking up from some paperwork.

I tell her that in a few minutes I'm going to be meeting with Ida Gutstadt. "We want to take pictures of Ida with her father's shirt," I add.

"Oh, no! That means we have to find the shirt!" she exclaims. "Let's wait until Pavel arrives. He'll know where it is."

I try not to worry as I wait for Ida to arrive.

A few minutes later, Ida comes rushing into the library. She is lean and elegant with shining pale eyes that look almost transparent.

"Sorry I'm late," she says.

After Ida and Adela greet each other, Adela immediately tells Ida that she has no idea where her father's shirt might be. Ida reassures Adela that the shirt is bound to appear. Adela isn't so sure. She unlocks her secret closet, where she keeps her stash of medicines and chocolates, and hunts around aimlessly.

"I just have no idea where it is!" Adela repeats. "I don't know where Pavel could have put it!"

Now I really do begin to worry. Could they really have lost such an irreplaceable garment? Why isn't it being stored in a more secure place?

Not a moment too soon, Pavel Tennebaum appears. A very tall, very serious young man, Pavel is Adela's trusted assistant in the office.

"Pavel, where's the shirt?" Adela asks. "Ida's father's shirt?"

Stopping just short of rolling his eyes, Pavel says there's no need to make a fuss. He knows exactly where the shirt is. It's on the top shelf in the secret closet. No one else could have retrieved the shirt without a stepladder. But Pavel, the tallest Jew in Cuba, lifts an arm and finds it.

Ida is as relieved as I am. She takes the shirt from Pavel and gently hands it to me.

"Here's the shirt." And she adds, "The shirt my father wore in Auschwitz."

The shirt is striped and long-sleeved and the fabric has become flower-petal soft from many washings. I hold it only for a moment, afraid to have it in my hands, and set it down on the table between us.

"I donated my father's shirt to the Patronato about five years ago," Ida says. "It wasn't going to be of any use to anyone if it stayed in my house."

"Did your father bring the shirt to Cuba?"

"Yes, he brought the shirt and the pants with him to Cuba. The pants developed holes and my mother threw them away. But he'd wear the shirt when he felt cold. I'd ask him, 'Why do you wear it, if it makes you sad?' He liked to wear it. He'd watch Russian war movies while wearing the shirt. They showed those movies here a lot during the early years of the Revolution. He'd torture himself watching those Russian war movies. His eyes would fill with tears. It bothered me to see him like that. His life was sad. He chose to hold on to the sadness. The sadness had put down roots inside him."

"What did your father tell you about his experience in Auschwitz?"

"He refused to speak about his time in the camp. What I know is that he was from Lodz and my mother was from Pioterkov. They were married in 1941 in Poland and my sister was born in 1942 in Siberia. They were in the Warsaw Ghetto. My father was taken to Auschwitz in 1944. My mother was in hiding with my sister. My father wasn't liberated from the camp. He managed to escape from a train while being transferred between wagons. He was in the camp for several months. Then he was in hiding until the war ended."

"When did your family get to Cuba?"

"My father, my mother, and my sister arrived on May 4, 1948."

Ida rustles through her handbag and pulls out an old passport. "Look, I brought the Polish passport, so you could see it. This is the passport my mother and sister used to enter Cuba. I was born twenty-five days after they arrived."

"How did your parents adjust to living in Cuba?"

"Somehow my father was able to communicate with Cubans and he set up a printing press. He produced labels for condensed milk cans. After the Revolution he taught Russian. He was very worn out. He was twenty years older than my mother. He felt too old to start again somewhere else. So he decided we would stay. My mother said it was the only thing she couldn't forgive, that he'd decided we should stay in Cuba."

"Was your mother against the Revolution?"

"My mother was never happy in Cuba, period. She didn't feel any affinity with Cubans. Sometimes she'd call me and I'd say to her, 'I'll be there in a little while.' And she would say, 'Drop what you're doing and come now.' What she couldn't stand about Cubans was that they weren't punctual, they were too informal. She never adapted. She lived in Cuba for fifty-two years and never adapted. My mother spoke Spanish as if she'd just arrived from Poland. In our house we all spoke Yiddish. When my parents didn't want me and my sister to understand what they were saying, they spoke in Polish."

Ida rubs her temples and closes her eyes. When she looks back at me again, she says, "They're all gone. My father died in 1974, my mother in 2000, and my sister in 2001."

She herself is divorced. She has two daughters. One lives in Cuba and the other in the Dominican Republic with her husband and two children.

"Did you have a Jewish upbringing?"

"As a child, I remember that my father was very Jewish. I'd go with him to Adath Israel on Saturdays. But not my mother. She used to say she was an atheist. When my father died, my mother refused to let him be buried in the Jewish cemetery. My mother and my sister are buried there in Guanabacoa, because I made the decision. My father had wanted to be buried in the Jewish cemetery, but my mother didn't allow it. She said God didn't exist. If God existed, the terrible things that happened in the war wouldn't have happened. 'So many died,' she would say. 'A true God wouldn't have permitted such a thing.' She was very negative. In my mother's house we never smiled."

Although she considers herself a revolutionary, Ida has drawn closer to her father's Jewish spirituality than to her mother's atheism. "Returning to my roots has been good for me," she says. "There isn't a conflict anymore between the Communist Party and religion. I feel good at the Patronato. I feel good when I come to Saturday services. I remember my father when I'm here. It also makes me sad. I'm like my father. I do things that make me sad."

It's almost one o'clock when Humberto arrives, the hour when Ida teaches a computer course at the Patronato. Humberto starts snapping pictures: Ida holding the old Polish passport, and then one photograph after another of her father's concentration camp shirt.

But Humberto isn't satisfied with the light in the library and we step outside to the front of the building. He photographs Ida holding up the shirt. He gets close to Ida, he moves away, he tries different angles. And finally, when she thinks he's done, she folds up the shirt lovingly, as if it still holds her father's spirit, and nestles it between her hands and presses it to her body.

We go back inside to gather our things and Ida hands her father's folded-up shirt to Adela.

"Here, put it away," she says. And in the next breath, "Adela, do you think you could spare an aspirin?"

"Yes, of course," Adela replies.

Adela goes to the secret closet and brings out an enormous container of aspirin. She pours out a handful and wraps them in a piece of heavy brown paper.

"Here, take these. They're the stronger ones."

"It never fails," Ida says. "Touching that shirt for too long always gives me the most awful headache."

6

LOS PRINSTEIN

The Prinstein family, or los Prinstein, lives just four blocks from the Patronato, and it's a good thing because they spend so much of their time there. Any day of the week you can see David Prinstein's 1956 Chevy parked in front of the synagogue.

Marlen leads Shabbat services on Saturday, teaches Hebrew to the children in the Sunday school, and is one of the leaders of the Israeli folk dance group. In addition, she teaches in the provincial cities of Campechuela and Manzanillo, preparing children who are of bar mitzvah age and adults who wish to convert to Judaism. David leads Kabbalat Shabbat services every Friday and runs errands for the synagogue with his Chevy. They are both remunerated for their work through the Joint Distribution Committee.

Their children dedicate all their free time to the synagogue. Victor and young David (children from David Prinstein's first marriage) have become Torah readers since their bar mitzvahs. David, as well as Jessica, are both active in the dance group.

Jessica prides herself on having been chosen several times to be Queen Esther for the synagogue's Purim festivals. She adores wearing the donated tiara, costume, and elbow-length gloves, even when it isn't Purim.

But the member of the family who has attracted the most attention is five-year-old Moisés, who's become a poster boy for the Jewish revival in Cuba. By the age of three he had memorized the Jewish blessings for the wine and the bread. He recites these prayers without fail each week before the congregation sits down to the weekly chicken lunch at the Patronato following Saturday services. His dedication has won him the attention of American visitors, including Steven Spielberg. On his visit to the Patronato, Spielberg knelt and shook hands with Moisés, who failed to see what all the fuss was about.

As Marlen brews espresso coffee for us during a visit to the family's apartment, she says, "Sometimes I have to bring dinner to the Patronato and get the kids to wash up there. We practically live in the Patronato!"

The late afternoon sun pours through the open window, the sea visible in the distance. With sugary coffee in hand, I take a seat with los Prinstein in the living room. I think they must be a happy family, because they have no problem squeezing next to one another on the brown leather couches and armchairs that fill all the available space. I notice there aren't any traditional wooden rocking chairs. Leaning against one of the walls is an entertainment center that includes a large television, a VCR, and a DVD player, things not commonly found in Cuban households.

Marlen, who was trained as a lawyer and is a convert to Judaism, has an exuberant personality, and it is she who eagerly begins to tell the story.

"My family is extremely atheist," she says. "My parents are military people. Imagine, both of them worked for the Ministry of the Interior. They completely frowned upon religion. They're very Fidelista, they believe in the monotheism of Fidel."

She glances at David, who nods and smiles. "Go on," he says.

Marlen continues, "When David and I married, I went to his house and got to know his Polish grandfather, one of the few *polacos* left in Cuba, and that was how I started learning about the Jews. His grandfather had books in Hebrew and it shocked me to see these books in another language. The first Jewish ritual I witnessed was the *shiva* for David's grandfather. He died at the age of ninety in 1991."

David adds the next strand to the story. "I was a military man myself, a member of the armed forces. I had to keep quiet about my Jewish identity, even though it says on my record that I'm of Jewish origin. The one thing I always did was spend Passover with my grandfather. I was born in 1963 and was circumcised on the eighth day after birth, but I didn't have a bar mitzvah. By then my father had distanced himself from Judaism. He's part of the lost generation."

The "lost generation" refers to the middle generation of Jewish revolutionaries who broke with the religious traditions of their parents, letting Judaism lapse and synagogues fall into disrepair. Now it is their children who want to return to their heritage and recover the legacy of the Jewish immigrants.

I ask David if his father was involved with the Revolution.

"Oh, yes," he replies. "My father and my aunt were founding members of the Communist Party. But I'd go with my grandfather to the kosher butcher shop to get the meat." He pauses to reflect for a moment on these disparate influences, and then says, "When I joined the Jewish community, I didn't believe in anything. What do Jews believe in? Mainly the idea of one God, right? Slowly, very slowly, I started learning and started to believe."

David is a de-assimilated Jew, a Jew who could easily have remained assimilated into Cuban society and the Revolution, but who has chosen to be outspoken about his Jewish identity. While Marlen comes to Judaism as a convert, she has exactly the same motivations as David for choosing to identify as Jewish. Both have rejected revolutionary atheism, both have pulled away from the dominant political system, both have found the values of their parents to be spiritually unsatisfying, both have declared their inability to keep believing in the "monotheism of Fidel." Becoming Jewish was *their* revolutionary act; or, at least, it was more revolutionary than bowing unquestioningly to the Revolution that had been handed down to them. I think about how people like David and Marlen have been the soul behind the Jewish renaissance in Cuba. They took a risk, a risk born of a heartfelt spiritual quest, in choosing Judaism over communism, and ultimately reaped the religious and economic rewards of being aligned with the Patronato. Basking in their religious freedom, they built a strong Jewish family, a showcase Jewish family, giving visitors to Cuba hope that Judaism won't perish from the island.

"Show her the bar mitzvah pictures!" Jessica says.

From a shelf in the entertainment center, Marlen pulls out a big box with the photographs of Victor's 2002 bar mitzvah and young David's in 2004.

"We also have both of the bar mitzvahs on video," David says, pointing to a shelf with several videotapes neatly lined up in a row.

"Any time you want to see the videos, just let us know," Marlen says.

Victor, who has been listening attentively, says that his bar mitzvah was made possible through a donation sent by an American Jewish girl, and shows me a news clipping to prove it.

"With Her Bat Mitzvah Money, New Jersey Girl Helps Cuban Kids." The New Jersey girl, I learn, is Jennifer Recant, daughter of Will Recant, the director of the Latin American Division for the Joint Distribution Committee. She made the decision to donate $600 to help six young Cubans, including Victor, obtain Hebrew lessons and purchase ritual items, including prayer books, *tefillin*, and *tallitot*, for their bar and bat mitzvahs. Traveling to Cuba with her father, she was also able to be present at Victor's bar mitzvah. On her return to New Jersey, she commented to the reporter that one of the things that most impressed her about meeting the Jews of Cuba was seeing "how little they have," but how well they were able to make do. And she added, "We have so much here, but even a penny goes so far there."

7

IN THE REALM OF LOST THINGS

Alberto Behar Medrano, a computer engineer, lives with his wife, Carucha, in the house that belonged to his grandparents, who passed away more than twenty years ago. Located in a quiet neighborhood not far from Havana, the house opens onto the living room where big old rocking chairs rest on pink and brown tile floors so smooth and so spotless as soon as you enter you have an urge to walk barefoot. Alberto says that as a boy he liked to stare at the tile floors and ponder the arabesques of its design.

Here, you know the ghosts of the ancestors have not been shooed away.

This is how Alberto prefers it.

Carucha feels differently. She doesn't like to have old photographs hanging everywhere. She doesn't like to have to look every day at photographs of people who are gone, whether through the power of death or the power of diaspora. Either way, in the end it's the same—they are gone. But despite her objections, such photographs cling to the walls: there is one of Alberto's father, who passed away in 1987, and another of Alberto's aunt Regina who left Cuba in 1962 and has never returned.

Alberto confesses that there is something melancholy about such photographs.

"I know I'm being a masochist," he announces. "Always remembering those who are no longer here." He's like his grandfather, about whom he says, "The poor man, he kept every scrap of paper anyone ever gave him."

Alberto lifts his gaze up to the doorframe at the entrance to the house.

"You see that mezuzah? It was there always. My grandfather kept it inside the house, not outside. I've never moved it. It's exactly where it's always been. We haven't changed anything in the house. For better or for worse, we've kept things the same."

We follow Alberto to the bedroom. From the chifforobe he pulls out a velvet pouch with an embroidered Jewish star. Then he empties several drawers and boxes that are stuffed with old photographs and documents.

"This *kippah* belonged to my grandfather."

Inside the satin lining of the skullcap, the words, "Souvenir of the wedding of Isolina and Jaime." The date is clearly stamped: 1959.

Alberto holds up an old *tallit*, a prayer shawl that is slightly yellowed. It also belonged to his grandfather, a Sephardic Jew from Turkey.

Alberto remarks, "My grandfather was religious. That's why I like the work I do in the Patronato preparing children for their bar and bat mitzvahs. I feel that I'm passing the culture on to them. I'm maintaining Jewish traditions."

I've seen Alberto at the Patronato teaching the children, seen his enthusiasm and selfless devotion. He's the most spiritual Jew in Cuba, unwavering in his soul-searching. "I'm not an Orthodox Jew," he adds. "I wasn't brought up in that tradition and our conditions here make it impossible for us to live that way. But I remember how my grandfather would curse me when I'd turn on the lights on Shabbat. I would do it on purpose to pester him. He was religious. Not my father."

Alberto's father supported the Revolution. He spoke good Russian. But when he was dying, he asked to be buried in the Sephardic cemetery in Guanabacoa, across the train tracks. Alberto questioned his father's wish, reminding him that he'd never believed in religion. His father insisted he wanted to be buried where his parents were buried, together with other Jews. At the funeral, when asked to recite the Kaddish, Alberto said he had no idea what Kaddish was. It was the first time he'd heard of the existence of this ancient Jewish

prayer of mourning, which children are obligated to recite when they lose their mother or father.

"Did your mother die soon after your father?"

He looks at me as if I've uttered a curse.

"My mother is alive. She left for Miami in 1993."

He explains that his mother had heart problems and the medication she needed was difficult to find in Cuba. Once in Miami the family convinced her to stay, so she wouldn't have to struggle so much.

After his mother's departure, Alberto felt alone, abandoned. It was just him and Carucha—no one else remained. Both his grandparents had died, his father had died, his mother had left for Miami, and then in 1994 his brother left for Israel. Alberto's mother isn't Jewish, but the sadness of seeing her go led him to the Jewish community. Carucha, though not Jewish, gave Alberto moral support as he underwent circumcision, converted, learned to chant the Torah, and became not only the most spiritual person in the Jewish community but one of the most knowledgeable.

We sift through the pile of papers scattered on the bed. Alberto says, "Look, I have the results of my Aunt Regina's health examination. She needed this to be able to leave Cuba." He hadn't been able to throw it away. It was a bond, however flimsy, to the aunt he spoke to on the phone regularly, but never saw face-to-face.

Carucha now calls to us from the kitchen. Dinner is ready, she says. She doesn't want the food to get cold.

The dinner is delicious: chicken with black beans and rice, cabbage and tomato salad, a shot of coffee, and shredded sweet syrupy coconut that I can't get enough of. But I'm embarrassed to be receiving the gift of this lovely meal, for I've not come simply as a friend; I have come seeking a story to tell.

After dinner Alberto takes us into the narrow den off the living room. His father's hand-colored photograph hangs on the wall, greeting all those who enter. The window faces an alley and two low shelves are lined with LPs.

"This was my father's little corner. He sat here on the big chair and I on a wicker chair next to him. In the afternoons, after work, he'd come here. My father especially liked the tangos of Carlos Gardel."

Alberto removes an LP from the shelf and plays it on his father's old Victrola. It is Gardel, singing a tango in French. Alberto, standing beneath the photograph of his father, grows melancholy, and I no longer have the heart to ask any questions. I let the music fill the silence and I wait. But Carucha, sitting in one of the rocking chairs in the living room, must know these silences very well, must know when to pry Alberto loose from the nostalgia that both sustains and wounds his soul. She calls to him softly. "Come, Alberto, let's sit here, let's leave the music for another day."

In the living room we sit in the rocking chairs and as the night enfolds us, the tile floors with their swirling arabesques seem to rise up over our feet like waves. Perhaps because over the last few hours we have dwelled so fully in the realm of lost things, we get to talking about several young people from the Jewish community who have left for Israel in the last month. Alberto notes that they have already found jobs and are making money and this encourages others to leave.

"Jacob Barlía is leaving and taking his mother with him," Alberto tells me.

I can't help gasping. It is incredible, this news. In all the years I've known him, Jacob has been an active member of the Centro Sefaradí, attending services on Shabbat with his mother and serving as treasurer of the synagogue. How can he leave? He of all people? He's one of the pillars of the community. But that's how it is in Cuba. From one day to the next, a pillar crumbles, disappears. And yet miraculously there are always Jews left in Cuba to keep the whole edifice from toppling.

I turn to Alberto, now pensively staring at the tile floor as I imagine he did as a child. I can't imagine he will ever leave Cuba. He is responsible for too many memories. He isn't an accidental memory keeper, like many of the Jews I know in Cuba. He has chosen to carry the burden of memory, or rather not simply to carry it, but to lift it high, the way the Torah is lifted during Shabbat services to receive kissed prayers. Yet to outsiders unable to understand such deep ties to the island, Alberto's commitment to being in Cuba can seem absurd.

Later in the evening Alberto recalls an awkward meal sponsored by a visiting Jewish-American mission. His dining companion, one of the members of the mission, dug into a huge platter of lobster in a way that Alberto felt constituted a boast about the man's greater financial power and greater freedom from Jewish dietary regulations, which stipulate that shellfish isn't kosher. As the man ate the forbidden luxury food while Alberto ate an inexpensive chicken dish, Alberto thought the unwritten message was: "I as a Jew from the United States can eat lobster, but you here in Cuba, we're going to give you a lot of matzah to eat."

The man wanted to know, as all foreign visitors do, how much Alberto earned working as an engineer for the Cuban phone company. When Alberto told him what his monthly salary was, the man practically burst out laughing. The curious thing was that Alberto quoted a higher salary than he earned, but it still amounted to the equivalent of twenty dollars, which he knew was a pittance by American standards. Out of pity, the man tried passing Alberto a wad of dollar bills, but Alberto refused to accept the money.

As he tells the story, Alberto trembles with fury. "The man was wondering how this horse could survive on that amount of money. He'd come to Cuba to see how Indian we Cubans are. I was a little Indian. A dying species."

I find myself staring at the floor tiles, uncertain of what to say. Alberto seems close to tears. The humiliation of the encounter hangs like a dark cloud in the room.

At last Alberto continues, "And I say to the man, 'You may be the American and I the Cuban. But you know what? You're the one who should feel small next to me.'"

At the time I didn't remember it, but afterward I found a passage in Eduardo Galeano's *Book of Embraces* that I wished I could have shared with Alberto that night. It was a vignette based on an observation made by the anthropologist Ruth Benedict. She had learned that in Vancouver the Indians competed for the claim of greatness by seeing which of their leaders were most adept at destroying their possessions. They burned their canoes and from the cliffs they threw their blankets and pots to the sea. Galeano writes, "The winner was the one who rid himself of everything."

8

HOW TO PACK YOUR SUITCASE

Alberto Mechulam Cohen is always in a hurry. He has so much nervous energy he can't sit still, even though he encourages me to take a seat in the living room as soon as I come in. Meanwhile, he keeps pacing.

Mechulam—no one ever calls him by his first name—has retired recently from his job as a pediatric neurologist. He has a scruffy demeanor but a kind gaze, always looking intently at you with harried eyes over his large glasses. He is a man who finds it natural to worry about the needs of others. For years, every time I ran into him in the Patronato, he'd ask if I could spare some sanitary napkins. They were constantly running short on their supply and the young women, who needed them most, were too shy to ask the foreigners for them. So Mechulam asked; he didn't tire of asking.

Mechulam's wife, Rebeca Paison Weiner, wanders in from the kitchen, offering me a slice of *pudín*—homemade bread pudding. She asks if I'll also have some *garapiña*.

"You're going to give her *garapiña*?" asks Mechulam.

"I'd love some," I say.

"But you know what it is, don't you? It's a drink made from pineapple rinds left to soak in water for five or six days."

I tell him I've had it before and I like it.

He shrugs and says, "I forgot you were born in Cuba."

Rebeca returns with the *garapiña* and Mechulam watches me intently with his harried eyes as I sip the foamy drink.

"So do you want to know the story of how the *escuelita* got started?"

The *escuelita* is "the little school," the name by which everyone refers to the Sunday Hebrew school, where both children and adults receive classes in Jewish education, which are offered by the more knowledgeable members of the community. I urge Mechulam to tell me the story, but he's staring as I take another sip of the *garapiña*.

"Don't drink it if you don't like it," Mechulam says.

I assure him I like it, but I can tell he doesn't believe me.

"So we started the *escuelita* in 1985. There was a period here—a Stalinist period—when people were afraid to enter a church or a synagogue. It wasn't easy to get the *escuelita* going. The Jews who left for Miami didn't want to send us money because they said they didn't want to help Fidel. Everything is more difficult here."

In the end, the Lubavitch organization sent a teacher, Rabbi Appel, from Brazil. Mechulam went door to door telling people about the plan to open the *escuelita*. He worked together with a fellow Cuban Jew, Moisés Asis, who now resides in Miami. It was known who was a Jew because people were listed on a census to receive Passover products. And there was shared knowledge, at least in Havana, of who the Jews who had stayed after the Revolution were. But people were so distrusting and apprehensive, in the era before religious freedom, that many slammed the door in Mechulam's face. Eventually they were able to open the school with twelve children.

"Now we have ninety students. Every week a new student joins. All we ask is that they have one Jewish grandparent. We teach them about our traditions, we teach them Hebrew and Israeli folk dancing. The school meets only on Sundays, because we don't have private schools in Cuba. Of the 700 people who've left for Israel, at least 200 attended the *escuelita*. But when we started out, a lot of people didn't even know they were Jewish. 'Is this a Jewish church?' they'd ask. 'Tell me your name,' I would say. Someone would reply 'Tomás' and I'd give him a Hebrew name and slap a *kippah* on his head. We didn't have candles for Shabbat, so we lit matches. We hustled to get everyone notebooks and pencils. I was always hustling to get shoes for everyone."

Mechulam explains that they have to be able to help people with their material needs in order to attend to their spiritual needs. "I'll say, 'Here, have this T-shirt.' Not in order to buy anyone's devotion, but that's just the way it is. It hasn't been easy. There's just a few of us, but we're stubborn."

In the middle of our conversation, the phone rings. Rebeca hands the phone to Mechulam. When he learns it's Jeff on the line, Mechulam jumps from his seat and says it's an important call that he must take.

"Be sure to give the shoes to me personally," Mechulam shouts. And then despair creeps into his voice as he's about to hang up. "Don't leave the shoes in the Patronato! If you do, they'll never get to me."

I had finished the *pudín* and the *garapiña*. Rebeca immediately takes my plate and glass, in the ultra-polite way that hosts always do in Cuba.

"Did you really like it?" she asks.

"Yes," I say.

"And it's all kosher," Mechulam announces proudly.

All the visiting Lubavitch rabbis feel comfortable eating at their house, he says, because Rebeca keeps a kosher home.

I notice that Mechulam and Rebeca have a poster hanging on their wall of Rabbi Menachem Mendel Schneerson, the spiritual leader of the Lubavitch. Before his death in 1994, some of Schneerson's followers proclaimed him the Messiah. He had spurred a vast missionary movement to bring secular Jews into the fold of Jewish orthodoxy that continues to this day.

When I ask Mechulam about the impact of the Lubavitch on Cuba's Jews, Mechulam shrugs and says that no one in Cuba is fanatical about Judaism. He himself doesn't hesitate to tell visiting Lubavitch rabbis that he doesn't approve of how they discriminate among Jews, allowing only children born of Jewish mothers to attend the special summer camps in Cuba that they organize and fund. In Cuba, this makes no sense, he tells the rabbis, because almost all the children are Jewish on their paternal side, and like their parents, they are converts.

Whatever critical things Mechulam has to say about the Lubavitch, they are balanced by enthusiastic remarks about their religious energy and generosity. Nor does he object when Humberto asks if he and Rebeca might pose next to Schneerson's picture. As Mechulam explains, they owe a lot of gratitude to the Lubavitch.

"Look, I'm sixty-nine years old. I retired a year ago. Our daughter, Ester, was in Israel for five years and she just arrived in Miami. Our son, Moisés, left for Buenos Aires ten years ago. The Lubavitch helped him get out. He studied with the Lubavitch. Now he's married, so he doesn't come back to Cuba that often, but he still returns once a year. He's the manager of a textile firm, but he says he wants to start his own business. He doesn't want to be an employee anymore. He was always very sharp, very enterprising. And he's ambitious. What ambition can he have here? We're here because we have this house. Everyone's always praying for the old folks to die, so they can finally get the house. But you should see how the old people take care of themselves when they come down with a sniffle! Young people need privacy. That's our most serious problem in Cuba—there aren't enough houses. Many of my friends are doctors who only have a room to sleep in."

Now that Mechulam is retired he goes to Adath Israel every morning on his bicycle to attend religious services, even though it's thirty kilometers away from his house. He jokes that he goes because otherwise his wife will find more chores for him to do at home. He says it would be easier to get around if he had a motorcycle. But old people need to exercise, right? He tries to participate in all the synagogues equally; he attends Friday night services at the Patronato, and on Saturday mornings he goes to the Centro Sefaradí for Shabbat services.

"We continue to exist today. We have the *escuelita*. We have three synagogues functioning here in Havana. It's true that a lot of people go to the synagogue because they want to leave for Israel. And at Adath Israel, at the end of the month, they give you a bag filled with rice, beans, vegetable oil, tomato sauce, sardines, and tuna. So people go and pray. If they go three or four times a week, they get that bag of things at the end of the month. Some people get a little bit of money too, only the ones who need it the most."

My hand is getting tired from writing and I pause to take a rest. I smile at Rebeca, who has been present during this last part of the conversation and listening quietly. I want to bring her into the conversation, but she has her own idea of what she needs to know from me. She asks what I plan to do with all the notes I'm writing and all the photographs Humberto is taking.

I tell her we hope to produce a book about the Jews of Cuba.

"People have come from all over the world and interviewed me," she says. "They say they're journalists, writers, filmmakers. They say they're researching the history of the Jews of Cuba. But I've never received a copy of any of the articles or books they've written or the movies they've made."

"I promise I'll bring you our book," I tell her. But I can see she doesn't have any more faith in that vow than Mechulam has in my praise for the *garapiña*.

In the photograph Humberto takes of Mechulam, he is holding an old picture of himself as a robust, kerchief-wearing pioneer and member of the Hanoar Hatzioni, a Zionist organization that backed the kibbutzim movement. Holding the picture up for the camera makes him sigh and reminisce for a moment about his youth. Reminisce isn't the right word, though, because reminiscences are rose-colored and he isn't romantic about the past.

He tells me about his Bulgarian maternal grandmother who prepared yogurt and sweets made of roses. But in the same breath he says his father left two sisters behind in Istanbul when he came to Cuba in 1923. He never knew what had become of them after the war. On the very same day in 1961 that news finally arrived of their whereabouts, a motorcyle ran his father down and killed him.

I ask Mechulam what he learned from his father.

Without hesitating, he replies, "A lot of Jews chose to stay here in Cuba. They liked the climate. They liked living near the sea. But the first thing they taught you as a child was how to pack your suitcase. My father taught me by saying, 'Climb up on the table. Okay, now jump! Go on, jump!' Then he'd say, 'You shouldn't trust your father. You shouldn't trust anybody.' They taught you to pack your suitcase, taught you as soon as they could."

Mechulam looks at me impatiently. "Anything else?" he asks. He's pacing again.

I thank him and thank Rebeca and we take our leave. Mechulam walks us to the door and says he's sorry he has to rush, but he has an appointment. There's a man named Jeff waiting to give him a donation of shoes. Shoes for the Jewish people of Cuba.

9

ENRIQUE BENDER'S
BLUE-GREEN EYES REMIND ME
OF MY GRANDFATHER

The first time I saw Enrique Bender Solztein at the Adath Israel synagogue, I felt a little spooked—because he seemed to me like an apparition.

Enrique looks and even sounds like my maternal grandfather, Máximo Glinsky. My beloved Zayde had blue-green eyes, the sweet temperament of a man who could lull cranky babies to sleep, a head of cottony white hair, and he spoke Spanish with a Yiddish accent. Enrique is shorter than my grandfather was, but apart from that, I feel he's the closest I'll ever come to feel the aura of my Zayde.

When I see Enrique again in March 2006, I'm in Cuba as a part-time study leader with a Jewish group from South Florida. Although I'm not staying at the plush Hotel Parque Central with the group, I've agreed to give a few lectures and attend lunches and dinners whenever I can. The morning I see Enrique, the group has invited me to lunch at La Guarida, an expensive gourmet restaurant that opened in 1996 and has become so well known it has even been written up in the *New York Times*. The restaurant was the set for the Academy Award-nominated movie *Strawberry and Chocolate,* about the friendship between a straight male revolutionary and a gay critic of the Revolution. A few blocks from the Parque Central, it is located in a building just dilapidated enough to be charming. I have to admit I love the food at La Guarida and I'm happy to get a free meal there whenever I can. So I agree to meet the Jewish group from South Florida at the Hotel Parque Central, where they're staying, and accompany them to lunch.

But I have the morning open and so I decide to go to Adath Israel and see if I can find Enrique. After services I hang around, turning down the breakfast that everyone else is hungrily eating, to save my appetite for lunch at La Guarida. I talk to Enrique and we make plans for me to visit him the next day at his home in San José de las Lajas.

"I live very far from Havana," Enrique says. "How will you get to my house?"

I assure him I will be able to get to his house. I don't want to tell him I will go in a taxi that will cost the equivalent of several times his monthly pension.

I say goodbye and he asks which way I'm walking. I tell him vaguely that I'm meeting some people at the Parque Central. I only mention the park as the meeting place, because I'm too embarrassed to tell him I'm going to the Hotel Parque Central, one of the most expensive hotels in Havana, and then going to a fancy lunch at La Guarida.

To be sure I'd arrive on time, I'd thought to catch a taxi, but Enrique offers to walk with me to the Parque Central. He tells me it's close and we'll be there in a few minutes.

Walking side by side, he and I set out through the throbbing streets of La Habana Vieja. People walk every which way. Cars zoom by, their drivers, mostly men, looking at women's backsides instead of the road. Every time we need to step down from the curb, Enrique grabs me by the elbow in a gentlemanly way and we smile at each other.

We reach the Parque Central and he says, "Where now?"

Hesitating, I point to the Hotel Parque Central.

"A very good hotel," he says.

I tell Enrique I'm not staying at the hotel myself, that I'm getting together with people who are staying there. I'm going to a meeting, I say. Work, I add. It's not completely a lie. I am giving lectures to the Jewish group from South Florida. And joining them for deluxe meals at the best restaurants in Havana is part of my job, isn't it?

"Until tomorrow," he says. "You will definitely come to see me in San José tomorrow?"

Enrique looks at me expectantly with his blue-green eyes and speaks to me in that Yiddish-accented Spanish I can't believe I'm hearing again. And all around us the buzz of Havana street life, all around us the royal palms of the Parque Central, tall enough to scratch the sky.

"Yes, for sure, I'll be there tomorrow," I say.

"Then I'll wait for you," Enrique replies.

We prepare to part ways and that is when I notice how he's dressed—clean but ragged oversized pants, striped polo shirt pulled over a checkered shirt to keep warm on this slightly chilly day, old sandals with their thick tire-rubber soles, which he's wearing with threadbare socks. He's not my Zayde, I realize then, he is a man in need. I have never before done such a thing in Cuba, but I reach into my purse and pull out a bill, $5, $10, whatever I find first, and give it to Enrique.

I fear I've offended him, but I see the tears welling up in his eyes.

"You don't need to give me anything," he says.

He's as embarrassed as I am.

"It's to help you get home to San José."

"Gracias," he says.

And we go our separate ways.

At the door of the Hotel Parque Central, I look back and I can no longer see Enrique. He has merged into the Cuban crowd. Should I have invited him to lunch? Why didn't I? Why did I think that was out of the question? He's a Jew and I'm meeting up with other Jews who want to learn about Jews in Cuba. Wouldn't it have made sense to bring him along? Shouldn't I facilitate such encounters, however awkward they may be?

I get on the Havanatur bus with the retired Jews from South Florida and when people start asking where we're going and why, I switch into my tour leader mode, grab the microphone, and tell the story of La Guarida, its connection to the movie, *Strawberry and Chocolate,* its write-up in the *New York Times,* everything I think the group will find fascinating and exotic. Everyone is freshly showered after their morning tour of Old Havana and they are in a jovial mood. As soon as we arrive at La Guarida, snapshots are duly taken of everyone posing in front of the revolutionary slogans on the main floor of the building. On the second floor, clothes are hanging out to dry amid the crumbling columns, and another round of snapshots are taken there. Finally we climb the last flight of slippery, rundown marble stairs and enter the restaurant's main dining room. Cuban art and antiques hang on the walls. Wax candles melt prettily in their candelabras. There is eggplant caviar, tuna marinated in sugar cane and coconut, Chilean wine, a soothing flan. Nothing could be better. I want to float away. And everyone in the group is much too gracious. They tell me they've learned so much about the Jews of Cuba from my lectures. But I'm feeling like a fraud, thinking of Enrique Bender's blue-green eyes welling up with tears as we said goodbye in the Parque Central.

The next morning I go with Humberto to visit Enrique at his home in San José de las Lajas. He wasn't exaggerating when he told me he lived far away. The town is a good forty-five minutes from the city of Havana in a functioning car.

At the door of his house, Enrique greets me with worried eyes. "You came by taxi! Oh, no, that is too expensive!"

He invites us in and says, "I'm prepared for your visit." From a small plastic bag he pulls out several old family photographs, as well as his Polish passport, which has torn and split into two pieces.

He points to the place of birth on his passport. "I'm from Ostrolenka," he says. "A beautiful town. I wonder what it looks like now."

I look at the name on the passport: Enoch. The name he lost.

"Tell me, Enrique, when did you arrive in Cuba?"

"I came from Poland when I was thirteen. I left my family behind—my mother, my brother. I came in 1938. The 17th of October of 1938. Three months before the war began. The war began in 1939. And I never heard from my family again."

He shows me a family photograph from Poland, when his parents were young and optimistic and he and his brother were little boys in shorts and matching sweaters.

"My father came in 1929. Then he sent for me and my brother in 1938. My mother didn't want us to leave, until the neighbors said, 'Look, Hannah, at least send the older boy, and that way he can get you out later.' But then the war began and I couldn't do anything. My mother stayed in Poland. So did my aunts and uncles and my brother. I never heard from them again. I've gone to the Polish embassy four times and they say they don't know anything."

He struggles to get the photographs and passport to fit again in the plastic bag, where he wants to return them for safekeeping and maybe for another spell of forgetting.

I drop my notebook and pen and clasp the bag to help him. He smiles and thanks me and then we're both at a loss for what to say next.

I glance around the room and see that at the center of Enrique's pink-walled house there is a pastel-colored photograph of his wife, Candelaria, who passed away years ago. The photograph is propped on the television set and has a garland of plastic gladiolas.

I ask Enrique to tell me about his wife and he says, "She was a very good woman. She helped me so much."

Just remembering his wife brings a smile to his face.

"And do you have children?"

"Yes," he says. "One son is in Israel, the youngest. My older son is a doctor and he lives in Playa, a nice neighborhood in Havana. He's doing very well." He breaks out laughing and adds, "He likes women a lot, so I don't see him that much."

The one who looks after him is his daughter, Lourdes. She's an English teacher and also lives in San José de las Lajas. She has her own problems as a diabetic. But he can count on her. His daughter is the one he can count on.

Enrique points to the bicycle parked by the pink wall next to the entrance. "And I still work," he says. "All my life I've worked."

"What kind of work?"

"I used to sew shoes. Now I make covers for bicycle seats."

When I ask Enrique if he'll show me how he produces the bicycle seats, he scurries over to a desk on the other side of the living room and tugs at the curtains to let in the light. Then he opens a drawer of the hutch, pulls out scissors and strips of leather, and dons enormous black-framed glasses. He sits down at the sewing machine and for the next fifteen minutes he sews feverishly until he completes an entire bicycle seat cover.

When he's done, he shows me how the cover fits neatly over the bicycle seat.

"I'll keep working," he says. "Until the police or the Comité tell me I can't anymore."

He makes the bicycle seat covers when he doesn't go to Adath Israel for religious services. It's an entire day's trek to go to the synagogue and he returns home exhausted. On the nightstand next to his bed he has three alarm clocks, all set to ring at two in the morning. He says the clocks go off one after the other and he awakens. Then he takes a series of buses that land him at the doorstep of Adath Israel by six in the morning. He waits until the synagogue opens, at seven or eight. This is his routine on Monday, Thursday, and Saturday. He'd go every day, if he could.

Enrique winks at me. "Let's see if you can send me a motorcycle from over there, where you live. A motorcycle a rich person doesn't want, a broken-down motorcycle they've thrown away. Send it to me here. Then I can go to synagogue every day."

"I'd have to send you a motorcycle helmet too," I say, trying not to miss a beat.

In the same joking spirit, Enrique says, "Oh, yes, and the helmet. We don't have any helmets here. When you send me the motorcycle, be sure to send me the helmet too!"

It's time to go, but I don't want to leave. Even Enrique's jokes remind me of my grandfather, who was always poking fun at the pretensions of others. Reluctantly, I tell Enrique that we have to leave. But he is concerned that he has nothing to offer us. "Do you have enough time to go with me to visit my daughter Lourdes?" he asks.

I say we still have a few minutes—even though Humberto is glancing at his watch and the driver is getting tired of sitting around.

We all get in the car and drive a few blocks to his daughter's house.

Enrique introduces us to Lourdes as friends from the synagogue.

"Oh, of course. How nice," Lourdes says and welcomes us inside.

Lourdes is the exact image of her mother—her face is moonlike, round and iridescent. Her eyes are a shade darker than her father's. Although a full-bodied woman, she's as proud of her curves as any island Cuban woman and wears a stretchy strapless top. And I notice the Star of David around her neck.

Once we're seated in her living room, she perches herself on the armrest of her father's chair and gently scolds him. "Ay, Papi, you had guests and you didn't tell me! I would have prepared something special for them. Why didn't you tell me?"

Enrique shrugs. "I didn't know if they were really coming."

I guess Enrique never believed I'd travel such a long distance to see him.

Lourdes shakes her head. "What a pity." She turns to me, "And when will you be back, so I can make lunch for you?"

I tell her I don't know. Maybe in a few months, or a year.

"Ay, no," Lourdes exclaims. Then she thinks for a moment and says, "Do all of you like yogurt?"

"Please don't go to any trouble. We have to leave soon."

"It's no trouble. Please wait."

A moment later Lourdes returns from the kitchen carrying a tray on which she has set several tall glasses filled to the brim with yogurt. She gives one to me, Humberto, the driver, and her father.

"There's a yogurt factory in town," she says. "So the yogurt is very good. Some say it's the best in Cuba."

I have to agree the yogurt is exquisitely rich—more like ice cream than yogurt.

"It's delicious. Thank you."

Lourdes looks playfully at her father. "Can I tell her what you always say about this yogurt?"

He nods, his blue-green eyes twinkling.

"My father says it's Fidel's yogurt. He calls it the yogurt of the Comandante, because it's so good!"

And Enrique laughs. "Yes, the yogurt of the Comandante, that's what we're having. If it's good, it's got to be what the Comandante himself eats."

10

THE DANCING TURK

Pilar Little Bermudez hides her years very well. When we go to visit her at her Vedado apartment, she wears a dress with an orchid print, gold earrings, and a gold necklace. Her white hair is freshly brushed. As she says, "Even though I'm ninety, the moment I wake up I get dressed and put on my makeup."

Certainly some of the credit for Pilar's longevity must go to her daughter, Flor Najmías Little, a retired social worker, who takes impeccable care of her mother. Throughout our conversation, I can't help noticing how Flor never sits, but stands protectively, like a bodyguard, behind Pilar.

"This is everything I could find," Flor says, pointing to the photographs, passports, citizenship papers, and memorabilia spread out on the dining table. As I sort through it all, Flor remarks, "For the longest time I held on to my father's comb. It had his hair stuck in it. I held on to it until just the other day. I still have his eyeglasses. My father was Moisés Najmías Maimón. In Turkey the family uses the *h* and here we use the *j* in Najmías. My father came to Cuba in May of 1925."

Flor stops herself, realizing suddenly she isn't being a good host.

"Would you like a *cafecito*?" she asks.

We say yes and Flor smiles and disappears into the kitchen.

Now Pilar continues with the story. "I was born in 1914," she says. "My husband was about twenty when he came to Cuba. He was nine years older than me. He was born in 1905, but he always liked to pretend he was younger."

Returning with the coffee, Flor adds, "My father's father had died of cholera, so his maternal grandfather raised him. He came alone to Cuba. Afterward his brother came, but he didn't like Cuba and went back to Turkey."

Pilar holds up a picture of herself as a young woman with a young Moisés looking dapper in a white suit.

"He was such a good dancer," Pilar says dreamily. "He loved parties. There used to be a place on the Malecón, near the Hotel Riviera, and I'd go there with a chaperone, because you couldn't go by yourself in those days. We liked to watch everyone dance. 'Look at that guy. He's not Cuban. Look how well he dances to the American songs.' This was in the late 1930s. Two, three years later I went to the Centro Asturiano. They held dances every Saturday. But I didn't want to go. I didn't think anyone who could dance went there. But my mother talked me into it. There I am, standing next to the orchestra when I see him again, all dressed in white. He looks at me and keeps walking. Then he comes back and looks at me again. The third time he holds out his hand. I thought to myself, 'Well, at least this one will know how to dance.' And we danced the entire night."

Pilar puts on her glasses and examines the picture more carefully. "Oh how the years ravage us!"

"When you met him, did you know Moisés was Jewish?" I ask.

"I had no idea," Pilar replies, and adds that they were married in 1943 in a civil wedding.

"My father never denied he was Jewish, but he didn't go to synagogue," Flor says. "He was poor, but he paid his membership fees at Chevet Ahim. I remember the blue metal cans for Tzedaka. They came around asking for money for charity. He gave all year long."

As a single man, Moisés thought he was free of family pressures when he chose to marry Pilar, a woman not from the Jewish tribe. But the one relative he had in Cuba, a cousin, would not forgive him.

Flor tells the story: "He had a cousin whose marriage had been arranged in Turkey. When I was born, my father went to his cousin's house with the news. This cousin looked at him and said, 'Was the girl born very retarded?' She said that because she thought my mother was a mulata. She thought my mother wasn't white. And who was *she*? Just a Turkish woman whose marriage had been arranged by her family. And her son was as dark as my mother."

A few years later, Moisés and Pilar had their son, Luis. Flor recalls her brother being circumcised: "My mother wasn't Jewish but my father found someone to do it. This was a violation of Jewish law, but with money you can get a monkey to dance."

Pilar is unwilling to remember anything that will make her sad. She continues to gaze at the photograph of her and her husband in their youth. Finally she says, "He sold fabric. He was a peddler. He bought the fabric on Muralla Street."

According to Flor, her father never learned to write in Spanish, but he was good at arithmetic and this helped him to become a successful peddler. After the Revolution, he stopped peddling because the government took away his merchandise.

"He didn't support the Revolution, but he was fifty in 1959 and he thought he was too old to leave. So he learned to repair jewelry."

Flor goes to her bedroom and returns with a pair of gold earrings. "My father gave me these earrings. I keep them locked away. You can't wear your jewelry on the street here. You risk your life if you do."

Her father died in 1986, and losing him drew Flor back to her Jewish heritage. She started attending services at the Centro Sefaradí and tried to convince her husband to participate in her quest. She says he remained an atheist, a revolutionary, and a Communist Party member. But it hasn't caused a split between them. He goes to Party meetings and she goes to the synagogue.

Pilar has followed in Flor's path. In 1996, during a group conversion ceremony, they both formally became Jewish. Flor took the name Rachel as her Hebrew name. Pilar took the name Sarah.

"I'm religious in my own way," Flor says. "When I don't go to Kabbalat Shabbat services on Friday night, I worry that my week won't go well. I start to fear that someone will get sick in the family. Or that we'll have a terrible fight at home. Turks are very superstitious and I'm the daughter of a Turk."

Being superstitious, it worried Flor that just before her father died, he asked to be buried in the Sephardic cemetery in Guanabacoa, but she had buried him in the Colón cemetery, the main Catholic cemetery of Havana. As soon as she started participating in the Centro Sefaradí, she made arrangements to have her father's remains transferred to the Jewish cemetery.

"I brought his remains to Guanabacoa myself, in my car. I kept my promise to my father, even if I didn't do it exactly as he had wished."

II
MONDAY MORNING IN LUYANÓ

Sara Elí Nassy and her daughter, Victoria Cohen Elí, were regulars at Shabbat services at the Centro Sefaradí and over the years I had often sat and talked to them at the lunch following services. These conversations always followed the same pattern: Sara would try to tell me about her life, while Victoria excitedly interrupted and tried to tell the story for her mother, who eventually would lose her patience and yell at Victoria to let her speak, which in turn would leave Victoria in a catatonic sorrow. I soon learned that it's no secret in the Jewish community that Victoria is schizophrenic. And that Sara, the loving mother, had always valiantly stayed by her daughter's side. Their relationship, from the start, struck me as tender in its intimacy and terrifying in its claustrophobia.

I liked them both and had often wondered how they lived. I'd been promising for a long time to visit them at their home in Luyanó, a Havana neighborhood just beyond the old city. One Monday morning I decided I would pay them a visit. Sara and Victoria don't have a phone, so I knew I was taking a chance by heading over unannounced, but I figured that on a Monday morning the two women would be home.

Neighbors peer through half-shuttered windows and open doors as Humberto and I walk past. "Who are you looking for?" someone asks. And when I say "Sara and Victoria," I'm told, "Go to the last door."

I knock softly. "Who is it?" The voice is Victoria's. "Ruth." I say. "From the Centro Sefaradí."

Victoria flings open the door and seeing us she becomes deliriously happy.

"Come in, come in," she yells, for she is incapable of speaking without shouting. "We're so grateful for your visit!" Then at the top of her lungs, "Mamá! Look who's come to visit us!"

Sara, a wisp of a woman at the age of ninety-two, floats in from the kitchen at the back of the house and greets us warmly. Behind her is Victoria's older sister, Dora, who visits every day to help her mother and Victoria, though she herself suffers from severe depression. In lieu of a greeting, Dora looks despondently at us and says, "We don't have water today. There's a problem with the cistern. We won't be able to offer you anything. We don't have a single clean glass in this house."

Victoria immediately pipes in, "We're always the last ones in the building to get water. That's the way it is. Oh well, what are you going to do? But please, sit down!"

We huddle in the front room, where one of the walls has burn marks from a Hanukkah menorah that caught fire a few years ago. I tell them I'd like to know about their lives.

Sara begins to speak, but Victoria interrupts, "She recovered from cancer! My mother recovered from cancer! My mother is the best. She's the greatest companion I could ever have!"

"Now please let me speak," Sara says to Victoria, who immediately quiets down. She turns to me and says, "I don't have a lot to tell you. As a young woman I learned how to sew. I sewed for others and I embroidered. I can't work anymore because my eyesight is gone. I only see a little from one eye. I married Abraham Cohen Behar who loved me. But he died young. I have two daughters and a granddaughter who has three children. I was a little girl when we came from Turkey. My mother said we were from Istanbul. We lived in Havana, then we went to Camagüey, but we didn't like it there, so we came back to Havana. My husband died young. He was fifty years old when he died. He wasn't religious. But I have faith in Judaism. On Yom Kippur we always light the candles and we fast for the entire twenty-four hours and every Saturday we go to the synagogue."

Victoria chimes in. "We go to the Centro Sefaradí every Saturday! They have a little bus that picks us up and brings us back. If it weren't for that little bus, we couldn't go."

Sara continues, "My husband—did I tell you his name was Abraham Cohen Behar? And my mother-in-law, she was as good as bread."

And Victoria again, "My father was a member of the Caballero de La Luz Lodge, the B'nai Brith Lodge, and the Otero Lodge. He sold clothing. My father was a socialist. He didn't have enemies. He was a socialist and he supported Israel. When he was alive, there was no war with the Arabs. That whole mess started later. He always talked about Israel. And he didn't have any enemies."

Dora, who has been listening to the back-and-forth talk of her mother and sister without batting an eyelash, now haltingly remarks, "I worked in the maternity ward in Guanabacoa. I became a medical technician."

"I was studying to become a nurse!" Victoria announces in her booming voice. "The Revolution had just begun. But I couldn't go on because of my nerves. I've been sick with nerves for over forty years. Once in a while, I can fall asleep without taking any pills. What else can I tell you? I'm single and a señorita."

Is it possible that the Revolution drove Victoria mad?

But how fortunate she is, I think, that her mother has lived to a ripe old age and has cared for her. Not that Victoria necessarily sees things that way. She guards her mother. She never lets Sara out of her sight. When we ask if we can take their picture in their bedroom, Victoria sits close to her mother, while Dora sits further away, keeping her distance. The symbiosis of Sara and Victoria has probably been in place forever—the mother protecting the daughter from her demons, the daughter protecting the mother from her frailty and her mortality.

Two months later, in July 2005, when Sara angelically goes to sleep and doesn't awaken, I can see Victoria weeping her heart out. But I want to imagine that she also finds comfort in the thought that she cared faultlessly for her mother, that she was the most faithful daughter she could ever be, that she did what every mother desires from a daughter—she saved her mother from having to live under the curse of solitude.

12

DANAYDA LEVY'S SCHOOL REPORT

I have known Danayda Levy since she was two years old. In the early 1990s I'd see her with her father, José, who diligently brought her to the Patronato for Jewish schooling at the Sunday morning *escuelita*. A white Jewish father with a black Jewish daughter was not a common sight around the Patronato in those days and Levy had to put up with more than a few cold stares. He and Danayda's mother, Florinda, had separated shortly after Danayda was born, but Levy didn't abandon his daughter. On the contrary: she was a daddy's girl, the beloved daughter of his elder years, and he strove to bring her up Jewish at a time when he, the son of a Jewish father and a Catholic mother, was reclaiming his own Jewishness. After Levy became the president of the Centro Hebreo Sefaradí, the synagogue became a second home for Danayda. It was Levy who prepared Danayda for her bat mitzvah.

The first time I formally videotaped an interview with Danayda, she was eleven years old. She dressed up for the interview. I remember she had on a new blue skirt and matching print blouse. She pulled her hair back with plastic butterfly barrettes and smelled of violet cologne.

Accompanying her father to synagogue throughout her girlhood, Danayda developed a strong sense of her Jewish identity. She is the color of café con leche, a typically Cuban color. I wondered if she'd had a difficult time asserting her identity and asked if she'd had problems in school identifying as a Jew. She replied forcefully that everyone at her school knew she was Jewish, accepted her as a Jew, and it had not caused any problems. "Maybe for an enemy or two," who already held a grudge against her, it was a problem, but otherwise she didn't know of anyone who didn't respect her Jewish identity.

I was impressed by her confidence and maturity. Whenever I visited Cuba, I tried to spend time with Danayda at her home in the Chinese neighborhood of Havana, where she lived with her mother and half-sister in a spare apartment that was always sparkling clean. They had built an upstairs addition, as many people do in Havana, by constructing a *barbacoa*, a false ceiling, and squeezing a small room into the space above.

I had never been to the upstairs room, but one day I arrived when Danayda was alone and in the midst of ironing her school uniform. I followed her upstairs and watched as she ironed the white blouse and mustard skirt that all Cuban schoolgirls wear in middle school. I wondered how many young women were left in the world who still washed and ironed their uniforms each day?

As she ironed, Danayda had a story to tell me.

"At school we were told to do a report about any country in the world. So I chose Israel. I wrote about geography, culture, politics. I went into depth about religion—death customs, weddings, bar mitzvahs. I did it by myself. Everyone else worked in groups."

She put down her iron and turned the blouse around, looking for wrinkles around the seams.

"The professor said Tel Aviv was the capital of Israel and I said it was Jerusalem. He said I'd get 98 points if I wrote it was Jerusalem and 100 points if I wrote it was Tel Aviv. I told him to give me the 98 points."

"What did your father have to say about this?"

"My father spoke with the teacher, but he continued to claim the capital was Tel Aviv. When a geography teacher heard about my report she said she'd bring in a book that listed the capitals of every country. If the book said Jerusalem I'd get 100 points. The book said Jerusalem and I got the 100 points."

13

MAY DAY WITH

A JEWISH COMMUNIST

It's May Day 2005 and Fabio Grobart Sunshine has graciously agreed to let us accompany him to the Plaza de la Revolución. We want to photograph Fabio amid the crowds who'll be waving little Cuban paper flags and celebrating the Revolution.

I can't think of another Jew in Cuba with whom it would be more appropriate to attend this annual civic ritual. Fabio is often called Fabito to distinguish him from his father, also named Fabio Grobart, a Polish Jew (born Yunger Semjovich) who arrived in Cuba at the age of nineteen and committed himself to the struggle for Cuba's liberation, helping to found the Cuban Communist Party in 1925. After the various leftist parties were consolidated into the Communist Party of Cuba in 1965, Grobart, the father, was elected to the Central Committee, a position he held until his death in 1994. Honoring his role as a senior member of the Communist Party, it was Grobart who introduced Fidel Castro at party meetings. Castro liked to call Grobart *el polaquito*. When they embraced, Castro towered over "the little Pole."

At 6:30 in the morning Humberto and I arrive at Fabio, the son's, apartment building. Before I even knock, Fabio opens the door wide and greets us. Although already in his mid-sixties, his red hair and freckles give him a youthful springiness.

"I think we have time for a *cafecito*," he declares, and brews espresso coffee for the three of us.

As we're leaving his apartment he asks if I've brought a hat. When I say I haven't, he tells me I can't go to the plaza unless I have a hat.

"Here, wear this," he says, tossing me a white baseball cap. "Otherwise your brain will bake in the sun." He slips on a Yankees cap.

On our walk to the plaza, we join others on their way there. The atmosphere is festive. Grandparents stroll with grandchildren and groups of friends walk arm in arm. Fabio knows everyone in the neighborhood. People wave hello and shout greetings.

At the plaza, vendors are selling rolled-up paper cones of roasted peanuts, one of the folkloric street foods that has survived from pre-revolutionary days. "Maní," they yell. "Maní tostao!"

The little Cuban paper flags are being given out for free. I've always wanted one of the little flags—it's a sentimental desire, a narcissistic nostalgia for patriotism, because of the photograph I've seen of myself as a child with just such a flag in my hands. I go to the woman who is magically producing the flags, pulling them like rabbits out of a huge cardboard box, and get one for myself while Fabio smiles approvingly. When I take the flag in hand, I discover that the wooden handle to which the flag is attached is homemade and rustic—you have to be careful how you hold it or you'll get splinters.

People are carrying all sorts of revolutionary banners, and seeing us with a camera, they hold them up in the air and urge us to take their pictures. Fabio meets up with an acquaintance wrestling with a large banner honoring Che and immediately rushes to help, grasping the edge of the banner as it flaps in the breeze.

After a while Humberto says he's gotten enough pictures of Fabio and takes his leave. I decide to stay with Fabio and wait until Fidel Castro begins to speak. The sun is out and scorching. I'm very glad Fabio has lent me the cap.

At first I find it exhilirating to see such a huge number of people in the plaza. So many Cubans gathered together! This is what I lost not growing up in Cuba, I think, this sense of unity. But a strange fear grips me and soon my heart is beating frantically in my chest. I cast a hopeful glance at the Red Cross trucks stationed along the major pathways, imagining they'll revive me if I pass out.

What a terrible revolutionary I'd be. I'm scared to death of large crowds.

When, at last, Castro appears, Cuban flags rise into the sky. Fathers lift their children onto their shoulders, so they too can wave their little paper flags. I want to wave my flag too, but I have never held any flag up in the air and I feel self-conscious. The best I can do is just hold on to it and try not to get any splinters.

Castro promises to be brief, but people know better. They make themselves comfortable; some have come prepared and spread blankets on the ground to sit.

"All of humanity is hungry for justice. That's what all of you are demonstrating by being here today!"

"Fidel, Fidel, Fidel!"

Fabio and I listen for a while. Partway through the speech we both agree we're tired and set off again to his apartment.

As we walk I try to be the anthropologist and ask him about the situation of the Jews in Cuba.

Fabio has an immediate reply. "Here the Jews are overseen by the Office of Religious Affairs. They're not viewed as a social community—like the Chinese or the Arabs. They're viewed as a religious community. Maybe the Joint [the Joint Distribution Committee] won't give money to Communists—that's why the Jews have had to come together as a religious community. But in Cuba we know how to be Jewish, with or without religion."

I ask him how he feels about the young Argentine community leaders, sponsored by the Joint, who come to Cuba for periods of two and three years to teach the Jews of Cuba about their heritage.

Again he has an immediate reply. "Those *argentinos*, they're just kids, and they come and try to force their religious perspective on us. But Karl Marx was Jewish and he was against religion."

Fabio also doesn't like the way the various synagogues in Cuba, supported by international Jewish organizations, try to attract lapsed Jews by offering material aid in exchange for religious devotion.

"So I'm going to start believing in God because they give me a bottle of cooking oil? People who've never believed in God, now because of a bottle of oil, suddenly believe in God?"

He pauses and continues, just as fiery, saying the role of Jews is to do good works for all of humanity. To be Jewish isn't about being religious or being a Zionist. Being Jewish is about being a revolutionary. On this point he agrees completely with his father.

"And is your father buried in the Jewish cemetery?" I ask.

Fabio shakes his head. "No, he isn't. My father always said he didn't want to be buried in the Jewish cemetery. He wanted to be with his brothers in the Communist Party. He doesn't have a tombstone. Just a plaque with his name and a red star. Revolutionaries don't even have a place where they can lie down to die."

"And how was he as a person and a father to you?"

"He had total confidence in me and was transparent in everything he said and did. He was my first and greatest friend."

Upon reaching Fabio's building he invites me to lunch. Both of us have worked up a sweat from the walk and Fabio buys a large bottle of Materva soda from the lady on the first floor of his building who has a private business in her home. We take it upstairs to his apartment and gulp it down in ice-filled glasses.

"Here, make yourself comfortable," Fabio says, and turns on the television in the living room. He sets up a fan on a table next to the television and turns it on high. He tells me to relax and cool down while he prepares lunch.

Fidel has not yet finished his speech at the Plaza de la Revolución. Now and then he pauses to take a breath and his audience responds, "For the solidarity of all the people of the world! For peace! For Fidel! For the revolution! Long live the First of May!"

After watching for a while, I wander into the kitchen and find Fabio making an omelet with sliced potatoes. He passes me some plates and silverware, and I set them out on a corner of the dining table. The table is piled high with books, journals, and papers. Boxes bulging with more books, journals, and papers are strewn about the apartment. This is the home of an intensely busy scholar—Fabio is a professor of economics at the University of Havana and he publishes and lectures widely. He's also just returned from a conference in Quito about Latin America and the world economy. But Fabio's apartment isn't simply the messy abode of a typical professor. There are things he keeps inside his four walls that make his a distinctly Cuban apartment. Two bikes are crammed into the dining room, along with a bicycle tire, and assorted car parts, grimy with soot and oil. On the sideboard an image of Lenin leans against a vase blooming with little Cuban paper flags from previous May Day rallies. The first time I visited Fabio with Humberto, I remember Humberto took one look at the clutter in the apartment and whispered in my ear, "It's obvious that a woman doesn't live here."

It's still hot, even though the fan is blowing and the door to the balcony is open. On this day there are no breezes from the ocean. While cooking Fabio has taken off his shirt, as men do in Cuba when they're at home. We have already begun eating when he asks if I mind if he eats without his shirt on. In truth, I feel embarrassed seeing his bare chest. But wanting to be the polite and ever-tolerant anthropologist, I say it's fine, that I know it's the custom in Cuba.

With a straight face, he says, "It's nice when the women also follow the custom."

After recovering from my surprise at this flirtatious line, I burst out laughing and he laughs too.

"You don't mind if I joke around with you?"

I tell him I didn't mind. I'm glad to be laughing. I realize I've been needing to have a good laugh to let go of the anxiety I've been feeling since my fainting spell in the plaza amid all the revolutionary zeal.

Suddenly I remember the paranoid advice my parents always give me before I travel to Cuba. "Ruti, no hables de política." *Don't talk about politics.* They fear if I say the wrong thing to the wrong person I could end up in jail, or worse. And I understand their fear. No matter how often I travel to Cuba, I always feel a touch unsure of things when I'm there, doubt lingering in the back of mind about whether I'll be able to get out again. I don't completely relax until I go through security and I'm on the other side, waiting for my plane back to Miami.

But I wish I could tell my parents that, for the time being, I'm okay, not worried in the least. A Jewish *comunista* gave me a hat to wear so I wouldn't get sunburned at the May Day rally. He invited me to lunch. Then he made me laugh by flinging my own anthropological language back at me. *It's nice when the women also follow the custom!*

From the living room I can hear the television reporting live from the Plaza de la Revolución. Fidel has finished his speech.

14

THE WHISPERING WRITER

In the Jewish community of Cuba there is only one famous writer and his name is Jaime Sarusky.

He is very soft-spoken, but not shy. He just seems to be whispering every time he talks, as if he's perennially in a crowded movie theater and raising his voice would be a disturbance to those around him. There's a sweetness to his expression and when he smiles he scrunches his eyes and winks impishly.

Jaime's father was from Poland and his mother from Byelorussia. They met and married in Cuba, settling in a rural town in Ciego de Avila, but both died young, leaving Jaime to be cared for by uncles in Havana who had little understanding of how to nurture his creativity. In the early 1950s he was set up by a prospective father-in-law to run a store in Marianao, a suburb of Havana, but he resisted the imposition of this "dowry." He sold the store, started writing, and moved to Paris. In Paris he coincided with other young Cuban Jewish intellectuals escaping the Batista regime, including Saúl Yelín, who was the founder of the ICAIC, the Cuban cinema foundation, and José Altshuler, an engineer, who continues to live and work in Cuba.

Along with these other intellectuals, Jaime returned to Cuba in 1959. He was involved in the revolution as a writer and a teacher, and became a member of the editorial board of the magazine *Revolución y Cultura*. A journalist and novelist, in 2004 he won the Cuban National Literature Award, which is the island's most prestigious prize for writers. Although he has written essays about the role played by Jews in Cuban history, he doesn't consider himself a

Jewish writer who primarily writes about Jewish themes. Rather, he refers to his writing as chronicles that explore the traces left by even more invisible immigrants, Swedes, Japanese, Americans, and Yucatec Mayas, who came to Cuba during the era of the building of the railroads.

I hadn't seen Jaime Sarusky in quite some time and when we meet again in 2005, the first thing I do is congratulate him on receiving the National Prize for Literature.

He smiles and scrunches his eyes.

I tell him about my project and ask what text I should use to accompany his photograph.

"You can use the speech I gave when I received the award. It's on the web site. There are also articles and reviews of my work," he adds.

He mentions an article that appeared in a Swedish magazine, and another about his presentation at a book fair in Argentina. Like other esteemed writers in Cuba, Jaime is able to travel without difficulty and he has access to a wider spectrum of information than ordinary Cubans.

Suddenly I fear that there's nothing I can ask him to talk about that he hasn't already talked about, nothing that isn't already available on the Internet.

A little desperately, I ask, "So what does it mean to you to be a Jew in Cuba?"

In his whispery voice, Jaime responds, "I'm not religious. I go to the synagogue very infrequently." He pauses to catch his breath. "Jews need a community in order to be Jewish. You need at least ten people."

It's not exactly an answer to my question, so I try again.

"Maybe you don't write about Jewish topics, but people know you're Jewish, right?"

"Yes, my friends all call me *polaco*. Here in Cuba it's like saying *Jew*. I don't deny I'm Jewish. The interesting thing is most of my Jewish education happened as an adult, not as a child. It was later in life, for example, that I learned Jews don't bring flowers to a grave, they bring stones."

"So you don't mind that your friends call you *polaco*?"

"Only my old friends call me *polaco*. But if someone who doesn't know me were suddenly to call me *polaco,* I might get upset. Those who call me by that

name in an affectionate and sympathetic way, that's a completely different thing."

"Jaime, tell me why you stay in Cuba."

"I was raised in Florence," he replies. "Not the Florence of Dante or Machiavelli, but the Florence in Ciego de Avila. I lost both my parents when I was a boy and that created a need in me to be rooted. I've traveled all over the world. I was in France for five years, but I never thought I'd live anywhere but in Cuba."

15

THE THREE THINGS JOSÉ MARTÍ
SAID ALL REAL MEN MUST DO

I'm able to make an appointment to see Enrique Oltuski Osacki on a Friday afternoon at his office in Jaimanitas, close to the Marina Hemingway, after several phone calls to his wife and several to his secretary. It's an accomplishment that at the last minute I've managed to pin down a time to meet the highest-ranking Jew in the Castro government. A Cuban-born son of Polish immigrants, he was a buddy of Che Guevara and one of the leaders of the July 26th Movement in Santa Clara. Since 1971 he has been vice minister of the fishing industry.

I am leaving Cuba the next day. I am always coming and going to Cuba, and I have much to do before my departure, bags to pack, people to say goodbye to yet again, but I try to be patient when his secretary asks me and Humberto to wait in the hallway when we arrive for our appointment. As we wait, I start to feel uneasy. I had hesitated to contact Oltuski in the first place, leaving him for the end of my list. I wasn't sure I ought to be seeking out someone so entangled with the dominant political culture. Maybe I was succumbing to the old fear my mother had instilled in me about being brainwashed by the *comunistas*. But I worried about the consequences, even if I felt too naïve to even try to imagine what the consequences might be of appearing to flirt with people in power. I'd met Oltuski ten years earlier and found him charming, though it had also been stressful. That time I'd gone to his home and I had to listen to him tell me his life story as he sat under a life-size poster of Fidel Castro.

A half hour later, we are called into Enrique's office. In the large, airy room, a desk sits smack in the middle. Above it is an enormous map of Cuba, framed in glass. There is a seminar table on one side of the room and a green velvet print couch and two sunken chairs on the other side. The picture windows at each end let in the vastness of the sky and the gauzy sunshine of the end of the day.

Enrique, at seventy-six, is slim, svelte, neatly dressed in a beige shirt and brown pants, and his turquoise eyes shine with the vigor of a man who has lived his life without regrets. After we greet one another, he asks, "Do you like the sea?" When I say yes, he tells me to sit in the chair to the right, so I can face the sea.

Before I can say anything, he remarks, "Next week we celebrate the anniversary of our nationalization of the phone company."

He asks if I've heard of ETECSA, the Cuban phone company.

"Yes," I say.

He replies proudly, "I was the one who suggested we nationalize it."

These days, Enrique says, he has four jobs. He is vice minister of the fishing industry. He is involved in a project, together with the former minister of culture, to recuperate everything that can be known about the history of Cuban independence leader José Martí. He is a writer of books. And on Sundays he puts on his farming clothes and goes out to his yard and tends to his tomatoes, his green peppers, his trees.

He asks, "Have you read my books?"

I admit that I haven't.

He smiles and seems not to hold it against me.

From his desk he pulls out an English translation of one of his books, *Mi Vida Clandestina: The Secret Life of a Leader in the Cuban Revolution,* so I can have a look at it. Enrique tells me that when he received the first copy of the book he sent it to Fidel and Fidel called him up and told him he'd learned a lot from his book.

I smile a polite anthropologist's smile, keeping my Fidel-phobia under control, and leaf through the pictures.

Enrique says, "In my books you'll find everything you want to know about me. I write for the youth, so they'll know why we became revolutionaries. I want them to know what it was like here before. How people in Santa Clara walked barefoot through the streets. My family had money, so if someone became ill we went to the hospital. But there was no hospital for the poor."

While Enrique speaks, the wind pounds against the windows and the old air conditioner huffs and puffs. I look out at the sea and look back at Enrique's eyes, the same turquoise color, as if his eyes have become more turquoise from staring at the ocean for so many years.

Enrique continues, "As a child I spoke Yiddish. My culture was Jewish culture. But in school I learned Spanish. I learned about another history that wasn't the history of Moses, but the history of José Martí. That's how I became Cuban. I pulled away from Judaism to become a free thinker. I wasn't a *polaco* or a Jew anymore. I was *cubano*. Now I have four children and they all live in Cuba. You better watch out! The four of them are members of the Cuban Communist Party!"

Enrique laughs and I laugh along with him a bit awkwardly. Clearly he recognizes my position as a Cuban American, recognizes that I might feel uneasy about talking to a staunch communist like him, whose four children have followed in his path.

As I think about what he's said, what fascinates me even more is how Enrique draws a parallel between the history of Moses and Martí. For all Cubans, the nineteenth-century independence leader and poet José Martí is a hero of sacred importance. Since Martí lived in the United States while organizing Cuba's liberation (for which he would pay with his own life), Cuban exiles in Miami identify with him. At the same time, Martí's struggle to free Cuba from Spanish domination was unfinished because of the postcolonial intervention of the United States in the Spanish-American War; it is this aspect of Martí's legacy that inspired Fidel Castro to view the Cuban Revolution as a *revolución martiana*, a revolution that would complete Martí's.

Before the Revolution, Jews in Cuba looked upon Martí as a thinker who admired Jewish values. Martí had also drawn upon American Jewish legal and financial assistance to wage his freedom struggle against Spain. In 1954, a homage to José Martí in Yiddish was published by the Jewish Cuban community in honor of the centennial of his birth, and in 1960 *Vida Habanera* published an article on the parallel lives of José Martí and Theodore Herzl, the founder of Zionism. Enrique seems to be drawing on both the revolutionary and pre-revolutionary Jewish views of Martí as he contemplates how he became Cuban and Communist and passed that inheritance on to his children.

After a pause, Enrique says, "What do you think? Am I a Jew? Or an ex-Jew?"

Since I don't know what to reply, he continues, "Let me tell you a joke I once heard from a Jewish reporter. What did the five most famous Jews give to the world? Moses gave us the law. Christ gave us love. Freud gave us sex. Marx gave us politics. And Einstein said it was all relative."

We laugh and drink the shots of espresso the secretary has brought us on a tray.

Our conversation has now gone on for a while and Humberto is concerned that the light will fade as dusk approaches.

The three of us stand and glance around the office, trying to see where we might take Enrique's picture.

Might we photograph him next to the portrait of José Martí?

Enrique immediately agrees.

As he poses for the picture, he remarks, "There are three things Martí said all real men must accomplish in their lifetime."

"Have a child.

"Write a book.

"Plant a tree.

"I'm happy to say I've done them all."

16

EINSTEIN IN HAVANA

José Altshuler Gutwert and Ernesto Altshuler Alvárez are an unusual father and son. For one thing, both are accomplished scientists. José Altshuler, the only child of a Polish mother and a father from Belarus, is an electrical engineer by training who grew up in Old Havana. By the time he finished high school in 1947, he had decided to become a Communist. He supported the Revolution and was a key advisor in the development of telecommunications in Cuba. He became president of the National Space Commission and the Cuban Society of History of Science and Technology. In turn, his son, whom he named Ernesto in honor of Ernesto (Che) Guevara, became professor of physics at the University of Havana in 1989.

Like many multigenerational Cuban families, José and Ernesto live in the same apartment, together with their wives and Ernesto's young daughter. Their apartment is around the corner from the new staging area across the Malecón, with its massive statue of independence leader José Martí holding a rescued Elián in his arms. Political rallies against the American government are held there almost daily.

When Humberto and I arrive, we are immediately ushered into the book-lined study of the apartment. José tells me to sit in the big rocking chair, so I'll be comfortable, and he sits in another rocking chair facing me. Ernesto takes a seat on the small sofa. After a few minutes, José's wife, Mercedes, brings us tea and quickly excuses herself, saying she has to keep an eye on her grand-daughter.

"We are two different generations," José begins. "I am older, so I should be the one to start."

José asks what it is I want to know, and when I say I'm writing about the Jews of Cuba, he says, "I remember that on Lamparilla Street, near Compostela, there lived a sculptor and that was where the leftists gathered. I was very young but I went with my parents. During the years 1936–1939, the time of the Spanish Civil War, we knew this was a war against fascism. Then the Second World War started and it was horrible. Even more horrible than we could imagine. When we heard about the Nazi savagery and how they were specifically killing Jews, my father, who was always an optimist, said, 'This can't be,' but my mother said, 'That's how it is, it's taking place.' I remember going to the Parque Central in 1945 with my father and seeing Russians and Germans arguing with one another."

In that era José said it was imperative for Jews to boldly assert their Jewishness because the fascism was so blatantly anti-Semitic. But leftist Jews like his parents went to Yiddish cultural events at the Kultur Farein to connect with other Jews, not to the synagogue. The Yiddish radio station, which was Communist in orientation, played imaginary dialogues between a nonbeliever and God, in which the nonbeliever would say, "I'll exchange everything in the next world for a bit of happiness in this world."

He vividly remembers that one of the luxuries his father most enjoyed was going to a Jewish bakery on Acosta Street once a month and buying delicatessen meat and sweet cakes. He loved *pan polaco* ("Polish bread"), which was basically a roll. "Give me a *polaco con mantequilla,*" people would say, "a Pole with butter."

José's parents struggled financially, but José viewed this as a blessing: "One of the things I have to thank my parents for is that they never had any interest in making money. The only thing they cared about was me and that I be able to study."

In a manila folder titled "Jews in Cuba," José keeps a copy of a text written by Cuban anthropologist Fernando Ortiz, *Defensa cubana contra el racismo antisemita* ("A Cuban Argument against Anti-Semitic Racism"). José says that as a Cuban Jew he feels proud of this document because it was published a few months before the war began in 1939 and signed not only by Ortiz but by Afrocuban leftists of the era. As José points out, although people often say that anti-Semitism doesn't exist in Cuba, they rarely know why that's the case. He is convinced anti-Semitism didn't gain a foothold in Cuba because of the leftist antiracist movement. Scholar-activists like Ortiz and his allies understood that the struggles against anti-Semitism and racism were linked struggles.

After the Revolution José hoped Jews would stay in Cuba to fight against all forms of racism. He organized an event to commemorate the anniversary of the uprising in the Warsaw Ghetto—the leaflet reads *A todos los Hebreos de Cuba* ("To All the Jews of Cuba")—but by then it was 1962 and the vast majority of the Jews had already chosen to flee the island.

José is done speaking. He gets up from the rocking chair and tells Ernesto it's his turn. Ernesto sits and waits for me to begin asking questions. Not knowing what to say, I ask him what's new in the realm of physics. He brightens and tells me it's the World Year of Physics (2005) and events are being held globally to commemorate Einstein's miraculous year of scientific breakthroughs. Cuba is participating, he adds, marking the seventy-fifth year since Einstein's visit to the island in 1930. He helped organize an exhibition at the Casa Humboldt in Havana and was glad it had turned out well.

"And there's something else I'm doing," Ernesto says, with an air of mischief.

He opens up a rolling suitcase and takes out a bronze bust of Einstein and a smaller bronze standing figure of Einstein. He puts them on the edge of his father's desk and says, "I'm lobbying for the idea of placing a statue of Einstein on the *escalinata* [stairway] of the Physics Department at the University of Havana. It's a very central location in the city. The statue would be life-size and in bronze. It would be an interesting attraction. But I've had to become a showman to try to get financial support. There's an Israeli involved in the production of grapefruits in Jagüey Grande and I've spoken to him, but I haven't gotten a response. We need $14,000, which for us is a lot of money."

Ernesto strokes his beard, which Ernesto Guevara, his namesake, would surely have approved of.

"It's funny, Einstein is always portrayed as an old man, but he made most of his discoveries when he was young. Anyway, here I am, my ancestors were total failures at making money, and I want a statue of Einstein in Havana. It's a new experience for me, a metaphysical experience, trying to raise the money to do this. I guess there's a Jewish element to it all. I feel proud that Einstein was Jewish."

"So you do feel Jewish?" I ask Ernesto.

Ernesto sighs. "I have very little contact with the Jewish community. But there are a lot of Jews in science. I'm 50 percent Jewish; my mother isn't Jewish. I don't know whether Jews are a people, a religion, or a bunch of interesting intellectuals. Like my old man, I think being Jewish is a cultural thing. I've always had the impression that Judaism requires you to study a lot. Since the religion is so demanding and Jews have been persecuted for such a long time, they don't know what else to do, so they study physics. Here, when there's no water and the electricity goes out, there isn't anything else to do but study physics."

A year and a half later, in the fall of 2006, I sent Ernesto an email asking about the Einstein statue. He wrote back immediately from the Ecole Super-iéure de Physique et de Chimie Industrielles in Paris. He said he would be returning soon to Cuba, where a lot of work awaited him as the new dean of the physics department.

He'd had no luck raising the money for the statue.

He directed me to the web site for the World Year of Physics in Cuba where he'd posted a paragraph entitled "A dream that didn't come true."

Ernesto writes: "Albert could not 'return' for the 75th anniversary of his visit to Havana. What a pity."

17

SALOMÓN THE SCHNORRER

I've known him for years, over a decade. While other people come and go, he's one of the most consistent faces in Havana's Jewish community.

He's the community's resident schnorrer—Yiddish for freeloader, moocher, beggar. He specializes in asking foreigners—especially women—for handouts. He'll present a foreign woman with a wilted rose, or any flower he finds while wandering around the city, utter a few flattering words, and ask for a gift in return. If he sees a visitor struggling to find his or her way back to the hotel after a visit to one of the synagogues, he'll offer to escort them and then wait around for a tip.

He spends his days roaming from one synagogue to another, eating the meals provided at each, and asking for people's leftovers and chicken bones to take home, he always says, to his dog. I've been told he isn't as poor as he appears, that he deliberately dresses like a tramp to win sympathy, that he performs his Jewishness by donning a *kippah* as soon as he's in range of Jewish visitors. I can't say whether these rumors are true. I've never been to his home. I do know he speaks English perfectly. He's smart and cunning, and he's capable of being very charming.

One day I decide not to brush him off. What he wants, I realize, more than anything, is to be noticed, to be seen. Overjoyed at my attention, he whips out a Brazilian magazine with a story about the Jews of Cuba, in which his picture appears.

"Look, that's me!" he says.

Not in the least afraid to be vain, he adds, "Lots of people have taken my picture. Someone also took my picture for a newspaper in Holland."

He's around the synagogues so much that I'm sure he's been photographed countless times by Jewish visitors and journalists from all over the world.

It dawns on me that in a way he and I are not so different from one another. I too roam from synagogue to synagogue, talking to people, asking to hear their stories, observing, taking photographs, accepting hospitality. We anthropologists are also schnorrers, sponging off of others to find tales to tell of our travels.

On some level, I think the schnorrer of Jewish Havana knows that he and I are in the same boat, because after carefully wrapping up the Brazilian

magazine in a plastic bag, he says to me, "Come to Adath Israel on Thursday. Don't miss it! Mr. Fisher from Canada will be there. He distributes things one by one, to men and women. He's come to Cuba thirty-two times. Really, don't miss it. I know you'll like it. You can take pictures."

I tell him I'll be there, and then I think after so many years I've never stopped to ask him his name.

"My name is Salomón Bonte Lederman," he tells me.

Just in case I might forget, he asks to write it down in my notepad. With a strong hand, he writes his full name out for me.

"I was born in Romania in 1924, on the 12th of March. In Bessarabia, a little village. I came to Cuba in 1931 when I was seven years old. I studied Yiddish in a school that used to exist on the corner of Jesús María and Cuba. That was where the old Adath Israel synagogue was located. I'm the only one here who knows Yiddish perfectly. I can read *and* write Yiddish; I'm the only one."

I ask him to write some words in Yiddish in my notepad and he agrees.

"What did you write?" I ask when's done.

He smiles devilishly and says, "*Estoy enamorado de tí.*" And then in English, he says, "I love you, Ruth!"

18

MR. FISHER'S
TWICE-YEARLY GIFTS

It's Thursday and I take Salomón Bonte Lederiman's suggestion and go to Adath Israel to witness the visit of Mr. Fisher from Canada.

The synagogue is Orthodox and the men and the women sit separately. Religious services begin early and at nine A.M. the pews are already almost all full. Usually there are plenty of seats on a weekday morning. I see people praying, but most are half-dozing, distractedly looking around.

I choose a pew in the back, joining two old women who are deep in conversation. One whispers to the other, "All these people heard that el señor Fisher would be here today. That's why they've come."

While Mr. Fisher leads services on the men's side, the women in my pew turn to me and ask who I am. I tell them I'm from Cuba, but I live in the United States. I tell them I've come to visit, to learn about the Jews in Cuba. Then I ask who they are.

Berta Esquenazi Benador, sitting next to me, tells me her name and gives me her address. She watches as I write the information in my notepad. Then she says, "I don't have a phone. I was a fool not to install it when I could have. At the time I thought I was leaving the country."

I turn and ask the woman to Berta's left what her name is.

She takes my pad and writes: Dinah Elena Nudelfuden Perelmuter. She gives me her address and the phone number of a neighbor.

Berta says, "Elena was born in Poland. I was born in Sagua La Grande. My family came from Turkey. From Istanbul."

"Do you always attend services at this synagogue?" I ask.

Berta nods. "I come to ask God to give me health and to give my son health. I like to come here because they help us a lot. Here they give you more than at the other synagogues. They give us breakfast every day. And a meal on Friday and Saturday. They attend to us very well. On Mother's Day they gave us a set of glasses and silverware. They give us money too. The older people get ten dollars every month. They give us clothes, shoes, everything. Every month they give us vegetable oil, ten cans of tomato sauce, three cans of tuna fish, two cans of sardines, black olives and green olives, two packages of chickpeas, two packages of lentils, two packages of pinto beans, and two packages of white beans. They give us all those things. It's more than they give at the Patronato. And a nice breakfast they serve us. I've been coming here for ten years and they keep helping me just the same."

Elena reaches inside a plastic bag and pulls out an ancient passport. She passes it to me and says, "I'm going to be eighty-four in September. This is my Polish passport, the one I came to Cuba with." It is worn and frayed at the edges but the photograph of her and her mother is still clear and shows the fear and uncertainty in their eyes.

I admire the passport, learning that she always carries it with her, and ask if I can photograph it.

"Yes," she says. "Afterward, not now."

"Quiet," a woman orders from the pew in front of us. "The Torahs are coming!"

The procession of men carrying the Torahs quickly passes by and Berta and Elena squeeze around me to kiss them, following the Jewish tradition of showing devotion to a sacred object.

When the service is over, Elena says, "Now el señor Fisher will give out the things he brought for us. He gives us underwear. He gives us deodorant. First he gives things to the men. Then to the women. He comes in January and in May. Twice a year."

Sure enough, just as Elena says, the tall and grinning Mr. Fisher comes sauntering over to the women's side, the men following. The men take their seats in the front pews and the women move to the back. The scene feels like elementary school. Mr. Fisher calls the men to the front, one by one, placing underwear, a tube of Colgate toothpaste, socks, soap, deodorant, a disposable razor, and a handkerchief in their hands. Then the women are called up, one by one. They receive underwear, Colgate toothpaste, soap, deodorant, socks, and a kitchen towel.

I don't know what to think as I watch. It all seems carnivalesque and yet at the same time it's endearing to see Mr. Fisher holding up men's underpants and women's panties and trying to judge if the size is right by dangling the garment in front of each person's body. While he might have simply dropped off the treasure trove of things at the office and asked the Adath Israel leadership to distribute them to the members of the congregation, he has chosen to put his gifts directly in the hands of people in the community, perhaps to be sure that the things get to those who need them. Now that the Cuban rationing system can't provide the wide variety of goods it once did, Mr. Fisher fills the space vacated by the government, at least for those Jews who know about his twice-yearly visits to Adath Israel. Clearly he's taking pleasure in giving. And the recipients are genuinely grateful. Everyone says, "Thank you." Some say, "May God bless you." And I hear someone exclaim, "This is a country where, even with money, it's not always easy to find these things."

Salomón, the schnorrer, is there, of course, holding his own trove and cheerily taking in the pageant of fellow congregants passing by with their arms full. "Aren't you glad you came? I told you this would be interesting for you. Take pictures. Take pictures. It's no problem to take pictures today. It's not Shabbat."

And then I see a woman whose name I don't learn. There is a look of such anguish in her expression that I can't think of anything to say to her and just watch

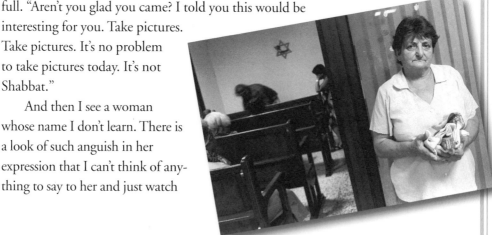

mutely as Humberto snaps her picture. "It hurts," she seems to be saying. "It hurts to have you see me in this condition, but you insist on seeing me, so go ahead and look."

She is holding Mr. Fisher's gifts and it seems like she's about to weep.

Mr. Fisher didn't foresee the possibility that a woman might break down in tears after receiving his gifts. That must be why he provided handkerchiefs to the men, but not to the women.

19

BECOMING RUTH BEREZNIAK

Hours later, in the kitchen of the Adath Israel synagogue, there is an intoxicating aroma of boiled milk from the *café con leche* offered to the congregants after morning services. Nelsy Hernández Reyes is alone and sitting at an empty table, lost in thought.

"Do you have some time to talk?" I ask.

"Yes, I do. Come, sit down."

I take a seat next to Nelsy and she smiles brightly. She is looking healthy and strong. The last time I saw her she was at home recovering from breast cancer.

"What can I do for you?" she asks, watching as I pull out my notepad and pen.

"Nelsy, I would love to know the story of how you became involved with the Jewish community."

She sighs in response, as if I've asked her to tell a long story she doesn't know how to begin to tell. Finally, she says, "I've been part of the Jewish community since 1979, when I married Abraham. I used to help him here at the synagogue. And I helped him with the cemetery. I have good handwriting. I wrote up the minutes of the meetings."

"Did you convert when you married him?"

"No, not at all. The first conversions after the Revolution took place in 1993. That's when I converted. And then Abraham and I were married under the *chupah*."

Her husband, Abraham Berezniak, was one of the leaders of the Jewish revival in Havana. He was the only child of a Polish Jewish father and a mother who converted to Judaism. Abraham was brought up religious. He celebrated his bar mitzvah at Adath Israel in 1959, coming of age the same year the Revolution began. His father had intended to leave Cuba and then at the last minute decided to stay. The synagogue became a refuge for him and eventually for his son as well. Abraham attended services daily at Adath Israel during the 1980s, when atheism was the norm in Cuba and only a few elderly Jews kept up religious traditions. He also managed the records of the two Jewish cemeteries in Guanabacoa, served as the kosher butcher for all of Havana, and each year he distributed the matzah for Passover. He took it upon himself to rescue Torahs from the synagogues that shut down, which is why Adath Israel has Torahs from Poland as well as from Turkey, and the Torahs that belonged to the United Hebrew Congregation (the American temple). Abraham became the president of Adath Israel, presiding over the decision to affiliate the synagogue with the ultra-Orthodox Lubavitch movement. He was in his early fifties when he died, in 1998, due to kidney failure.

Nelsy edges closer and says, "I chose the name Ruth as my Hebrew name. Abraham showed me her story in an encyclopedia. Seeing what Ruth did, without being born Jewish, I thought to myself, I can do that too."

"What did you know about Judaism before you met Abraham?"

Nelsy laughs. "I didn't know anything! I had no idea what a synagogue was. But the world is so small. One of my aunts had married one of Abraham's uncles. No one had any idea he was Jewish. He died young, of the same disease as Abraham. But before then, they had a little store in Oriente and he used to give me things from the store all the time. So the years passed, and my aunt, who was remarried by then, runs into Abraham and tells him she has a beautiful niece who has just returned from studying in the Soviet Union. Out of curiosity he comes to visit. And that's how it all began. I was working in Holguín, close to my family. I didn't want to leave. But Abraham persisted."

Abraham convinced her, a country girl, to go to Havana with him. Her life took a turn she would never have predicted.

Nelsy says, "There was a time when hardly anybody came to the synagogue. Abraham worked hard. It helped me to help him. Now I can't live without coming here. When I was ill and getting chemotherapy, it was good to come to the synagogue. It made me feel alive. On Fridays we have 60 people coming to services and during the fiestas the Lubavitch join us and we get 160 people. We're following the path Abraham wanted us to follow. We're continuing in the Orthodox tradition. Being as kosher as we can be."

Nelsy feels that her lack of religious background helped her to be open to the idea of becoming Jewish. Both her parents were atheists. "I never went to church, never took communion," she says. "My father and mother fought in the Sierra Maestra. I lived in Jíbara until I was fifteen. It's picturesque, but very underdeveloped. I studied psychology and education in the Soviet Union for five years. I'm a professor of pedagogy. Thanks to the Revolution, I am who I am today."

"What do you mean thanks to the Revolution, you are who you are today?"

"Well, I was born in the countryside. I was from a humble family. If it hadn't been for the Revolution, I wouldn't have come to Havana, I wouldn't have gone to the Soviet Union. I'll always be grateful for that. And Abraham also was grateful to Cuba. His kidney transplant didn't cost him anything. He got all his medications for free. Thanks to the government he lived for another fifteen years. What he never lost was his faith. His world was the synagogue, but he wasn't disaffected. And for someone like me, who started out poor, you have to feel grateful."

We're so immersed in our conversation that we don't see Nelsy's son, Yacob Berezniak Hernández, standing in the doorway of the kitchen.

Yacob, half in jest, but also half serious, proceeds to scold his mother.

"How can you be telling her all that about being grateful to the Revolution? Don't you realize that everything you're saying is going to be heard in the United States?"

I can understand Yacob's apprehension. He and his mother are carrying the mantle left by his father at Adath Israel. That mantle has spiritual and economic underpinnings that depend on external support from the Lubavitch and other Jewish organizations in the United States, Latin America, and Canada. Nelsy's praise for the Revolution might seem like they're biting the capitalist hand that feeds them.

But Nelsy is not about to take any of her words back. She looks her son in the eye and says, "This is how I feel, I owe everything to the Revolution. It's the truth."

"What about you, Yacob?" I ask. "How do you feel?"

From the doorway, Yacob says, "I had Jewish roots planted inside me from my earliest days. I was two years old when my father started bringing me to the synagogue. I celebrated my bar mitzvah in December of 1994 and haven't stopped coming here since then. After a while, this place becomes a part of you."

Yacob turns away, his attention distracted by the sudden appearance of two men who look to be in their late twenties. They are dressed in shorts and sandals and introduce themselves, in English, as Jewish visitors from Boston. They were roaming around, they explain, and saw the synagogue. They hadn't expected to find a synagogue in Havana!

"Excuse me," Yacob says and leaves Nelsy and me in the kitchen.

I hear him switch effortlessly into English as he tells the Bostonians about the history of the synagogue, the daily religious services, the charitable assistance provided to the congregants.

The Bostonians listen intently and ask the usual questions—How many Jews are there in Cuba? Are people free to practice the Jewish religion? Is there anti-Semitism?

Yacob tells them there are a thousand Jews in Cuba, that people are free to be Jewish in Cuba, that there is no anti-Semitism.

"That's amazing, just amazing," I hear the Bostonians say.

Back in the kitchen, I am thanking Nelsy for taking the time to tell me her story.

Nelsy smiles. "That's my story," she says. "The story of Ruth Berezniak, as Abraham liked to say."

20

AFTER EVERYONE HAS LEFT

The shuttered door to the balcony is open and the evening breeze feels soft as a silk scarf. The last rays of sunshine want to illuminate the old photographs that Myriam Radlow Zaitman has spread out on the dining table in her apartment in the neighborhood of Santo Suárez.

"Everyone left, but we decided to stay," she says.

I have known Myriam since I first started traveling to Cuba in the early 1990s. She is the trusted secretary of the director of Casa de las Américas, the foremost cultural and literary institute in Cuba, headquartered in an art deco building two blocks from the Malecón. It includes a library, a gallery, and a bookstore on its main floor. On the second floor is the home of the journal, the literary press, and an office overlooking the sea where Myriam can be found every day of the week working at her desk.

Myriam was never a stranger. From the beginning, I knew I could stop by her office and say hello whenever I visited Casa to shop at the bookstore, attend a lecture, or see the latest exhibition. If she received an extra copy of a newly published book, she saved it for me until I returned again. It wasn't simply that she was Jewish, though that was part of the bond. We had other ties that connected us—not exactly kinship ties but something very close to kinship in the Jewish Cuban community. Myriam's sister Perla, who lived in Miami after leaving Cuba in the early years of the Revolution, is my Aunt Rebeca's best friend. In the years before easy Internet access, when I traveled back and forth to Cuba, I became a bridge between the two sisters, delivering letters and gifts for them. Perla would load me down with knapsacks filled with clothes and toiletries, while Myriam wanted me to lug bottles of rum and boxes of cigars back to Perla.

Then there was the tie with Myriam's husband, Luis Lapidus Mandel, an architect who died of cancer in 1995. Luis, who had shown me around Old Havana as the city was starting to come alive again with the restoration of the main plazas, was the nephew of Oscar Mandel, who became my grandmother's "boyfriend" while the two lived out their final widowed years in Miami Beach. Because of these ties, it was in the presence of Myriam and Luis, more than with other members of the Jewish community, that I would wonder what it would have been like if my family had stayed in Cuba. Around them, that strange expression often popped into my head—*There but for the grace of God go I.*

My Aunt Rebeca has often asked me about Myriam, wondering how it is that she continues to stay in Cuba "all by herself." Not only is Myriam's sister Perla living outside of Cuba, but so too is her sister Raquel and brother Samuel. "Myriam must really believe in the Revolution," my Aunt Rebeca always concludes.

Myriam hadn't expected to stay alone in Cuba. She was certain her parents would remain on the island too. Her father, Arón Radlow, fought against the dictatorship of Machado and was jailed numerous times before the Revolution. He was a dedicated communist and Myriam looked up to him. But in the late 1970s, he and her mother made what they thought would be a brief visit to Miami and ended up choosing not to return to Cuba. Their departure broke Myriam's heart. When the news of Myriam's father's death came by phone in March 1995, her husband was in the last stages of terminal cancer. Luis couldn't stop weeping at the news of his father-in-law's death and two months later he was dead too.

We eat a savory dinner of black beans, rice, and salad, along with potatoes roasted with beef Myriam has obtained from the kosher butcher shop. She tells me that she and Luis believed they could live a life founded on idealistic principles. Nothing was more emblematic of the hope they had for a better future than a photograph from 1974 of Luis and Myriam and their two daughters, Lydia and Batia, huddled together, the long arms of Luis gathering them closely. Myriam explains that in the picture they were posing in front of the campsite where students resided while in the countryside doing volunteer work. Even today, she notes, young people work in the countryside as part of their schooling to make them feel part of the national goal of improving life for everyone.

I think about that picture of a united family standing together on the soil of Cuba despite all the odds. The family has unraveled, or, more precisely, it has become transnational, as have so many Cuban families. Ten years ago, Lydia met and married a Norwegian man, had a baby, and settled in Norway. Four years ago Batia left with her son and went to live with her Aunt Perla, who had moved to Puerto Rico.

Although Myriam is able to travel and has visited her daughters and grandchildren in Puerto Rico and Norway, she knows it's not the same as having them nearby. Now more than ever, her family doesn't understand why she still stays in Cuba. They would get her out in a minute—but Myriam won't go.

"Yes, I get nostalgic for my daughters," says Myriam. There is sorrow in her voice, but then she says, "I have my work, and these days it's also easier to be in touch."

She clears the dishes and brings out the heavenly dessert combo that only tastes so utterly delicious in Cuba: a thick slab of the white hard cheese from Camagüey and a nectared guava paste she has made herself.

"Look how pretty," Myriam says, pointing to the fading light behind me.

With our fingers sticky from the cheese and guava, we step out to the balcony to watch the sun set over Havana.

It is more than gorgeous, the way the sun dives into the sea, the way the skyline turns pink, then turquoise, then black. At last the night spreads a blanket over the secrets of the city's inhabitants. It is enough to make you fall in love with Cuba all over again.

21

THE KETUBAH THAT
BECAME A PASSPORT

"We're trying to create paradise here in our home," Sara Yaech says as she invites Humberto and me into her freshly painted house on the outskirts of Havana.

We are barely inside and Sara is already offering us fresh mango juice.

"From our garden," she announces proudly, leading the way to the patio behind the house, where her husband, Pedro Mauriz García, is busily sweeping up the debris of leaves from the mango tree. Sara points out how he has built an outdoor fountain, planted flowers in pots, and hung a loveseat-swing between two poles. Their small garden is an enchanted space, far from the noise and grime and intense crowding of Havana's streets.

"We love to spend our time out here," Sara exclaims. "But let's go inside—I have some things to show you."

On the dining table Sara has arranged neat piles of photographs and documents.

"You want to see my parents' *ketubah*?" Sara asks.

The *ketubah* is a Jewish marriage contract traditionally written in Aramaic. Sara holds up a *ketubah* with elaborate calligraphy, a delicate border design, and an image of the Ten Commandments.

"It's very beautiful," I say. "It's good you've saved it."

"And we almost lost it!" Sara exclaims. "I rescued it from the flames." She shudders and asks, "Do you want to know the story? I'll tell you."

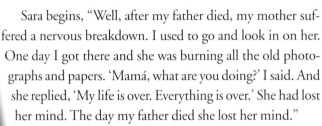

Sara begins, "Well, after my father died, my mother suffered a nervous breakdown. I used to go and look in on her. One day I got there and she was burning all the old photographs and papers. 'Mamá, what are you doing?' I said. And she replied, 'My life is over. Everything is over.' She had lost her mind. The day my father died she lost her mind."

Sara had recovered the *ketubah*, thinking of it as a document of sentimental value, a document that enshrined the love of her parents for each other. She saved it, along with the old photographs and other keepsakes that she salvaged from her mother's bonfire of memories, imagining that she'd show these things to her children when she grew old.

A curious thing about the *ketubah* was that it sanctified a marriage between a Jew and a convert. Sara's father, a Sephardic Jew from Istanbul, arrived in Cuba in 1920, and chose to settle in the town of Manzanillo. As Sara says, "I don't know what it was about Manzanillo, but the *turcos*—the Turks—all went to live there." Her father met her mother in Manzanillo. Chuckling, Sara remarks, "My mother used to say she got married late in life because she was picky. She was blond and had blue eyes. She looked around so much that she ended up marrying a *moro*—a Moor. That's what they called the Turks. They called them Moors. They were dark and had curly hair."

Her mother always spoke of having "renounced" her Catholic faith. She was the one who maintained Jewish traditions in their home. She made sure her three sons were circumcised. She even opposed Sara's plan to marry Pedro because he wasn't Jewish. Pedro's family was from the Canary Islands and Galicia. He was offended that Sara's mother didn't want him to marry Sara. Speaking in the racist ideology of the time, he quipped, "What's the problem? There isn't anyone black in my family."

Sara and Pedro had met while participating in the literacy campaign at the start of the Revolution. Along with hundreds of other idealistic young people from Havana, they went to the countryside to teach illiterate adults how to read and write. They married in 1965—by that time the difference in their religious backgrounds, though still an issue for Sara's mother, was otherwise inconsequential because the Jewish community had withered and a newly atheist society had been established.

I ask Pedro if he has since converted to Judaism.

"Not yet," he replies. And then he adds, "But I have to. Because when we die, she's not going to be in the Jewish cemetery and I will be somewhere else."

Sara nods. The hopeful glance she gives Pedro suggests to me that he's been promising to convert for some time but keeps putting it off.

Grasping the *ketubah* again, Sara runs her hand softly over the names of her parents, and says, "How do you prove you're a Jew? You need to have documents."

With those words, Sara launches into the story of how the *ketubah*, which she thought was just a keepsake, came to serve a practical purpose that changed the destiny of her family. In 1994, her daughter Jackie, a dental surgeon, was on a visit to Mexico. It was a time of unusual austerity in Cuba and Jackie decided she didn't want to return. But she was reluctant to defect because, as a doctor, that would have made it impossible, according to Cuban regulations, for her to go back to visit her family on the island. Then she heard about the Law of Return enacted by the Israeli government in 1950, which offers Jews and their families the right to settle in Israel and gain citizenship. She went to the Israeli embassy in Mexico City, announced she was Jewish, and asked for help in immigrating to Israel. The embassy was willing to assist her, but requested that she present family documents proving she was Jewish.

It occurred to Sara to send Jackie the *ketubah*. Two weeks later, with the ketubah of her grandparents as proof of her Jewish identity, Jackie was able to leave for Israel. Eventually Jackie returned to Mexico, married a Mexican Jew, and settled there.

But that wasn't the end of the story. That same *ketubah* became a kind of magical passport, a flying carpet, for several members of the Yaech family who chose to leave Cuba in the 1990s. Not only Jackie, but Sara's son, her nephews, and her brother all used it to prove they are Jewish and to gain the right to immigrate to Israel.

Sara says her family calls the *ketubah* their *carta de libertad,* alluding to the freedom decrees once granted to slaves in Cuba.

But she quickly adds, "Don't write that down. It's too harsh. Let's call it *una carta de salida*." An exit permit.

A *ketubah* that became an exit permit.

And tore the family apart.

Sara says that after her daughter and son left Cuba she wept so much it scared her. "My eyes were like a hose pouring water," she says.

A friend suggested she try painting, and that was how she found some peace of mind. Each day she fills canvases with images of her two grand-daughters, one living in Mexico, the other in Israel.

"Life in Cuba is hard," Sara says. "My son and daughter have paid for our visits to Mexico and Israel. So we see them now and then. My daughter gave me a Visa card and she deposits money in the account. She buys the oils so I can paint. We have enough to live. We take care of the house. My daughter says we're using the money very wisely."

It's time to leave, but I stop to take a last look at Sara's old photographs. One picture jumps out at me: a young Sara in a strapless party dress posing in front of a huge Star of David made completely of flowers. Seeing my interest, Sara retrieves another picture taken the same day showing a group of women in puffed-up dresses standing in a semi-circle on the swerving tile floor.

Holding up the two photographs, Sara says, "These pictures were taken at the Patronato. We were twenty-one young women and we had all turned fifteen in 1959. My birthday was in September. The *quinceañera* at the synagogue took place in November."

Although she saved the family passport from the flames, it is Sara who has been left behind. With a hint of grief in her voice, that no amount of time spent in her garden or painting canvases can fully heal, she tells me, "By 1960, 1961, everyone had left. None of those women are still here. The only one who stayed was me."

22

WHEN I SEE YOU AGAIN
THERE WILL BE NO PAIN
OR FORGETTING

Daniel Esquenazi Maya, a retired stevedore, has lived in the same rooftop apartment in Old Havana since 1957. He and his late wife used to rent the apartment, but the owners of the building left following the Revolution, and afterward Daniel, along with the other poor tenants of the building, no longer had to pay anything for their homes.

An articulate man who was active in the Jewish community long before others found their way to it, Daniel is one of the most photographed, filmed, and interviewed Jews on the island. And he deserves his fame. His parents were Sephardic Jews from Turkey and he was president of the oldest synagogue in Cuba, the Chevet Ahim, until it shut down. Now he is a daily participant at religious services at Adath Israel where his thunderous voice rises above all others when it is time to intone prayers and chants.

That voice has been trained through years of being a tango aficionado. Daniel spends his weekend afternoons singing tango at local cultural clubs in Havana. Tango is his great passion in life. Some of the neighbors, he says, think he's a madman on the roof singing tango songs. A "*polaco*," they call him, though he's Sephardic and born in Cuba.

I must confess that I am guilty of being part of the pack of onlookers who have turned Daniel into a celebrity. When I heard he was a tango aficionado, I asked Daniel to sing tango songs for my movie, *Adio Kerida,* which he did willingly. He crooned "Mi Buenos Aires querido" (My Beloved Buenos Aires) with the brokenhearted nostalgia of an immigrant, even though he's never been to Buenos Aires. In fact, he's never left Cuba.

He has more than two hundred records of Carlos Gardel, the great icon of Argentine tango. Enamored of Gardel since his youth, Daniel has turned an entire wall in his apartment into an informal shrine to the famed singer, who died too young in a plane crash at the height of his international popularity.

But Daniel is an organized romantic. All the songs in his collection are listed alphabetically in a binder. The titles hint at the moody joys and sorrows of the tango: "Como se canta en Nápoles" (How They Sing in Naples); "El mal que me hiciste" (The Harm You Did to Me); "Para quererte así" (To Love You Like This); "Que payaso" (What a Clown).

When I interviewed Daniel in 2001, his 1960 record player was still working. He played tangos for me from his collection and they sounded glorious, all their breathy drama still intact. He proudly gave me a Carlos Gardel album to take home as a souvenir. But five years later, when I visit him again at his rooftop apartment, he tells me he can't listen to his tango records anymore.

"My record player broke and there's isn't a soul in Cuba who knows how to fix it," he says. "It's nobody's fault. They don't make record players like this anymore."

Daniel is taking a stoical attitude to his loss, perhaps because he recognizes he's getting older and material possessions are of less use to him now. I see suddenly how gaunt he has grown, how his hair has thinned, how he struggles to get up the last flight of shaky wooden stairs to his rooftop apartment.

"I still enjoy my record collection," he says. "I remember all the tangos. I can hear them in my head."

Memory has become Daniel's record player. Memory and imagination. Tango has given him the ability to imagine how exile feels. Tango has given him the ability to put himself in the place of people not at all like him, people who've left their homes and are endlessly searching for a way to return.

Mi Buenos Aires querido
Cuando yo te vuelva a ver
No habrá más pena ni olvido.

My beloved Buenos Aires
When I see you again
There will be no pain or forgetting.

I can see Daniel singing this song on his rooftop, even though he's never known exile, never left home. He knows about a different sort of loss: seeing people leave all around him. And he knows that after everyone has left what remains is solitude.

Now and then, I will dare to think he's singing that Buenos Aires song for me. It was through Daniel that I first learned about the tango, first knew of Carlos Gardel, first heard the tango sung, first felt the desire to dance the tango. Like Daniel, I love the tango, love it for its obsession with lost things, love it for its inconsolable goodbyes.

III

Traces

23
TRACES

Upon the Jews still in Cuba has fallen the responsibility of preserving the scattered bits and pieces of Jewish life, the archaeological relics that have survived. At times willingly, at times reluctantly, they have become memory keepers.

They are the keepers of the mezuzahs that still cling to the thresholds of Jewish houses in Cuba.

They are the keepers of the Torahs brought from Turkey, which are conserved in the Centro Sefaradí in Havana. Their breastplates are beautiful works of filigree silver, with crowns and mini-arks that have little doors that open, revealing tiny Torahs inside.

They are the keepers of the prayer books in the synagogue, which speak to God in Hebrew and Spanish.

They are the keepers of old family prayer books that have turned brown with age and smell like rain.

They are the keepers of the wine cups, Shabbat candle holders, and hand-washing jugs left by Jews who have died or immigrated. Yacob Berezniak holds on to all these objects that were given to his father, Abraham Berezniak, who passed away.

They are the keepers of the leather chairs with embossed Jewish stars and Lion of Judah designs made for a bar mitzvah celebrated at the Centro Sefaradí on the eve of the family's departure from Cuba. The chairs have remained there ever since, waiting for the family's return, and are only used during religious services.

They are the keepers of the ornamental box that has always sat on the same shelf at the Adath Israel synagogue, where Elda Sevy Botton, a social worker, attends services every morning.

Matilde Farín Behar keeps a menorah that has been in her family for as long as she can remember. It belonged to her father, who was the last Jew to go to synagogue in Santiago de Cuba before it shut down in 1979. He was old by then and walked with a cane, but after the loss of the synagogue Matilde says he aged even more quickly.

The oud, a Middle Eastern instrument brought by a Sephardic Jewish immigrant from Turkey, is preserved by his niece Matilde Elí and her children. Sephardic songs in Ladino were sung with the oud as accompaniment. This oud is the only one that survives on the island. It is considered a national treasure and cannot be taken out of Cuba.

Traces remain, as well, of old Jewish stores, now the property of the state. Casa Jaime, a store owned by a Jew in Camagüey, preserves the original marble-tiled floor. Jaime—the Spanish version of Chaim—became a common name among Cuba's Jews.

And traces remain of customs that can be presented to the camera, but will not be passed on to the next generation. It is Leon Baly Levy, in a distant seaside town, who still remembers, "We came from Turkey to Campechuela on the 20th of June 1952. I was twelve years old. In Turkey we didn't use candles to welcome the Shabbat. We lit the oil in a bowl. This is how we used to welcome the Shabbat in Turkey."

How does one classify a trace such as this: an electricity bill that still arrives in the name of a Jew, Aron Wolfoicz, who has been gone from Cuba for half a century? Who knows if he is living or dead?

Having the right piece of paper, as Jews know all too well, can be a matter of life or death. Even during the upheavals of the Revolution, Jews in Cuba held on to family passports and documents of Jewish belonging. This immigration document, her youthful picture pinched by a rusty paper clip, belongs to Raquel Rodríguez Rodríguez, who immigrated to Cuba from Istanbul and settled in Remedios, a sleepy town with two churches and no other Jews midway between Cienfuegos and Caibarién.

Amidst a table piled with *ketubahs* and old citizenship papers, Raquel Rodríguez Rodríguez's grandson, David Langus Rodríguez, is guarded by a great-grandmother who stayed behind in Turkey. From under the glass frame she looks into the future with an eerie, penetrating stare, watching over the boy tenderly.

Dinah Elena Nudelfuden Perelmuter carries her family's Polish passport with her wherever she goes, as if it at any time she might be asked to prove her Jewish heritage.

José Levy conserves his father's Turkish passport. It's the only thing he has left of his father, he says. He had also kept the shirt he wore to his father's funeral, which he tore in grief, as is customary for Jews to do. And then one day his house was robbed and the thieves even took the ripped shirt.

It's not a document, but Jacobo Behar Behar, in Santiago de Cuba, guards like a diamond the one picture he has kept of his Sephardic mother in her youth, holding her image carefully in the palm of his hand.

But it isn't just documents from the past that people have found important to keep. To be a Jew you need new documents. Two young brothers, Victor and David Cabrero Pernas in Camagüey, already know this to be true. With conviction and sincerity they display their conversion documents—documents that prove they have been ritually circumcised and formally converted by a court of three rabbis. These papers certify, as well as pieces of paper can certify anything, that they are truly Jewish.

And then there are all the mass-produced receptacles from the capitalist world, not documents exactly, but Jewish flotsam and jetsam that arrive each day with the American Jewish donations coming to Cuba. What to do with those

things? Keep them? Throw them away? Isaac Nissenbaum Braitman tells me he keeps the empty jars of gefilte fish and horseradish, the empty bottles of kosher wine. He doesn't know why. He just does, as if they were a talisman from another world, a world where food is never in short supply. The role of the Jew in Cuba is to receive these gifts and treasure them.

Isaac has discovered that the heavy cardboard box from the round matzahs the Lubavitch distribute at Passover makes a very good hand-held fan if attached to a wooden stick. When I visit him, it's a hot day, so I try out the fan and agree it works very well.

After we photograph him, Isaac gives me the fan to take home as a souvenir.

IV

In the Provinces

24

SIMBOULITA'S PARAKEET

"It was like a tribunal of the Inquisition," recalls Julio. "They thought it was wrong for educators to have any religious affiliation. They singled me out for receiving matzah."

Julio Rodríguez Elí was a teacher for thirty-three years in Caibarién. He started his career working in a secondary school and kept moving up the ladder until he became a principal and a regional director of the schools he helped to found in the countryside. But in the years before the opening to religion in Cuba, his colleagues often questioned him about why he went to Havana to pick up the Passover matzah sent each year to the Jews of Cuba by the Canadian Jewish Congress. To avoid a confrontation, he gave up teaching. He now spends much of his time in his Soviet-era Lada. He has to baby it to keep it running, but he's able to drive neighbors and friends to and from Caibarién and Havana.

Julio holds no bitterness toward those who made his life difficult because of a few boxes of matzah. He is well liked in Caibarién for his lively character and wry sense of humor. He plays the saxophone every Sunday in the Municipal Band of Caibarién and never misses a performance. As he shows us around town, neighbors yell out "*Polaco*! What's new?" They stop to shake hands with him or to hear him crack a joke. All his life Julio has lived in this fishing town on the island's north coast, but people in Caibarién haven't understood the finer points of his identity. They all call him *polaco*, even though he's the son of Sephardic immigrants from Turkey and has no Polish ancestry to speak of. When I point this out to Julio, he shrugs and says he doesn't worry about it.

Even if they called him *turco,* it wouldn't be any more correct. He's not Turkish either. He's *cubano* through and through.

Before the Revolution, his father and his Uncle Isidoro owned clothing and jewelry stores in Caibarién. Julio takes me to see what's left of the old family businesses, which are now in ruins. He stops in front of his Uncle Isidoro's store, La Bandera Cubana (The Cuban Flag), and says that when Isidoro heard that his store was going to be nationalized and "given to the people," he flew into a rage and began throwing the merchandise into the street. He didn't stop until he was arrested by the police. "Pa'l pueblo todo!" he kept yelling. "Everything for the people!" Julio laughs. It is with wry humor rather than sorrow that he chooses to respond to the loss of his family's prosperity. As he puts it, "We so kindly donated our stores to the Cuban government and the Cuban government so kindly accepted our donation."

But on our return to his house, he continues on a more serious note. "I'm still here because of my mother and father," he says.

"Here" is the slow-paced town around which we're strolling, where fisher-men amble past on bicycles, freshly caught snappers strapped to their backs like knapsacks.

We've reached Julio's house and we're inside sitting on rocking chairs with the front door carefully left open so neighbors can see he's got nothing to hide. Then Julio tells me, "My father was going to leave when my Uncle Isaac left. But at the time people didn't think this system was going to last. And then my sister died. That totally destroyed my father. In 1980 my Uncle Isaac sent a boat to get us, but my father wasn't well. My sister's death had affected him even more than my mother. And I'd gotten married to María Elena and she didn't want to leave her parents. Back then, either the whole family left or the whole family stayed, so we stayed."

I ask Julio to tell me about his sister.

"Her name was Violeta. In Turkish it's Simboul. We called her Simboulita. She was studying biology in Havana. And she became ill. I don't know how, because she was always strong and healthy. I was the one who was asthmatic and skinny."

Violeta was twenty-five in 1977 when she died of leukemia. The question of where to bury her arose. The closest Jewish cemetery to Caibarién was in Santa Clara, but without the authority or the funds to attend to its upkeep, the few Jews left in the region had allowed it to deteriorate.

"Our cemeteries haven't been desecrated with anti-Semitic slogans like you see in other countries," Julio notes. "But they've been abandoned, since all the families left and the dead stayed here. And in Cuba building materials are in short supply, so people steal bricks and stones from the cemeteries."

What to do in such a situation? Julio's father wanted his daughter to be buried on Jewish soil, but only if that soil would be respected. Finally, he came up with a solution. Julio's father was a Mason—as were many Jews—and he was able to get a plot of land in the Masonic section of the Catholic cemetery in Caibarién. Simboulita was buried in that plot, which the family marked as Jewish. As Julio says, "We put up the Star of David and we made a family crypt there." After a few years, Simboulita was no longer alone; her father and mother, as well as an aunt and uncle, were eventually buried in the same crypt.

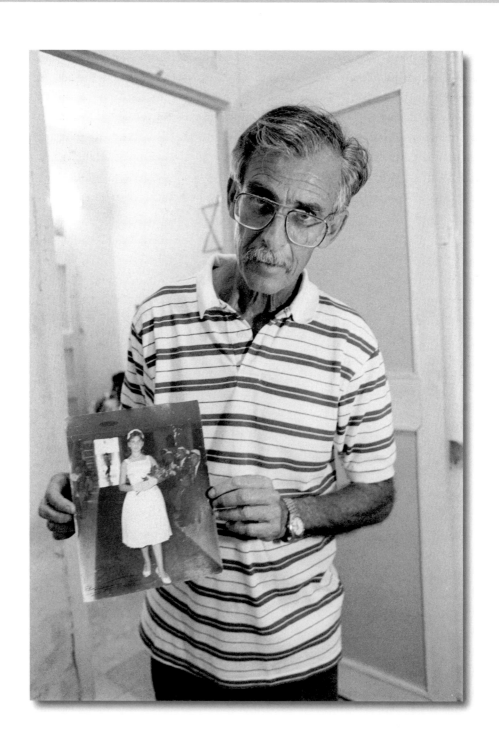

After hearing the story, I express interest in seeing Simboulita's grave. The words are hardly out of my mouth when Julio springs to his feet. "You want to go? Let's go." We get into his car and drive to the entrance of Caibarién. The cemetery is there, a vast web of crucifixes that rise over the horizon, the dead guarding the town's threshold.

Humberto and I follow Julio as he leads us through the crowded cemetery. He knows it well and whisks through the narrow pathways. We walk single file, trying to keep up. It is blazing hot in the middle of the day. Far from the entrance, past a maze of graves, in a corner that you would have to know was there to find it, we finally get to the Jewish crypt that Simboulita's father created for her in the Catholic cemetery.

My heart breaks to see where Simboulita lies buried—and to imagine the courage and fierce determination it must have taken to build her such a sheltering tomb, with a solitary Jewish star, at a time when it would have been easier to simply let her difference as a Jew go unmarked. Simboulita's stubborn

Jewish grave, hidden among crucifixes in the town cemetery of Caibarién, is one of the most moving memorials to Jewish endurance in the landscape of Cuba. No rabbi would approve of such a grave, but there was no rabbi around when Simboulita died. And for her grief-stricken father, it was a more loving gesture to carve out a space for her among the crucifixes close to home than to risk having his daughter's tomb vandalized or defaced in the abandoned Jewish cemetery in Santa Clara. If only visitors on Jewish tours to the island were taken to see Simboulita's tomb, they would truly understand the wrenching decisions Jews in Cuba had to make at a time when they felt alone in the world.

On our return to Julio's house, we are all thirsty, and Julio, as if to consecrate our shared experience of visiting his sister's grave, offers us leftover Manischewitz wine from his yearly Passover package.

And he remembers, "When my sister died, all of our grapevines withered. But would you believe it? Her parakeet is still alive. It's almost thirty years old."

From a bedroom deep inside the house I think I can hear Simboulita's parakeet singing. It is waiting for Simboulita to come home.

25

SEVEN JEWISH WEDDINGS
IN CAMAGÜEY

Julio reaches for a suit that has been in his closet for a long time . . . to be exact, more than four decades. He's been waiting for the right occasion to wear it, but that occasion never seems to come.

"I'd wear this suit, but it's full of moth holes," he says. "My Uncle Isaac was going to wear it when he left the country, but it turned out he couldn't take it with him. They only let people take two pairs of underwear, two pairs of socks, two of each thing. That was in 1962. It's a pity. The suit stayed here. And now the bugs have eaten it up. It's become a relic."

We have spent the night in Caibarién and we're visiting again with Julio Rodríguez Eli. He has a dilemma: he needs to figure out what he's going to wear to his own Jewish wedding. Julio and his wife, María Elena Gónzalez García, are already married by Cuban civil law and they have two children, Junior and Violeta. But in a few days they will be married in Camagüey's synagogue, together with six other couples. Presiding over this collective Jewish wedding in July 2004 will be Rabbi Shmuel Szteinhendler, the Argentine rabbi who has been overseeing the Jewish rebirth in Cuba since the 1990s with the support of the Joint Distribution Committee.

A few days later, when I see Julio and María Elena in Camagüey, Julio tells me he decided to wear a regular pair of pants and a regular shirt, as have all the other men. He whispers to me, "It doesn't really matter what we wear," and points to the large white-and-blue prayer shawls, provided by the Joint Distribution Committee, that have been given to each of the men. "With this *tallit* on, no one can see what we're wearing underneath."

But the Joint did think to provide funds for the women to be able to purchase new dresses. Each of the women wears a white dress made by a seamstress—in cotton, lace, or crocheted—and each of the women clasps a bouquet of white gardenias.

The old synagogue in Camagüey was turned over to the government after the Revolution, but a new one has been built with the support of the Joint Distribution Committee in another location in the city. It's long and narrow inside, with tall columns supporting wooden rafters, and filled to capacity with the seven couples getting married, their children and even some grandchildren, and members of the Jewish community of Camagüey. Whenever there is a festive occasion at any of the synagogues in Cuba, there is always a large turnout. Jewish Cubans, like all Cubans, love parties. But weddings are few and far

between in the Jewish community and everyone wants to get a glimpse of a mysterious ritual that no one has seen for decades. Plus there is wedding cake. Everyone looks forward to cake in Cuba. Cakes, for birthdays, weddings, and quinceañera celebrations, are considered hugely luxurious and yet indispensable items. The government has long provided all Cubans with cakes for such occasions through the rationing system.

Standing under the sacred canopy of a portable velvet *chupah,* which is attached to tall poles being held up by four young men (among them Junior, son of Julio and María Elena), the seven couples reaffirm their marriage bonds and their ties to the Jewish people and the Jewish faith. Each of the couples is made up of the same mix: men of Jewish heritage married to converted Cuban women. The couples say their vows one by one and exchange wedding bands, also provided by the Joint Distribution Committee.

It is a moving event, except that the rabbi, as rabbis tend to do, sermonizes for just a little too long about the miracle of the Jewish rebirth in Cuba while everyone is squished under the *chupah.* Between the crowding in the synagogue, the heat, and the restless children squirming in their seats asking when it's going to be over so they can eat cake, the seven-couple wedding starts to feel interminable. But the presence of so many Jews together in one place is a teaching opportunity for the rabbi, which he's not going to let go of easily, especially after the Joint Distribution Committee has flown him in from Chile, where he now lives. This may be why collective weddings are held periodically in Cuba—they are moments when religious authorities can bless the community for its devotion and reinforce its bond with the Jewish world beyond the island. And on the practical side, it's an efficient way to marry several couples at once in a country where there is no rabbi and people can't afford to throw wedding parties.

At the end of the ceremony, Rabbi Szteinhendler presents each of the couples with a signed copy of their marriage certificate, their *ketubah,* which certifies that they have been married by Jewish law, and should they ever choose to break their union, they will need to obtain a Jewish divorce from a court of rabbis.

And then, after all the solemnity, there finally is cake—triple-layered rum cake with meringue frosting that's melting fast in the heat and enough sugar flowers to rival the bouquets the brides were carrying.

It's cut very carefully, beginning with the bottom layer, so as not to disturb the little plastic husband and wife figurines balanced on top.

26

CHE WAITS FOR A NEW FRAME

An enormous portrait of Che Guevara used to hang at the entrance to Samuel León Profeta's house in Cienfuegos. It showed Che in the splendor of his youth, eyes cloudless, unsuspecting of the martyrdom that awaited him.

"Che Guevara is one of the greatest men who ever lived," says Samuel.

Given Samuel's admiration for Che, it is almost to be expected that in the family portrait from 2003, showing Samuel with his wife, daughter, and grandson, it looks as if Che is one more member of the family. It is Che's arms, rather than Samuel's, that seem to be embracing his wife and his daughter.

Samuel's Sephardic parents came from Turkey, and though his father was a rabbi, since his youth Samuel was passionately dedicated to the Cuban Communist Party and the Revolution. There is a "CDR" sign posted on the façade of his house, which means it is a meeting place for the Comité de la Defensa de la Revolución, the block association that watches the neighborhood. Samuel says in all the years he's worked for the Party no one has ever discriminated against him for being a Jew. The Comité can meet at his house one week and the next week he can hold a Passover seder. There's no contradiction and no problem.

Knowing Samuel's fierce loyalty to the Revolution, it comes as a surprise to me to return to Cienfuegos in 2005 and find that Che is no longer hanging on the wall.

"What happened to El Che?" I ask.

Samuel says that his daughter Raquel has done some repainting and

redecorating. Che is waiting until she can find a new frame big enough to fit his picture. The old heavy wooden frame doesn't match the new décor. But it isn't easy to find a large frame these days, he says.

"Where is Che in the meantime?"

"In the kitchen," Samuel says.

He leads me into the kitchen and points to the dark corner where the picture now hangs.

"You want to see it?" he asks.

I nod and he brings down Che in his old frame.

"It's full of dust," Samuel says. "Been back there too long."

Samuel leans the dusty Che against his knees. Che, now resting on the floor, seems deposed, no longer towering over everyone, humbly at the feet of Samuel's wife, Rebeca. It's a subtle thing, but when a daughter redecorates and can't find a place for Che in her father's living room, perhaps it means more than fashions are changing in Cuba?

Even Samuel seems to be having trouble finding a place for the trophies he's saved from the Revolution. Before we leave, he says he'd like to give me and Humberto a gift. He takes us into a bedroom off the living room and points to a stack of posters. They are crammed under hefty boxes at the top of a tall dresser. It will take a while to get the boxes down, Samuel remarks, but if we have time, he has some wonderful posters he'd like to give us.

"They're posters of El Comandante," Samuel tells us. "I have a lot of them. Beautiful posters of Fidel. From all the rallies and marches I've attended over the years. I just wish I could show them to you, so you could pick a few to take home with you."

I start to panic. I'm not sure what I'll do if Samuel insists on giving me posters of Fidel Castro. Will I say, "No, thank you," and try not to sound anti-revolutionary? Samuel's house is, after all, the headquarters of the CDR! Maybe he's testing me, I think. Testing to see how I'll react as a Cuban American. But my feeling about Samuel is that he's a true revolutionary and he's trying to give me something he and many other Cubans on the island would consider precious—historic posters of their enduring leader. But I couldn't possibly bring home posters of Fidel Castro. I choose to travel to Cuba while Fidel Castro rules, but I am the daughter of Cuban exiles and I cannot have posters of Fidel Castro in my possession. I guess I could ditch them. But maybe the posters are valuable? Maybe the wisest thing would be to keep them, sneak them through U.S. customs, and sell them on eBay?

It so happens that our bus to Havana is leaving in fifteen minutes and the friend of a friend who's taking us to the station has pulled up in front of Samuel's house and he's honking his horn.

"Next time," I say. "Save them for next time."

27

PEARLS LEFT IN CIENFUEGOS

"I find it interesting that Americans feel safe traveling to Cuba," I say as we drive through a lush landscape of palm trees in the air-conditioned lull of a Havanatur bus.

Aryeh Maidenbaum shrugs. He's a Jungian psychologist who organizes Jewish travel to Cuba for the Jewish Museum in New York.

"It's true, people are afraid to travel these days. Trips we organized to China, to Spain, got few takers. There was the fear of SARS in Asia, and after the war began in Iraq, and with Spain supporting the United States, people were afraid to go there. But people feel safe going to Cuba."

"That makes no sense! The United States has an embargo against Cuba. It's even called the Trading with the Enemy Act. Shouldn't Americans feel threatened in Cuba?"

"One thing about the system in Cuba, it keeps the country safe. The most difficult part for our groups is getting out of Miami. They check everybody's license at the gate, one by one. But people are willing to put up with that. Cuba is forbidden fruit, everyone wants to go. Since we began the program in 2000, the demand for the Jewish Cuba trip has been so high that I keep having to add more groups."

It is May 2004 and I'm in Cuba as a study leader for one of Aryeh's groups. The group I'm with is one of his extra groups, and my fellow travelers, sophisticated middle-aged and older Jewish New Yorkers, feel lucky to be in Cuba. For my part, I'm in awe of a few of the women. Their svelte bodies look like they've been preserved in amber and they're wearing Armani and Chanel to the Revolution.

Aryeh is a thoughtful man and he has put together an interesting program for the group, with time spent not only in the synagogues speaking to religious leaders, but also in the homes of visual artists learning about the Cuban art scene. He has chosen to bring everyone to Cienfuegos, so that his sophisticated New Yorkers can experience a more low-key reunion with Jewish Cubans. This is a good idea, because there have already been murmurings among people in the group that they were received in a cool and aloof manner by the Jewish Cuban leaders in Havana, that their presentations felt too "canned," that in Havana maybe they've become jaded by all the foreign attention.

And so we have traveled east from Havana to Cienfuegos, a seaside city whose elegant nineteenth-century architecture bears a French influence left by plantation owners who fled Haiti after it became free, and where there are thirty-six Jews, including the children.

Our Havanatur bus pulls up at the home of Rebeca Langus Rodríguez, who is the president of the Jewish community of Cienfuegos and a school-teacher, and she greets us warmly at the door and leads the entire group of forty-five people up a tall flight of stairs to her second-floor apartment.

Once upstairs, there aren't enough chairs in the living room, so the elders are given the seats of honor, while everyone else fans out, standing around the edges, or sitting cross-legged on the floor. It gets hot and crowded very quickly, but at the same time it all feels cozy, unlike anything the group has experienced so far.

I am asked to translate for Rebeca. Line by line, she talks, I talk, and the story unfolds—how she is the daughter of an Ashkenazic father and a Sephardic mother; how her mother still lives in the nearby town of Remedios with Rebeca's brother and his wife and child, the only Jews still there; how even in the heyday of the Revolution she never lost her attachment to her Jewish identity; but how it was difficult to practice Judaism before the recent open-ing to religion; how she is immensely happy that she and other Jews can be openly Jewish again; how her husband, Ramón, though he isn't Jewish and can't be circumcised because of a kidney condition, has supported her whole-heartedly in her quest to return to her Jewish faith, building the bookshelf with

the Star of David to hold the Jewish books that kind American visitors like our-selves have donated to their community; how even though they are a small community, the Jews in Cienfuegos get together and they study Hebrew and Jewish history every week; how her son David is now preparing for his bar mitzvah; how her little one, Danielito, already dreams of the day when he will have his bar mitzvah; how she is grateful for our visit; and how she hopes we will visit again, for now her home is our home too.

Rebeca is a woman who is easy to love—she speaks with genuine feeling and she smiles effortlessly. By the end of her emotional presentation not only is she in tears, but so too are most of the members of the group.

What happens next is hard to describe. Those who are seated on the floor jump to their feet, those seated in chairs collect themselves and rise with the force of a gale wind, and those standing come rushing forward. A stampede of giving ensues, but it all begins with one woman, tears flowing down her cheeks, taking off her pearl earrings and giving them to Rebeca, who whispers "gracias," slips them on, and hugs her. Soon everyone is putting money into

Rebeca's hands. The wad of folded dollars grows so thick that Rebeca can't hold on to it any longer and she deposits it next to the new menorah on her hutch.

Some members of the group have come prepared to indulge the Cuban passion for baseball; they rustle through their bags to retrieve balls and mitts that they hurriedly offer to Danielito, who is so astounded by the entire gift-giving frenzy that he virtually freezes in place.

I too am in a state of shock—proud, on the one hand, of my people, the Jewish people, for being so generous, so willing to help other Jews; but overwhelmed, on the other hand, by this crazy outpouring of emotion and charity. Is it redemption the gift-givers are seeking? To feel less guilty about the embargo and the way it is hurting regular Cubans? To be at ease with their American privilege knowing they can

share some of their wealth with people who will accept it graciously? Or is it a desire to affirm that the Jews of the diaspora are one people—that a Jew is a Jew wherever in the world he or she happens to land? None of the group members speak Spanish well enough to communicate with Rebeca and her family, nor can she and her family speak English, and so the whole interchange takes on a primitive quality, money and objects being thrust into the hands of the Cubans, who helplessly utter "gracias" over and over.

But no gift that day is as impassioned or intimate as the woman-to-woman gift of the pearl earrings. There is something enchanted about that gift—something almost out of a fairy tale. A rich woman tearing off her fine jewels to give them to a poor woman. "And they were good pearls too," as the woman will later tell her friends in the group, but not in the least bit arrogantly, rather to mean that she was glad she could give something of value to a Jewish woman in Cuba. As the giver realized, a woman in Cuba might not need pearl earrings, but she can still love having them. What is just as interesting is that Rebeca accepts the gift—which she might not have a few years ago, when women in Cuba wouldn't have dared to flaunt pearls in a society struggling to eliminate poverty and create equality. Although the pearls were given to Rebeca with spontaneous good will, does such a gift bring happiness, in the end, to a woman in Rebeca's position, or does it create longing for yet other unattainable things . . . for the matching pearl necklace?

After the last gift is given, after Rebeca, glowing in her new earrings, has said goodbye to each visitor as if they were an old friend, Aryeh assembles everyone and the group descends the stairs to the curb, where the Havanatur bus is waiting with the air conditioning on at full blast. I linger for a moment, and with the house quiet, I can hear the parakeets singing. "Where are they?" I ask, and David and Danielito take me to the kitchen and show me the parakeets, which Ramón, their father, raises for a living. There are dozens of parakeets, in every color, lined up in cages.

David takes out a parakeet and clutches it tightly in one hand. His little brother Danielito, just like a child, has observed the bewildering spectacle that took place at their house and he's wondering whether he and his family, like the parakeets, have it good or bad where they are. He strokes the parakeet's beak. "We can't let it go," he says. "Or it will fly away."

28

THE MOSES OF SANTA CLARA

Like a modern-day Moses, David Tacher Romano is filled with a sense of mission and purpose about the destiny of the Jewish people. Maybe part of his zeal comes from breathing the air of Santa Clara, the city in Cuba most closely associated with the legacy of Che Guevara. When Che was killed in Bolivia in 1967, the exact location of his body was kept a secret to prevent his admirers from turning the site into a shrine. After his remains were found and exhumed in 1997, they were claimed by Cuba, along with the remains of sixteen of his fellow combatants. They were brought to rest, with full military honors, in a mausoleum at the entrance to Santa Clara, the city from where Che had led his troops in the last decisive battle of the Cuban revolution.

I wasn't sure if David would agree to being photographed next to the monument to El Che. He doesn't claim to be a revolutionary. He says he's a Jew who lives in Cuba, a Jew who defends the right of Jews to live wherever they want. That is his revolution.

He laughs when I propose the idea of taking his picture with the bronze statue of Che looming on the horizon.

"Is that where you want to take my picture? You want my uncle in the United States never to speak to me again? Well, it doesn't matter. We can take the picture there, or wherever you want. My uncle doesn't speak to me anyway."

David, a husky man who can usually be found speeding around the city of Santa Clara on his motorcycle, has become one of Cuba's most passionate Jewish activists. A practical dreamer, his goal is not only to fortify the Jewish community in Santa Clara, but to teach all Cubans about the history of the Jews and the reasons why Israel exists.

These are quite ambitious goals, especially given that ten years ago, when the Joint Distribution Committee arrived and asked the dispersed Jewish families in the city to join together as a community, no one had any idea what they were supposed to do.

David vividly recalls those days: "They wanted us to be a community and have a president, a vice president, and a treasurer. So there we were, and I asked, 'Now what? I don't remember any Hebrew. It's been over thirty years since everything fell apart. What are we going to do? Sit here and stare at each other? What kind of Jewish meeting can we possibly have?' They'd given us a copy of *The Jewish Book of Why.* That one book was how we started."

The synagogue and the Torahs were gone, but the house of Virginia Yaech Bejar, the vice president, came to serve as their meeting place for Kabbalat Shabbat gatherings, at which initially they simply came together at sundown

on Fridays to mark the beginning of the Jewish sabbath and talk with one another.

As more books on Jewish religion and history arrived, David taught himself how to lead religious services, which always ended with strong embraces.

And afterward, if they were lucky, Julio Rodríguez Elí would bring two enormous smoked red snappers from Caibarién.

Yet the more they recovered of their Jewish heritage, the more they realized, as David notes, how in one generation so much could be lost. David's father and both sets of grandparents were Sephardic immigrants from Turkey and he celebrated his bar mitzvah at the Chevet Ahim synagogue in Havana. But his father, Isidoro Tacher Balestra, was a revolutionary and a member of the July 26th Movement. David speaks well of his father, describing him as a sincere and hard-working man, yet unwittingly he tore David and his younger brother, Victor, from their Jewish heritage. And tore them from their paternal grandparents, aunts, uncles, and cousins, all of whom left Cuba after the Revolution.

There was a synagogue on Calle de la Independencia, but the Jewish population declined so dramatically that a synagogue no longer seemed necessary. David's maternal grandfather, Victor Romano, the last treasurer of the synagogue, bore the responsibility of relinquishing the keys to the government. Then the Jewish cemetery in Santa Clara was given over to the government and soon after the surrounding walls collapsed. Children played ball amid the tombstones. Goats

pranced from grave to grave looking for pasture. Among the dead who suffered such disrespect was David's own revolutionary father, who died in 1986 and was buried in the desolate cemetery because there was no other Jewish cemetery in the region.

Fixing the cemetery became the first priority of the new Jewish community in Santa Clara. By 2000 that goal was achieved. But David felt they needed to do something more—they needed to build a Holocaust memorial, so that the memory of the six million Jews who perished in Europe would be preserved, even in provincial Cuban soil. He envisioned the memorial as not simply a site of Jewish mourning, but a place where people of every faith would be forced to reckon with the destruction wrought by fascism, so as not to let it happen again anywhere in the world.

To accomplish this, David needed money, but even more important, he needed help finding a meaningful symbol of the Holocaust to integrate into the memorial. Who could help him attain such a goal? The majority of the Jewish American missions rarely made it out of Havana into the provinces. All the attention was focused on Havana and the Patronato synagogue.

Just around the time David began to hatch his idea, Miriam Saul, a middle-aged empty nester in Atlanta, decided she needed to return to Cuba to fill a hole in her life. A Cuban Jew, she had left the island with her family at the age of eleven. She was active in the Jewish Community Center in Atlanta, where she teaches theater to kindergarteners and first graders enrolled at the day school. She had visited Israel several times, looking there for her spiritual home. But she still felt something was missing. When she went back to Cuba in 2000 with her sister, she found what it was—a connection to her native land and to the Jews who chose to stay during the mass exodus of the Jewish community in the early years of the Revolution. Her initial encounter with Cuba was so wrenching that when she returned to Atlanta she cried for three months. But then she wiped her tears and started going to Cuba more often. She took her brother and her parents, her three children, her husband, and seventeen cousins. With the support of the JCC in Atlanta, she organized the International Community Builders Project and was soon taking teens and adults on group missions to Cuba to help the Jews of the island. She became, in the words of her Jewish Atlanta-born husband, "a born-again Cuban."

In every Jew she met on the island Miriam saw her own reflection. As she came to realize, "It could be me down there. I'm lucky to be living here. It could be me down there starving and making $8 a month." Her purpose in life was now clear—to serve as a bridge between Jews in Cuba and Jews in the United States.

Miriam had noticed that most of the American help and media attention went to Havana. So she made it a point to get out to Santiago, Camagüey, and Santa Clara. She built relationships with the more humble Jews living at a distance from the celebrity spotlight. Meeting David Tacher, she knew she had found her match in Cuba. He wanted also to be a bridge, but from the other side. As David liked to say, the seeds of Jewish life on the island had been planted by the Jews who had fled Cuba. He never disparaged Jewish Cubans who lived in the United States. They were all people he considered part of the same big Jewish family. But the truth was that his actual family in the United States had broken relations with him, his brother, and his parents. Through Miriam he would recuperate, at least metaphorically, that lost family. Miriam, in turn, saw in David someone who needed her help and would know how to appreciate it. He was her most exact mirror: while she had become "a born-again Cuban," he had become "a born-again Jew."

In fact, it was Miriam who first described David to me as a modern-day Moses. Upon learning of his wish to build a Holocaust memorial in the Santa Clara cemetery, she immediately set to work. She contacted the U.S. Holocaust Museum in Washington, but the people she spoke to there were apprehensive, fearing the memory of the Holocaust might be trivialized, or worse, idolized. After a lot of paperwork and phone calls back and forth, it was agreed that the U.S. Holocaust Museum would donate 200 stones from the Warsaw Ghetto, each weighing twenty-two pounds, cobblestones from Chlodno Street. In 2002 Miriam brought two stones to Cuba, one for then-president José Miller at the Patronato, and one for David Tacher in Santa Clara.

David had a Cuban sculptor affix the Warsaw cobblestone to the side of the Holocaust monument. He also had a plaque created with an explanation of its origin. The inauguration took place on Sunday, October 26, 2003, in the Jewish cemetery of Santa Clara. He made sure the event was attended not just by the presidents of the different Jewish communities in Cuba, but by representatives of the various churches—Presbyterian and Baptist as well as the Catholic bishop of the province of Villa Clara. A Jewish American mission from South Carolina, in Cuba at the time, was also invited.

To create a living connection between past and present, David conceived of a series of rituals to take place at the inauguration. He had gone to Israel during the previous summer supported by Birthright, an organization that sponsors first-time travel to Israel for Jewish youth around the world, and that had asked him to serve as chaperone for the initial group of Jewish travelers from Cuba. David brought back desert sand from the Negev, and water from the Kinneret, the Sea of Galilee, and the Jordan River. A pine tree was planted with the Negev sand and the water from the three sources. From that moment on, all visitors to the memorial—I among them—would be invited to pour water

on the pine tree to help it grow and to express our desire for it to flourish in Cuba.

Miriam is slowly but surely delivering all the cobblestones to Santa Clara, where David eagerly awaits them. After delivering the first stone, she brought a group of twenty-eight people from Atlanta and was able to take another six stones. She urges the Americans who travel with her not to be passive consumers of Jewish Cuban life but active community builders. Her teen groups do volunteer work in the cemetery of Santa Clara, helping David to fulfill his dream of building a path leading to the memorial with the Polish cobblestones. With their assistance, David is achieving his aim: to bring Santa Clara ever closer to Warsaw and the memory of lost Jews. His provincial city in Cuba is now not only the keeper of Che's memory and his sacrificial death, but a tropical stop in the international circuit of Holocaust memorials and their shared grief.

I remember I had finished pouring water on the pine tree. I gave David back the plastic pitcher and he reached for the key in his pocket to lock up the cemetery, where goats no longer pranced on his father's grave. We were about to leave when David stopped to caress the letters on the granite memorial.

"Sadly, we now have a monument to the Shoah," he said. He stood as if riveted to the spot. "I can't tell you how moved people are when they see this monument. They weep and recite the Kaddish."

Although he's now a born-again Jew, there's still a tinge of Che's antimaterialism and revolutionary fervor in the way David sees the world.

He looked at me earnestly. "Every tear that is spilled here is worth more than all the money anyone could ever give us."

29

A CONVERSATION

NEXT TO EL MAMEY

Alberto Esquenazi Aparicio riding his bicycle in the city of Santa Clara is an ordinary Cuban doing his errands. I happen to know he's a Jew from seeing him at the Kabbalat Shabbat services the night before, so I wave him down. I start asking him questions by the El Mamey store, which has a freshly painted façade promising revolutionary victories, but nothing for sale inside. A soft-spoken man, Alberto is too polite to tell me that street corners aren't the best places to conduct interviews.

Long before the Revolution came along, Jews in Cuba sought to blend in. As Alberto remarks, "I thought my father was born in Cuba. His name was David Esquenazi Benestra. Then my grandfather told me, 'No, your father was born in Turkey, in Chorlú.' My father became a Cuban citizen and forgot he was from Turkey."

"And your mother?"

"My mother was Julia Aparicio. She wasn't Jewish."

Alberto and his sister were brought up with a mix of Judaism and Catholicism. After the Revolution they both pulled away from religion. Now he's returned to Judaism, but his sister hasn't.

"How do you feel being a Jew in Cuba today?"

"I feel very happy to be a Jew," Alberto says. "I converted on the 24th of February of 2003. I was circumcised a few months before. It was an emotional experience for me, one of the happiest days of my life. I was an incomplete Jew. Now I feel whole."

I ask him what it was like before the opening to religion in the early 1990s.

Alberto takes a deep breath before replying and looks around to be sure no one is approaching or snooping from a doorway.

"Before the opening to religion, the only thing people spoke about was the creation of the new man. It was taboo to talk about God. Jewish cemeteries were abandoned. Jews didn't get together or talk to each other. We didn't celebrate Shabbat. The matzah for Passover would often arrive late, in December or January. We were often afraid. They called us *polacos*. Me they sometimes called *sirio*—Syrian."

He waits to see if I have any more questions. I can't think of anything else to ask, so he pulls his cap down to shield his eyes from the afternoon sun and gets back on his bike. He rides away briskly, and when I glance at him again, he's very far down the street, looking like any other Cuban riding an old Chinese bicycle with an empty basket.

30
VILLA ELISA

    Sancti Spíritus is all flatland, or so it seems to me when I arrive there at the crack of dawn on a bus from Santiago de Cuba.

    José Isidoro Barlía Loyarte, a math teacher who acts as the president of the Jewish community of Sancti Spíritus, had given me his address on the phone. I hadn't bothered to ask for directions because I'd become spoiled enough to think we'd be able to take a taxi to his home. But outside the bus station there is only one means of transportation and it's a horse cart. Not that I have anything against horse carts. I don't mind riding on them at all, but I have a rolling suitcase and two heavy shoulder bags filled with notebooks, a laptop, and toiletries. I hesitate to try climbing onto the cart with all those things.

    Not knowing what else to do, I go back inside to the bus station, look for a public phone, and call up José.

    "Hello, José, we're here. But we can't find a taxi to get to your house."

    "Do you like to walk?" José asks.

    I say yes, but mention that I have a suitcase and some bags to carry.

    "It's six blocks to my house," he replies. "I'll come pick you up, but I don't have a car, so it will take me a few minutes."

    A half hour later, José arrives with his bicycle, walking slowly alongside it rather than riding it, as if he had all the time in the world. He straps my two shoulder bags to the bicycle and we proceed to walk down a long street that seems to stretch endlessly before us. I pull my rolling bag along, the wheels clacking in the still air of the morning.

We make a left turn and then a quick right. When we come within view of his house I am in awe. Never have I seen a house like this. Not in Cuba, not anywhere.

It is a pink stone house flanked on all sides by grillwork formed into Stars of David. There is a Star of David over the front window, the front door, the side gate. The front gate is inscribed with the words *Villa Elisa*. It is Jewish rococo in the tropics, the handiwork of a dreamer or a madman. With so many Jewish stars, the building should be a synagogue, but it's not. This is the house Salomón Barlía built in 1946 and which his son inherited and left untouched.

I am so completely fascinated by the house that I ask José to tell me its story before we've even crossed the threshold.

"So you want to know about the house?" he says, looking at me with weary eyes. "Let me put away the bicycle and we'll sit down and relax and then I'll tell you the story."

He leads us inside and we pass a Star of David hovering above the living room. We take seats in the patio at the rear of the house, where another Star of David adorns a staircase leading to the roof. One by one, the members of José's family emerge from the different rooms of the starry house: his wife, Daisy Bernal Mayea, a pharmacist, their daughters Anna Esther, Anni Frid, and Ivonne, their son José, and their granddaughter Claudia.

Rambunctious five-year-old Claudia is thrilled to have company and begs Daisy to give her the photo album so she can show it to me. No one can say a word until I have looked at all the pictures of her dressed up as Queen Esther at the last Purim party held in Sancti Spíritus.

"Very pretty!" I say, and Claudia beams.

"And this one is pretty too!" she says, by now so comfortable with me that she's sitting on my lap.

"Now Claudia, please let your grandfather talk," Daisy says, gently pulling away the photo album.

An envelope filled with negatives falls to the floor and I rush to pick it up and hand it to Daisy. But she hands the envelope back to me. "Keep them," she says. "There's nothing I can do with the negatives. It's too expensive to print pictures in Cuba. El Joint sent us the pictures."

José lights up a cigarette and takes a long drag. "So you wanted to know the story of this house? Of Villa Elisa?"

"Yes," I say eagerly. "I haven't seen another house like this anywhere in Cuba!"

José nods and Daisy looks at him with trepidation.

"The story is very simple: My father was married to a woman named Elisa Behar Tacher. She and my father were doing very well. The wealth came mainly from her family. He built this house for Elisa. This was her house, her Villa Elisa."

José puts out his cigarette and starts on a new one.

"Elisa died giving birth. It was their second child. Their first child had died two months after being born. And so my father built a big tomb for Elisa in the cemetery in Guanabacoa. In its time it really stood out. He had the marble brought over from Italy and the lines of poetry that were engraved on the stone were verses he wrote himself."

José turns to Daisy. "Bring the photograph, so she can see the tomb."

Even before Daisy comes back with the photograph, I can barely contain my excitement. My journey to Cuba began among the dead, as I searched for my cousin Henry and other Jews buried in Cuban soil, Jews who would forever remain on the island. The universe had presented me with a riddle—a beloved Elisa given a magnificent grave by her bereaved Salomón. The love story behind this grave seemed lost to memory, irretrievable.

"So it's your father who built that tomb? The one dedicated to 'My Elisa'? In the Sephardic cemetery in Guanaboca?"

"Yes," José says. "My father built it. I know it's a bit unusual."

"I've wondered about that tomb for years. You can't imagine how many pictures I've taken of it. But no one could tell me who Elisa was."

"Now you know: she was my father's first wife."

Daisy hands the photograph to José. He glances at it and says, "The tombstone had little angels on either side, but they were stolen."

After listening to José tell the story, Daisy is anxious to tell it from her side.

She slides into the plastic chair next to me, sits on the edge, and begins speaking with nervous energy. "When José and I married, I tried to keep the house the way it had always been. It was I who insisted on leaving everything intact."

Her voice cracks and tears fill her eyes. José looks on with concern and little Claudia says, "What's wrong? Why are you crying?"

Daisy hugs Claudia and fixes a determined smile on her lips. "I'm sorry. This story isn't easy to tell."

The tears return and she impatiently wipes them with the back of her hand.

"José and I fell in love when we were very young, but the elder Salomón did everything he could to try to dissuade José from seeing me because I wasn't Jewish. He selected a Jewish wife for José in Havana, but as luck would have it, that woman left for the United States. I promised the elder Salomón that if José and I married and had children I would be sure to raise them Jewish."

What makes Daisy cry is not only her father-in-law's disapproval of her, though it's clear that the sting of rejection remains an open wound, but the fact that he died before he was able to see that she didn't simply convert to Judaism. She did much more. She learned Hebrew. She studied Jewish history. And now it is she who leads monthly religious services at their home for the community of fifty Jews who live in Sancti Spíritus and Ciego de Avila. She spent months preparing her children, José and Yvonne, to chant their Torah portions for their bar and bat mitzvahs at the Patronato. She is more Jewish than most Jews. If only she could bring her father-in-law back from the dead, so he could see how loyal she was to her promise to him.

José lights another cigarette and asks for my attention with his weary eyes.

"There's one more thing I can tell you," he says in his steady school-teacher's voice. "When my father remarried, he demanded of his second wife, Zoila Estrella Loyarte, my mother, that she have a cesarean delivery to give birth to me."

José was born in 1952 and afterward his mother had to live the rest of her years in the house named for the first wife.

Now it is José and Daisy and their family who inhabit the shrine to Elisa, the haunted house of too many Jewish stars that eternally mourns a lost love.

Smiling wanly, José says, "I came into the world by cesarean. My father didn't want to lose my mother the way he'd lost his Elisa."

31
THE COVENANT OF ABRAHAM

David Pernas Levy is a man of unquestionable revolutionary credentials. He fought in the Escambray against counterrevolutionaries in the early 1960s, served in Angola in the late 1970s, worked for years as an adviser on economic and labor issues in the Ministry of Commerce, and cut thousands of pounds of sugarcane. Yet he lives in a dainty house in Camagüey filled with his wife Rosa Huerta Noy's collection of porcelain elephants, decorative plates, framed pastel landscapes, and plastic flower arrangements.

After he agrees to be photographed with his revolutionary memorabilia, he asks, "Do you think a lot of people in the United States are going to hate me because of this?"

He himself doesn't see why anyone *should* hate him. From his perspective, the passion he feels for the Revolution is the same passion he feels for Judaism. As he puts it, "The Revolution is for the good of all and Judaism is for the good of all."

But as the son of a mixed marriage, he came to his Jewish identity feeling that he was reclaiming a heritage that had been forfeited for the sake of the love that brought him into the world. He tells me that his parents were married in 1926, just four years after his mother arrived from Turkey. His mother was the first Sephardic Jewish woman to marry outside the tribe in Camagüey. "What she did was totally prohibited," says David. And she paid the price: she was disowned by her family and the Jewish community. Hinting at the sexual attraction that united his parents, he laughs and says, "The *turca* fell in love with the *cubano* and there was nothing anyone could do about it!"

"How can Jews not unite with other people?" David asks. "In Israel you can stick to the rule of only marrying within your own tribe, but once you leave that territory, love has no boundaries." As he puts it, "El amor no tiene fronteras."

Eventually, David says, his grandparents came to accept him, his three brothers, and his sister, but they kept their distance. If only his grandparents knew that now all of them have become Jewish, as have each of their spouses, and that the eldest, Roberto, lives in Israel with his children and grandchildren.

I ask David if he needed to convert, given that his mother was Jewish. He says he did have to convert because he wasn't circumcised as a newborn. And then I ask what is certainly an impolite question: "How old were you when you were circumcised?"

Fortunately, David isn't the least offended by my question. "Understand," he says, "that Abraham did it at ninety-nine years old. And I did it at sixty-seven."

"A circumcision at sixty-seven years old!" I exclaim. "How brave!"

Much as I would like to know about his experience, I stop just short of asking David for more details. Perhaps I'm a freak, but I'm utterly fascinated by the special commitment to Judaism made by grown men in Cuba, like David, who have agreed to be circumcised. Even if the foreskin is ritually cut in the hospital by a *mohel* under the supervision of a doctor, it must be a little bit scary, a little bit traumatic, to offer up your penis to the knife. But as a woman I'm too embarrassed to push the conversation further.

As if reading my mind, David says, "I had to do it." He speaks with conviction, but then he laughs out loud. "Abraham did it when he was ninety-nine. So if I did it at sixty-seven, I think I did it in plenty of time!"

32

SALVADOR'S THREE WIVES

We've come to Manzanillo to look for Jews. Salvador Behar Mizrahi, I've been told, is one of the registered Jews among the dozen or so who remain in this port city on the southern coast of Cuba. We arrive without warning at his home, and his wife, a gregarious woman in a housecoat, doesn't seem at all concerned that some strangers are asking to speak to her husband.

"What a pity! You just missed him. He took off on one of those horse carts that you see everywhere in this town. He's going to try to find us a leg of pork. It's not easy, I tell you."

We jump back in the car to go in search of Salvador, following his wife's vague directions, but by the time we find the house where he has bought the leg of pork, he's long gone. On our return to his house, Salvador is waiting patiently at the door. A lean man, his untucked shirt hanging loosely over his pants, he peers at us with curious eyes through an ancient pair of aviator glasses.

"Welcome," he says. "Come in. Sorry I missed you. I had to go on a little errand."

Inside, the walls of his house are painted a sun-baked pink. The living room is crowded with furniture—rocking chairs and an assortment of big stuffed chairs. The door to the back yard is open and light shines on the clusters of plastic flowers, which are everywhere, in vases and tacked to the walls.

"How may I help you?" he asks, leading us into the dining room, where a Sacred Heart of Jesus in an oval wood frame hangs on the wall.

I tell him I want to know about the Jews who lived in Manzanillo. I ask if he has any old photographs.

"Let me find my box," he says, and excuses himself. He pulls aside the curtain hanging over the door to his bedroom and returns with a bulging box.

"Would you believe it? This was me," he says, holding up a picture of himself flexing his muscles.

He was a body builder when he was young, and like other Jews in Manzanillo, he owned a store.

"After the Revolution, all the Jews left. I lost my store, but I decided to stay. I was a math teacher until I retired."

Sifting through the things in his box, he pulls out an old letter. It is from his two sisters, Sara and Miriam, who are in the United States. He shows me the return address and I do a double take—it turns out they live on West Avenue, a block away from where my grandmother once lived in Miami Beach. How strange are the bonds that unite us, I think—not to mention that he's another Behar.

Salvador starts to thank us for our visit, and I realize that he and his wife

are probably waiting for us to leave to have lunch—he must have stashed the leg of pork in the kitchen when he heard we had come to see him. He gallantly comes to the door to say goodbye and wish us well on the rest of our journey.

As I am walking away, he takes hold of my elbow. His grip is still strong. He whispers, "There's something I have to tell you. That was my third wife you met. My three marriages have been with women who aren't Jewish. What choice did I have? There isn't a single Jewish woman my age left here in Manzanillo."

33

A BEAUTIFUL PINEAPPLE

It is May 2005 and Julio César Alomar Gómez is at the synagogue in Santiago de Cuba arranging on a table some pictures and posters that will form part of an exhibit about the Holocaust for the next day's Yom HaShoah remembrance. The Joint Distribution Committee has provided him images of the Warsaw Ghetto, Auschwitz, and Kristallnacht, "La noche de los cristales rotos" (the night of broken glass), a pogrom carried out in 1938 in German towns, during which windows of synagogues, Jewish homes, and Jewish stores were smashed with sledgehammers while many Jews were beaten to death.

It is only recently that Jews in Cuba have begun commemorating Holocaust Remembrance Day. As I watch Julio carefully sifting through the fragments of history scattered on the table, I am struck by the mysterious ways in which Jewish cultural memory is transmitted from one generation to the next. Julio's ancestors didn't suffer in the Holocaust. He is a convert to Judaism. Jewish history has become his history by choice, as has the project of passing on the rituals of Jewish remembrance. The flight of the Jews from Cuba after the Revolution has left a vacuum that is being filled by people like Julio, dedicated converts who are planting the seeds of Jewish memory in the far-flung corners of the island. I've often thought that in Cuba's synagogues there should be a prayer recited every day thanking God for all the Jewish converts.

Julio has turned off all the fans so the pictures won't blow away, and it is getting steamy in the synagogue as we sift through the painful images of persecuted European Jews in woolen coats and caps. "Let's go upstairs and talk in the office," he says. "There's air conditioning up there."

We make ourselves comfortable around a small table, I pull out my notebook, and Julio proceeds to tell me his life story. From the way he tells it, his life began on the day he met his wife Matilde Farín Levy, a sister of Eugenia Farín Levy, the president of the Jewish community of Santiago de Cuba.

Julio says, "We were married on the 21st of December in 1984. We'd met in July of that year. Very casually. During carnival here in Santiago. Matilde wasn't someone who went to parties, but she'd gone with a friend. And a friend had invited me as well. We all spent the night together. After that I courted her feverishly until she married me."

Although raised Catholic, Julio says that after the Revolution he studied physical education and became an atheist. When he met Matilde he didn't believe in anything. Matilde lived with her two sisters and her mother. They didn't talk about religion, but on Fridays, in the privacy of their home, the women lit a wick in a little cup of oil at nightfall. The synagogue had closed in 1979, and since no one had a Jewish calendar, they couldn't celebrate the holidays. All they did was light the oil on Fridays. Julio says he would watch them but he never asked any questions. He also noted that unlike other Cubans, who would receive a ration of oil that was half lard and half vegetable oil, the family's ration was entirely in the form of vegetable oil. When he asked Matilde about this, she told him very simply that her family didn't eat lard.

It wasn't until 1993, when the Joint Distribution Committee sent two teachers to organize the Jewish community, that Matilde and her family finally spoke openly about their Jewish heritage. Julio found himself drawn to Judaism and began to study Hebrew and Jewish history. After the reopening of the synagogue in Santiago in 1995, he decided to undergo circumcision and conversion, along with eight other adult men and six boys. Subsequently, he and Matilde, together with seven other couples, were married in a collective Jewish ceremony under a *chupah*.

Julio now leads weekly Shabbat services at the synagogue. Alejandro, the only child of Julio and Matilde, is one of the regular Torah readers.

Throughout the process of becoming a Jew, what reinforced his commitment, Julio says, was his appreciation for Matilde as a person of good sentiments and extraordinary kindness.

It's touching to hear Julio speak lovingly of his wife. But I happen to know he isn't exaggerating about her goodness and generosity.

Earlier that day I'd stopped to visit Matilde. As soon as I saw her, I thought to myself that I ought to have brought her something as a token of my appreciation for the hospitality she and her family always offered me. A book, a box of chocolates—what would have been right? I didn't know. I wished I were more organized, like the official helpers from the United States who are always

drawing up lists of what Jews need in Cuba—diapers, eyeglasses, diabetes medication, vitamins—and systematically collecting all these things and getting them to the island.

I had come with only my notebook and pen, accompanied by Humberto and his camera, ready to pounce on anything of anthropological interest that Matilde might say or do. And Matilde, asking for nothing from me, had been ready with a gift.

"Here," she said, when I walked in to her house. "This is for you."

Humberto snapped her picture and then from her hands to mine she offered a beautiful pineapple.

34

THE LAST JEW
OF PALMA SORIANO

"It would have been better if you'd gone to Palma Soriano like everyone else, so you could see how people travel around here," Eugenia Farin Levy says. "But I know you don't have a lot of time."

She points to the truck we're passing on the road. A crowd of people are standing in its rear bed. They are clinging to the frame, if they can reach it, or to one another if they can't, so as to keep their balance as the truck accelerates.

Eugenia and I sit side by side in the van that belongs to the synagogue of Santiago de Cuba. It is ten o'clock in the morning and, just as she promised, Eugenia is taking me to Palma Soriano, a town an hour away from Santiago, so I can meet Jaime Gans Grin, the only Jew who still resides there. For the last twenty years she has worked in the provincial headquarters of the Ministry of Culture and she has explored every alley in the city of Santiago and every town in the Oriente region. If there are any hidden Jews to be found around these parts, Eugenia will certainly know who they are.

When I met Eugenia in 1995, during the reopening of the synagogue in Santiago, she was modest and unassuming. Now, as the president of the Jewish community in Santiago, she has become a confident leader and has published her own books about the history of the Jews in the region, while maintaining a united family.

"Don't judge Jaime by his appearance," she warns. "He's a jewel of a per-

son—*es una joya en su propio estuche*, a jewel in his own unique case." And she adds, "Don't be taken aback when you hear him stutter. He's a very learned man. He reads a lot. He's helping me write a book about the Jews in Cuba using maps."

Eugenia is taking me to Palma Soriano to meet Jaime because she has faith that I won't misrepresent him. She considers me a fellow Cuban Jew, she says, "one of us." Foreign visitors, she's certain, would draw the wrong conclusion if they saw the ruined state of his house and his forlorn appearance. It distresses her to read articles in Jewish American magazines that portray Jews in Cuba as backward, mired in poverty, and desperate to be saved by "missions" from the United States.

Arriving in Palma Soriano, I have to admit I'm glad for Eugenia's warnings. Jaime's house is dark as a cave, but more than simply gloomy, it's a house that feels abandoned. If a house can be shipwrecked, this house is shipwrecked. Two stuffed chairs, coated with a thick layer of grime, are the only furniture in the living room. The one touch of color is a fishnet bag of limes, which Jaime offers to me and Eugenia.

Jaime has a bed and clean sheets, as well as a television, thanks to Eugenia. She wants to move him to Santiago, but Jaime won't leave Palma Soriano. Once upon a time, his house, located in the center of town, had been among the plushest homes in Palma Soriano. In the front room, Jaime's parents, both Hungarian immigrants, had a well-stocked general store, with everything from sewing needles to mattresses. Attired in a white tuxedo, Jaime had celebrated his bar mitzvah in the synagogue of Santiago de Cuba in 1953. Six years later, the Revolution began and Jaime and his parents chose to stay. He never married. His parents passed away and he considered leaving for Israel, but this was back in the years when the desire to immigrate was viewed as a counterrevolutionary act. He made the mistake of speaking too soon of his dream to the postman, who turned him in to the authorities. Now he just wants to spend the rest of his years in Palma Soriano.

Although he's gaunt, Jaime's dark brown eyes shine with intelligence and this makes him handsome. He also looks younger than his years because he has a full head of hair. In his gaze I see decency, a brooding nature, and a recluse's terror of being humiliated.

Jaime does, indeed, stutter, but once he's charged up about a subject he speaks fluidly. When he learns I'm an anthropologist, he takes me into his library, a small room adjoining his back yard.

In the room it smells like the beach after a storm. The book bindings are coated with green mold, as if they've been rescued from the bottom of the ocean. Jaime, who clearly knows his way around his library, pulls out a Spanish edition of Claude Lévi-Strauss's *Structural Anthropology* and shows me his copy of *Pelea contra los demonios,* the classic work of Cuban anthropologist Fernando Ortiz. He collects history books, he says, and has an 1858 history of Cuba published in Paris. It is the first time I've ever seen the edges of a book worm-eaten into delicate lace. I ask if he has a favorite author and Jaime says it's Kafka. Who else? I think to myself—who else but the Jewish author who was excruciating in his depiction of our anxiety and petrified smallness before the invincible structures of the modern state?

Surrounding Jaime are the ravages of time and yet he's found a Zen serenity amidst the deterioration. It's almost as if he welcomes decay. I'm not surprised when he announces that he's an amateur archaeologist. From a room next to the kitchen he brings out boxes of objects he's collected—arrowheads, stones, shells, and buttons from military coats worn by Spanish soldiers in the nineteenth century. But this, he tells me, is only a fraction of what he has. He's donated his more precious finds to the municipal museum.

As I look at his collection, Jaime says, "When they discovered a pre-Colombian archaeological site in Palma Soriano, I dedicated myself to doing excavations on my own. I had the good fortune to find a clay pot bearing an anthropomorphic figure. That pot is now the most important piece in the municipal museum."

Maybe because I'm in awe of all the things he's kept, Jaime takes me into the front room of the house, once the location of the family store, which is now his bedroom. From a dresser he retrieves a box of old pictures and letters.

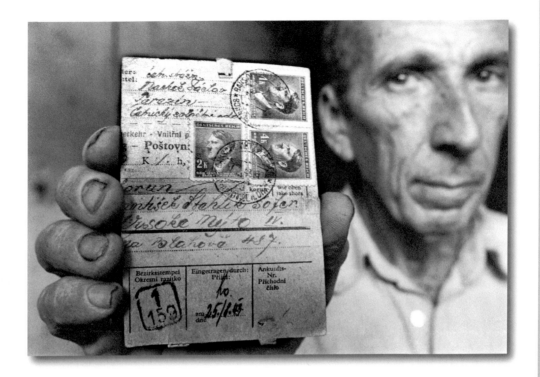

He clasps a photograph of a young couple. Then he holds up a letter. It is written in Yiddish. He says it's from relatives who were killed by the Nazis.

Humberto, who strives for a conscious invisibility during my interviews, patiently watching as I gather testimonies and waiting for natural pauses in conversations before he snaps a picture, now suddenly tells Jaime to be very still. Jaime holds the letter higher, as though it were a veil, and looks straight into Humberto's lens. As Humberto prepares to take the picture, he turns to me and says it's going to come out very well. The darkness and shadows are going to make for a very dramatic image in black and white.

We all gasp when Jaime reaches deeper into the box and shows us the postcard with the Hitler stamps.

"The writer of this postcard was dead by the time it arrived at its destination," Jaime says.

I start to feel as if this visit is anthropology at the end of the world. Here, in an isolated shipwreck of a house, the angel of history seems to have stashed away the fears that scare us to death, the fears that keep us awake at night, the fears that threaten to turn us into sleepwalkers.

Later, on the way back to Santiago, Eugenia will tell me that she's visited Jaime numerous times and she's never known he had this postcard in his possession.

"Jaime has shown you things he's never shown anyone. You won his trust," she will say.

I will wonder why I won Jaime's trust.

And I will find it strangely appropriate that the last Jew in Palma Soriano should have this document in his possession, which tore away brutally at my illusion that Cuba, a refuge for Jews, was the one place that Hitler—even Hitler's likeness—never got to.

Humberto photographs Jaime holding the postcard with the Hitler stamps, getting close enough to show his ripped-up nails, for Jaime spends long days wielding a machete. Then, as if glad to finally part with it, Jaime gives the Hitler postcard to Eugenia.

"Thank you, Jaime," she says. "You couldn't have chosen a better moment. Tomorrow is Yom HaShoah, the day of remembrance of the Holocaust. I'll show it to everyone in the synagogue."

Jaime nods and promises to be there—he'll get to Santiago standing on the back of a truck, if he's lucky, and if not he'll walk, but he'll be there.

I offer to take everybody to lunch, and we go to a cafeteria down the street from Jaime's house, one of those disappointing eateries now rampant in Cuba where you pay in "convertible currency" and get bad food and worse service and the air conditioning is turned up too high and everyone is drinking beer and shouting.

We all ask for fried chicken but Jaime chooses spaghetti napolitana. As he says, "Ever since I was a boy it's been my custom to eat like this. I don't eat chicken and I don't drink beer."

During the hour that it takes for our food to arrive we talk little. There is too much noise, too many people. Jaime lowers his head and his gaze. I feel him struggling to find safety in his recluse's shell.

To make conversation I ask what his daily routine is like.

He replies, "Once I'm up, I go to work on my plot of land. I work for a couple of hours. I mainly weed. Now I don't have much to do, because of the drought."

Awful as the food is, when it finally arrives we devour it.

Then it's time to say goodbye, except I can't bear to say goodbye to Jaime at the door of the awful restaurant.

I ask if we can go see his plot of land.

Jaime brightens and says to follow him. The land is just down the street.

This bit of Cuban earth is the main source of Jaime's livelihood. As a child of Hungarian bourgeois parents, he perhaps would have become a businessman in Miami if he'd left Cuba during the mass exodus of the Jews in the early years of the revolution. But staying in Cuba, he has learned to grow bananas and lemons and papayas and mangos and even sugar cane.

He gives me a strange fruit to try. It has a long pod like a tamarind and you break it open and the seeds taste like chocolate. The name of the fruit—*cañandonga*.

"I've never heard of this fruit," I say, biting into it.

Jaime says, "So you came to Palma Soriano just to try *cañandonga* for the first time."

Pointing to the stalks of sugar cane, I inquire, "Is there a sugar mill nearby?"

"Yes," Jaime replies. "The sugar mill is my mouth."

I laugh so boisterously at this remark I catch him by surprise. It's the first time that day I see him smile.

"May we take a last picture?" I ask. We'd taken many and I didn't want to wear out his patience.

He looks toward the camera and the loneliness of his expression is gone. Without thinking, he seeks the embrace of the banana tree and the wide arms hug him back.

35

THE MIZRAHI CLAN
IN GUANTÁNAMO

For years I'd been hearing about the Mizrahi clan in Guantánamo. They were all descendants of two Turkish immigrants, Isidoro Mizrahi Mizrahi and his cousin, Elias Mizrahi Nifusi. During the search in the early 1990s for all the Jews still left on the island, the members of this numerous clan were brought back to the Jewish fold. At the time they were so lapsed in Jewish ways that to celebrate the visit of their first Jewish religion teacher they roasted a pig. But the community soon found its way back to its Jewish identity. By the end of the 1990s, sixty-three Mizrahi from Guantánamo had made aliyah to Israel.

I had arranged by phone to meet with Rodolfo Mizrahi Tellez, who is the president of the Jewish community in Guantánamo, and his wife, Lisette Frometa Elías. As we pulled up to their house, they were waiting at the door, standing in front of a wrought iron fence that covered the entire façade. Both had taken time off from their jobs, Rodolfo with the electrical company and Lisette with the phone company, to meet with me.

Rodolfo has a boyish energy and jumpiness about him. "Come in," he says. "Let me show you where we hold religious services."

Lisette is more timid. She is dressed in the uniform of ETECSA, a short blue skirt and a white blouse with a scarf tied around the collar, though she's added black fishnet stockings to the outfit as a mark of her personal style. She murmurs hello and follows us as we climb an outdoor staircase attached to the back of their house. It leads to an upstairs room which has a Star of David on the wall, a podium, and stacks of white plastic chairs.

"What do you think?" Rodolfo asks.

I tell him it's a very nice temple.

"We have it thanks to El Joint," he says.

"How many Jews are there in Guantánamo?"

Rodolfo has an immediate reply. "We have twenty families, a total of sixty-eight people."

Even though there are many chairs available, we choose not to sit down to talk.

Lisette turns to me and says she too is named Ruth. That is the Hebrew name she chose for herself when she converted.

"Why did you choose that name?" I ask.

"Ruth was the wife of a Jew and she had to convert, just as I did," she says.

Rodolfo, who is the son of a Jewish father but not a Jewish mother, also

converted. As he says, "I chose Jacob as my Hebrew name. My Jewish grand-mother had wanted to name me Jacob, but my Cuban mother refused to allow it. My older brother is named David. With her first son, my mother agreed to the name and she let him be circumcised. But I was the second son and she chose to call me Rodolfo and didn't circumcise me. My younger brother also wasn't circumcised and wasn't given a Jewish name. His name is Carlos. I took the name Jacob and was circumcised at the age of forty-one. And a few months ago, Lisette and I were married under the *chupah* in Santiago."

I ask Rodolfo about his memories of Jewish life in Guantánamo. What he recalls, as so many Jews do in Cuba, is the matzah for Passover. There were always a few people who took the trouble to go to Havana and bring the matzah back each year when the shipment arrived from Canada. But at the time he didn't understand what the matzah was for. They ate it, but without performing a Passover seder. It was an enigma, which he only understood years later when the Jewish community took form.

His parents, I'd heard, were among the Mizrahi who left Cuba. I ask him if they are doing well in Israel.

Rodolfo shakes his head. "My parents live in Puerto Rico now," he says. "All my family made aliyah to Israel. Afterward they left for Puerto Rico and for Miami."

I don't dare ask Rodolfo if he's planning to leave in the near future, but I sense that he feels rooted on the island. He and Lisette are doing well. Lisette's family all live in Guantánamo, their house is impeccable, they are proud of the Jewish temple on their rooftop, they have good jobs, and they live a quiet life with their young daughter, Jennifer.

Lisette, who has been listening silently, excuses herself and says she has to go back to work. Rodolfo says he too should get back to work but he'd like for us to meet his aunt and his cousin. Do we have time?

Yes, I say, even though I know our ride back to Santiago is waiting. But I'm glad I choose to stay longer, because when I meet his aunt, Fortuna Mizrahi Esquenazi, I feel as if I am meeting a long-lost relative. She is cut from the same Turkish cloth as my Sephardic grandmother. I see similar dark eyes, a similar pensive gaze, I hear the sweet haunting allegretto of Ladino in her Spanish.

Fortuna shows me a picture of herself in her youth. Then she grows serious and says, "I was born on the 11th of May of 1932. We were a family of five brothers and I was the only girl. They said I was the *fortuna*—the fortune—of the house. But I didn't like my name. I was given the name for my grandmother Fortuna who came with Isidoro, my grandfather, to Guantánamo."

"Is this where you were born?" I ask.

And she says, now smiling, "Yes, I was born here."

"So you're a *guantanamera*?"

"Yes, I'm a *guantanamera*, a *guajira guantanamera*. Just like the song." And she hums a few lines from the famous Cuban song.

Somehow, in my quest to find the Jews of Cuba, I hadn't expected to hear a Jewish woman use those words from the song, "Guantanamera, guajira guantanamera," to define her identity. I hadn't expected a Jewish woman in Cuba to say of herself, "I'm a woman from Guantánamo, a country girl from Guantánamo."

Cubans have defined themselves in terms of the Guantanamera song for over a century, since their struggle for independence ended with the intervention of the United States and the imposition of a naval base in Guantánamo. But never had I associated the lines from the Cuban song, which incorporates verses from the poetry of José Martí and is virtually a national anthem, with a Jewish Guantanamera. Meeting Fortuna in Guantánamo was another lesson in how Jews came to be entangled with Cuban history.

Reluctantly, I say goodbye to Fortuna, thinking it's impossible I'll have another encounter in Guantánamo that will move me as much as meeting her has.

And then I meet Rodolfo's cousin, Luis Mizraji Abucre.

We have barely walked in the door and Luis pulls out a huge tray of freshly sliced pineapple from the fridge. He's had a throat operation and has trouble speaking, but he is very effusive with his body language. He insists I eat a few slices in his presence. I tell him the pineapple is delicious and he says that he's

going to give me the entire tray to take back with me on the car ride back to Santiago.

On the lace tablecloth in the kitchen Luis has spread out the family photographs. There is a large studio photograph of his mother and a very small sepia-toned photograph of his grandmother, whom he never knew because she stayed behind in Turkey. When I say I'd like Humberto to photograph him holding one of the photographs, he immediately reaches for the picture of his mother.

It is getting late and we are taking our leave when Luis's wife, Alicia Savón Rojas, arrives home with their granddaughter, Hizzaday Misraji Cisnero. Dressed in the short red skirt, white blouse, and kerchief of the Young Pioneers, Hizzaday looks like she just stepped out of an iconic photograph: the revolutionary Cuban schoolgirl. But I soon learn that her situation is not so sanguine—her father, the son of Luis and Alicia, has left for the United States, and she lives with her mother in Guantánamo. Maybe the abundant love of her grandparents steadies Hizzaday, because she is gentle and graceful. She has been taught to be polite to guests and gives me the requisite kiss hello before giving a hug to her grandfather Luis and "uncle" Rodolfo.

Hizzaday is so polite that when I ask her to clasp in her hands the photograph of the Sephardic great-great-grandmother who stayed behind in Turkey, she does so willingly, being careful to hold the photograph from its edges, as if trying to caress it, as if a firmer hold might hurt the memory of the ancestor who is looking so trustingly toward a future she can't imagine, a future that will include a black Cuban schoolgirl in a red Pioneer outfit. Hizzaday, I notice, bears a very strong resemblance to her Sephardic great-great-grandmother.

For me, this is a quintessential photograph. A black Cuban schoolgirl holds the Jewish past in her hands, but she also represents the possibility of a Cuban future—a future where Jewish memory is safe. As safe as it can ever be.

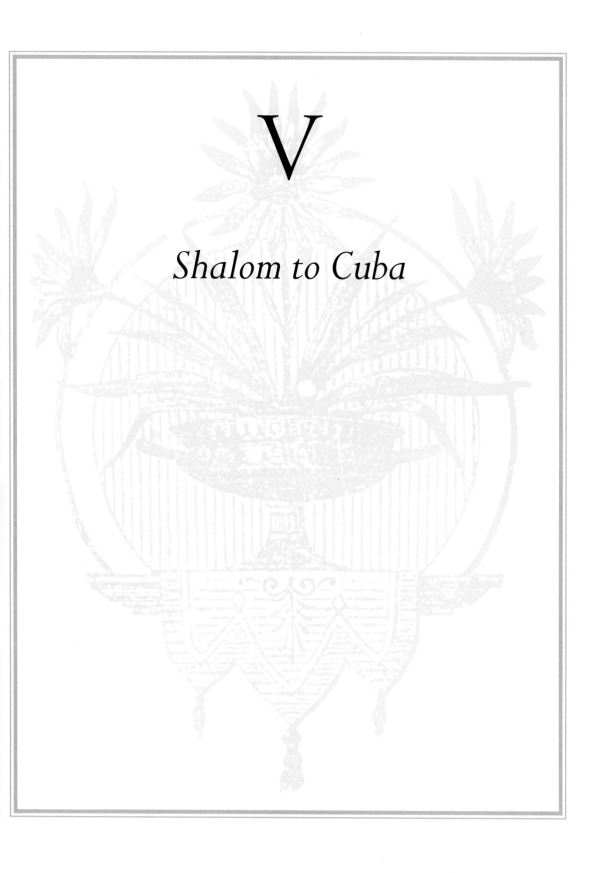

V

Shalom to Cuba

36
DEPARTURES

The Jewish community in Cuba is elusive. Inhabited by people who can turn into ghosts overnight. You never know who among the Jews still there—people that on the surface appear to be standing with two feet solidly planted on Cuban soil—have filled out papers to leave for Israel. Most of the time you find out someone is definitely leaving on the eve of their departure. Often you don't know until they have crossed over. I guess people worry about being jinxed, or about the evil eye. Then the moment comes and they get on a plane for the first time in their lives and cross the ocean, hoping for a better future in the Jewish homeland.

Nothing is easy in Cuba and it takes a while for the travel papers to be in order. Departure dates are postponed two and three times. In the meantime, people wait and wait, dare not speak of their worries, continue to report to the synagogues to show that their Jewish allegiance is sincere, and try to learn another couple of words of Hebrew. The months drag on with nothing to do, for people are forced to quit their jobs or their studies once they announce that their departure is imminent.

I watched an older couple wait for their exit permits to arrive. Their three children had already left for Israel. After the meal following religious services at the Centro Sefardí, the father of the family would yawn, put up his feet, and take a nap. Maybe those naps made the waiting go by faster. Eventually he and his wife also left.

And so while American Jews continue to go to Cuba on "missions" in hopes of communing with Jews still on the island, the Jewish community is continually losing members who are choosing to leave their native land for Israel.

With the much-heralded Jewish rebirth that has taken place on the island, why do so many Jews choose to leave Cuba? For the same reasons that Cubans in general leave. They leave because of their condition as Cubans. Cuba's Jews are able to leave as Jews, but they don't leave because they are being persecuted for their Jewish identity or faith. Jewish hatred is nonexistent in Cuba. The majority of Jews in Cuba are no different from most Cubans—they too have never traveled outside of Cuba, never flown on a plane.

Although socialized health care, education, and food rationing assure all Cubans an austere yet decent life, those who leave want to live by the norms that exist in the developed world. Memories of underdevelopment have not gone away in Cuba: housing is limited, salaries are pitifully low, there is no freedom to travel. Add to that the frequent electrical blackouts, food shortages, the lack of reliable transportation, and the control of information, including barriers on surfing the Internet.

But I don't want to give the impression that Jews in Cuba only have social and economic motivations for immigrating to Israel. There is a strong spiritual dimension to the exodus as well. The Jewish renaissance on the island is real, very real, and it is the force behind many of the departures. As Cuba's Jews have become knowledgeable about their own identity, whether as returning Jews or converts, they have also become better able to see the limitations of being Jewish in Cuba. Not only is the Jewish community on the island minuscule, there are few resources for Jewish learning and intellectual growth, and the survival of the community depends on donations from the Joint Distribution Committee, B'nai Brith, and other international Jewish organizations, as well as personal donations—or tzedaka—from foreign Jews.

For the last fifteen years, Jews in Cuba have been rubbing shoulders with Jewish Americans and Jewish Latin Americans and Jewish Canadians, who suddenly appear for a few days and just as suddenly disappear, well-meaning people who make generous offers of aid. I think these encounters created a culture of longing among Cuba's Jews as they were brought back into the fold of the mainstream Jewish community. Although grateful for all the big-hearted expressions of charity, seeing these privileged Jewish outsiders only increased their resolve to get to Israel and work hard so that one day they too could be givers rather than takers, and perhaps even be able to visit Cuba in the carefree role of tourist. The joke circulating around Cuba in the 1990s was that if you asked a child what he or she wanted to be when they grew up, the answer was, "a tourist." Many Jewish Cubans have fulfilled that hope, returning as tourists, sometimes just three or four years after settling in Israel. They return and visit family, travel around the island seeing all the towns and cities they were never able to see when they lived in Cuba, and even, as I have witnessed, get married in high style at the Patronato, without need of anyone's largesse. In turn, they motivate others to follow in their path and leave.

Those who leave for Israel know it will be hard to adjust to a new language, to a demanding work ethic, to a Jewish calendar in which Sunday is not a day off, and to the unpredictable violence and continual state of war that they have heard about in the news. But they have been told that life overall is better in Israel, that food is plentiful, well-paying jobs are easy to get, the education system is excellent, and good health care is available for all. If they had to foot the bill themselves, they could not even begin to dream of going, for on a Cuban salary it would take several lifetimes to accumulate the funds needed to make such a trip, but the Jewish Agency of Israel pays for their airfare, passport, visa, and housing at an absorption center, while also providing a stipend for their first year as new immigrants. What more can a penniless Cuban ask?

The State of Israel offers this benefit package to Cuba's Jews as part of its utopian ideal as a nation to bring about the ingathering of all the Jewish tribes in the diaspora. Yet it is unclear whether Israel is gaining many permanent citizens by taking in Cuba's Jews. Only a handful of the Cuban immigrants stay in Israel, acquire an Israeli identity, and send their children to the Israeli army. Israel is too radically different a society for them to feel at home there as Cubans, and so inevitably the Jewish promised land becomes a stepping-stone to reach Miami, the Cuban promised land.

The move from Cuba to Israel is a means of jumpstarting one's transition from life under communism to life under capitalism. The immigrants from Cuba find a certain degree of cultural understanding in Israel, which has experienced a mini-version of this transition through the growing privatization of its kibbutzim. For ambitious young people who feel stymied in their career goals in Cuba—and who may already have glimpsed Israel's promise through an earlier visit funded by the Birthright program—the idea of starting fresh in Israel is much more inspiring than it is scary. Many idealistic young people who fall passionately in love with their Jewish identity and with Jewish history and culture—becoming dedicated teachers in Cuba—eventually choose to leave for Israel. Still, it is painful to leave their families, to leave the island community which nurtured them and badly needs their presence in order to survive.

Since 1992, when the first four young Cubans left, followed by the 1994 group of seventy Cubans who departed quietly for Israel through a program called Operation Cigar, another six hundred have followed. The Cuban government initially kept this exodus secret, so that it wouldn't appear that special immigration privileges were being given to Cuba's Jews. But even after the news was made official in the world press in 1999, the Cuban government continued to receive payment for each Jewish immigrant who leaves the country, in the form of exit visas, which are paid for by Israel.

There were many people who left for Israel—or were about to leave for Israel—while I was at work on this project. When Humberto took their photographs, we thought of them as Jews of Cuba. We had no reason to think of them any other way. But are they still Jews of Cuba if they've recently said goodbye to the island? Should I erase them from this story because they're no longer standing on Cuban soil? Did they trick us into thinking they were there—body and soul—when really they weren't? When does a Jew of Cuba stop being a Jew of Cuba? On the airplane? Landing in the new country? After a few years away? Or does the process of no longer being a Jew of Cuba start before then—as soon as the paperwork is filled out? Or earlier—at the first flashing thought of departure? At the first dream of living in a nation of Jews? At the first desire to acquire more of the material things the world has to offer?

Only yesterday these Jews were Jews of Cuba. Now it is their absence that haunts these photographs. These photographs, rather than marking a sense of presence in Cuba, have become fugitive documents of loss. They are a testimony to how quickly the seen can be transformed into the unseen.

Salomón Botton Behar, a veterinarian who was also vice president of the Jewish Community of Santiago de Cuba, posed for a photograph in his home with his wife and daughter. When I'd visit, Salomón always took me back to my hotel in his motorcycle, so I wouldn't have to take a taxi. He'd warn me not to utter a word if we were stopped by a policeman, because he'd get

into trouble for transporting a foreigner. He'd drop me off a block away, or around the corner, for safe measure. He knew the city of Santiago like the back of his hand. He and his family left for Israel in 2004 and they now live in Miami.

María Luisa Zayon, who goes by the nickname Malu, told me she was leaving for Israel the very next day as we greeted each other at the entrance to the Patronato. I was in Cuba on that occasion as a study leader with a group from the Jewish Museum in New York. Three fashionably dressed members of that group appear in the background. Malu left for Israel in 2004.

Baly Baly Garcés liked to show off the tattooed Jewish star on his leg. In this photograph you might mistake him for one more tourist, but at the time he was still living in Havana. He left for Israel in 2005.

Vicente Dorado Levy and his sons, Mario Vicente and Ruben, posed with a Beatles album. At the time, they were making plans to celebrate Ruben's bar mitzvah in the synagogue in Santiago de Cuba. Ruben knew his Torah portion perfectly. A year later, in 2005, they and Olguita, wife of Vicente and mother of the boys, left for Israel.

Isaac Rodríguez Gónzalez, or Junior, who is also known as "polaco007," was a brilliant physics student in Cuba. He left for Israel in 2005, where he is continuing his studies at Hebrew University in Jerusalem. His father, Julio Rodríguez Elí, his mother, María Elena Gónzalez García, and his sister, Violeta, stayed behind in Caibarién.

Isaac Rousso Lilo stood at the center of this photograph like an anchor trying to keep a boat from sinking. He embraced, on one side, his wife, Flora Viota Coll, and older daughter, Beatriz Eugenia, and on the other side, his younger daughter, Tamara, and son-in-law, Houwer Friman. At the time, they were all living together in the same apartment in Havana. Tamara and Houwer left for Israel in 2006.

Jacob Barlias, the son of a Jewish father, and his mother, a convert to Judaism, never missed a Shabbat at the Centro Sefaradí. They left for Israel in 2006.

I thought of Pavel Tennenbaum as a permanent presence at the Patronato, where he
worked as Adela Dworin's personal assistant. He
was in daily contact with the Jewish American
missions, gathering the donations as they arrived.
As reticent as he is tall, I was never able to
exchange more than a few words with him. He left
for Israel in 2006.

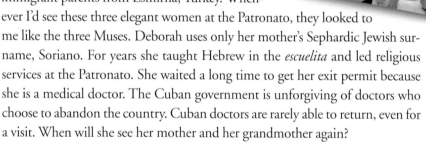

Deborah Soriano poses with her mother, Miriam
Morales Soriano, and her grandmother, Karina
Soriano Albo, who holds a photograph of her
immigrant parents from Esmirna, Turkey. When-
ever I'd see these three elegant women at the Patronato, they looked to
me like the three Muses. Deborah uses only her mother's Sephardic Jewish surname, Soriano. For years she taught Hebrew in the *escuelita* and led religious
services at the Patronato. She waited a long time to get her exit permit because
she is a medical doctor. The Cuban government is unforgiving of doctors who
choose to abandon the country. Cuban doctors are rarely able to return, even for
a visit. When will she see her mother and her grandmother again?

Before leaving for Israel in January, 2007, Deborah wrote me a note via
e-mail:

> *Dear Ruth:*
>
> *The greatest event of my life is getting closer and closer, the dream that I
> have nursed for 4 long years and that is about to come true. I'm full of appre-
> hensions and reasons for my heart to break but my hopes and dreams are greater
> than my sorrows. I don't know if I'll still feel like this after I pass through the cli-
> mactic moment of my departure, I hope that God will give me strength and
> firmness, and also that he will keep me company on this difficult and practically
> uncharted road on which I'm embarking. I'm going to start my life over again
> in the only place in the world I know aside from mi Cubita bella, my beautiful
> little Cuba, but I'll never know it as well as I know this island.*
>
> *A big kiss, we'll see each other very soon.*

Claudia Conde Ruíz, the little sister, will be leaving Caibarién for Israel with her parents and grandparents in 2007. Her older brother, Freddy, can't leave because he is of military age. For the last few years their house has served as the headquarters of the Jewish community of Caibarién, a fishing town where twenty Jews were still living until just the other day. Their grandmother, Sara Berta Levy Molina, was the community's president. Now the responsibility will fall to her eighteen-year-old grandson, Freddy, to keep watch over their house with the Star of David made of wrought iron. Who will remind Freddy to cover the television with the lace coverlet when no one is there?

As the president of the Centro Sefaradí, José Levy never stood in the way of congregation members who wanted to leave for Israel, but for his part, he planned to stay "until the last chapter was written," as people like to say in Cuba. He hoped his daughter, Danayda, felt as he did. He tried not to notice as she came of age and her eyes became foggy with clouds of other places where Jews she knew had gone—Israel, Canada, Spain—that she also dreamed of

departing to. Then in October 2006, at the age of seventeen, Danayda married
her sweetheart from the neighborhood. As a minor, she asked Levy and her
mother, Florinda, for permission to leave for Israel with her husband. Neither
parent felt they should hold back Danayda, and so they have grudgingly signed
the documents that will allow her to cross the ocean. As José Levy told me, "I
think Danayda didn't want to make that long voyage alone."

Danayda always told me that she would never leave Cuba without her
father. She knew if she left she'd miss her mother. But with her father, it was
another matter; he couldn't stay behind. "If I leave, my father has to come too,"
she'd say. But she was a girl then. She is a woman now and she is leaving him.
Hopefully not forever. Hopefully he will follow. Hopefully. As she waits for her
plane ticket out of the island, clouds of other places fill her eyes and she imag-
ines it will not be so terrible to say goodbye.

37

MY ROOM ON

BITTERNESS STREET

"Por favor, quiero la habitación Ruth," I say to the receptionist at the front desk.

"Yes, of course, we've already set the room aside for you," the thin woman with the languid eyes replies. "You'll be the first guest to stay in that room."

I thank her, wondering how it is that she and apparently others at the hotel have anticipated my desire to stay in the room named Ruth.

"Maybe you don't remember me. I'm María Elena, I'm married to Alberto Zilberstein, the president of the Adath Israel synagogue."

It takes me a moment to place María Elena. We have talked little, but I have seen her at the synagogue and know her to be among the women recently converted to Judaism who avidly attend religious services. She probably never expected to end up a Jew when she and Alberto were young revolutionaries studying together in Russia.

"I'm sorry, I didn't recognize you in the uniform," I say.

"Don't worry, I could tell you didn't," she replies. "There are a few of us from the Jewish community working here—Marlen as a cashier in the store, Joan as a porter, Wilber as a waiter. We all feel a little funny in our uniforms."

"So this is going to be a Jewish hotel?"

"That's the idea," María Elena replies. "For Jews who come to Cuba to feel at home. We've been asked to light the Shabbat candles on Friday night."

María Elena straightens her collar, then reaches into the cubby behind her. "Here, let me give you the key to your room. Room 206. The Ruth room."

When María Elena hands me the key to "my" room, we both smile politely, but I'm embarrassed by the awkwardness of our encounter—she, an educated member of the Jewish community of Cuba now working as a receptionist in a hotel, and I, suddenly a tour leader requesting a room from her, a room she couldn't stay in, even if she could pay for it, because by law Cubans are not allowed to stay in any hotels that have been turned over to tourism.

Insofar as it's possible, I try not to set myself apart from other Cubans in Cuba. I want to try to lead the most Cuban life I can when I'm back on the island. Over the years my home in Cuba has been a modest room in a house that belongs to a close friend of my former nanny, Caro. I'm used to sleeping with the windows open and waking to the sun in my eyes and dogs barking and roosters crowing (urban roosters that thrive on any patch of unoccupied terrain in Havana). I'm used to buying mangos and papayas in the outdoor markets, and I'm used to waiting, as Cubans do (but not as patiently as they), when there's no water or the lights are out.

Yet, unlike Cubans on the island, I come with dollars, I can afford to buy bottled water, I can take taxis. Not only that. I can exit Cuban reality at any time, I can change the channel, leave. This is the greatest privilege I have as a child of Cuban immigrants—that I can come and go to Cuba. And I'm still granted political immunity because I left as a child. People will say, *A ella la sacaron de Cuba*—"She was taken out of Cuba." Since I didn't make the choice to leave, I am innocent, I can be trusted.

But the last thing I want is to go back to Cuba flaunting my privileges, expecting Cubans who stayed on the island to serve me and clean up after me. I don't like to stay in hotels in Cuba. Hotels are for strangers and I don't want to be a stranger in Cuba.

Until the mid-1990s, all Cuban Americans traveling to Cuba were obligated by the Cuban government to stay in hotels. The government wanted to cash in on the wealth that the "worms" of the Revolution (now welcomed back as "butterflies") brought to the island. But the aim was also to keep us apart from our fellow Cubans, so we wouldn't ruin their socialist purity with our capitalist turpitude. After a while, as tourism increased, the government relaxed its policy. Returning Cubans could stay with family or friends—though such visits still have to be cleared by local authorities and are carefully monitored.

Once it became possible for me not to stay in hotels, I vowed I'd never stay in a hotel again while I was in Cuba.

Then at the turn of the new century I began to receive invitations to travel to Cuba on all-expense-paid trips in the role of "study leader" for American groups. My role was to serve as a professor-on-call for Americans hungry to see Cuba after decades of minimal information about the taboo island. I'd be the one to answer all their questions about Cuba, from why the cows are so skinny to why it is that Cubans don't hate the American people. I succumbed to the temptation, telling myself it would be good for me as an anthropologist to see the tourist side of Cuba. I became a study leader on group trips organized by the American Museum of Natural History, the Jewish Museum in New York, and Puentes Cubanos in Miami, before the "people to people" licenses that made most of these trips possible were revoked by the U.S. government in 2004.

Traveling with Americans who spent thousands of dollars to visit Cuba for one or two weeks in deluxe comfort, I enjoyed the hot showers and slept in air-conditioned rooms in five-star hotels. I ate and drank in ways I had no idea were possible in Cuba. There was imported Norwegian smoked salmon for breakfast and exquisite French wine with dinner. I rode on pillowy tour buses where you didn't feel the potholes and sat as if on a throne above the gritty streets, watching at red lights as fellow Cubans gazed back at me, packed like sardines onto airless double-wagon buses called *camellos*, or "camels," for which they had waited hours.

I'd gotten so expert at being a study leader—and, I admit, also so spoiled by the experience of traveling in luxury—that I agreed to organize a trip in May 2003 for a group of scholars, writers, and activists who had never been to

Cuba and wanted to see the country through my eyes. To make arrangements for the trip, I had gone to Cuba a few months earlier. I knew that several members of my group wanted to stay in the famed Hotel Nacional, but I hoped to find a smaller hotel in Old Havana near the Cathedral, the Plaza Vieja, and the Parque Central. By coincidence, a friend who is an expert on the history of Old Havana took me on a walking tour during that visit. He showed me around the old Jewish neighborhood nestled near the harbor of the city, where Jewish peddlers once went and collected their wares from the ships to sell door-to-door. When we reached a building wedged into the triangular corner of two streets, he smiled, and said he had a surprise for me. He told me the building was going to be the site of a Jewish hotel.

I looked at him quizzically. "A Jewish hotel?"

"Yes. The Hotel Raquel. It will be ready in six months."

"But how? The building is still half in ruins."

I pointed to the piles of rocks and cement at the entrance, the wooden supports around the balconies, and the sparkles of sawdust that rose into the air and caught the beams of sunlight that entered the building through the tall shuttered windows.

"Eusebio Leal is behind this project. They'll have it ready."

I knew Eusebio Leal was the official historian of Havana and that he was at the helm of the bold restoration projects in the colonial center which were giving back a semblance of its former splendor to the most voluptuous city of the Caribbean. UNESCO had named Old Havana a world heritage site in 1982, providing seed money for the initial restoration of the crumbling buildings in the area. In turn, Leal created the state-owned company Habaguanex to reinvest tourist profits in more renovations. Although local residents were being pushed out, Cubans took pride in the gentrification of Old Havana. "Leal did that," they liked to say, pointing to restored plazas, churches, and hotels, as though Leal had done the work with his own hands.

Signs were posted saying not to enter the hotel-in-construction, but we paid no attention. My friend and I tiptoed around the columns of the lobby, waving hello to the workers as if we belonged there. One of the workers knew my friend and he took us upstairs. There was a man hammering small bronze placards into the walls next to the door of each room. I peered over his shoulder and saw the placard he'd just finished putting up: it said "Ruth."

"Look, it's your room!" my friend said.

I might have nodded, enjoyed the quirky irony, and walked away, but I decided then I needed to come back and occupy that room. On more than one occasion, when academic audiences had asked me to define my identity as a scholar, I had called myself a diasporic anthropologist. A stay in the Ruth room, I thought, offered me a golden opportunity to experience in the flesh— and anthropologists always want to experience things "in the flesh"—what it means to be an anthropologist of the diasporic sort.

But I didn't want to foot the bill for this fieldwork jaunt. So I decided I'd bring my group to the Hotel Raquel. As a tour leader, I was entitled to free lodging. Why not use my little bit of privilege for the sake of anthropology?

Six months later, the Havanatur bus drops me and the group off at the Plaza de San Francisco de Asis, one of the showcase restoration sites overseen by Leal and filled daily with tourists wandering about snapping pictures.

"What are these buildings?" someone asks.

"That's the Lonja del Comercio, the home of the old Cuban stock exchange. There's a luxury restaurant on the ground floor and the rooftop has one of the best views of Havana."

"And that church?"

"It's a Franciscan convent dating from the sixteenth century. They hold classical music concerts there almost every afternoon."

"Can we go to one of the concerts?"

"Yes," I say. "It's on the program."

I summon my patience. "Okay, everyone, now follow me," I yell.

As we trudge across the cobblestone plaza, I try to seem confident, but the truth is I'm not sure how to get to the Hotel Raquel. I know it's a few blocks from the plaza, but I don't mention I have a terrible sense of direction. I can't read a map and I'm capable of getting lost a few blocks from my house in Michigan. I find my way around places only if I have landmarks to guide me. I know that to find the Hotel Raquel we need to get to the Benetton store.

And, fortunately in this case, Benetton isn't difficult to find. I see the green sign on the display window all the way from the other side of the plaza. The store caters to tourists and resident foreigners, for no ordinary Cuban could possibly buy anything there. Only once had I entered the Benetton store myself. I'd been on the verge of buying a blouse that in the United States I would have put on my credit card without thinking twice about it. But since American credit cards aren't valid in Cuba, if I wanted the blouse I had to pay cash for it. In Cuba, where everything must be paid for in cash, I am perpetually afraid I will run out of money. The inherited paranoia grips me—what if Fidel dies and people revolt and I have to flee, what if I have to pay my way out of the island and don't have enough money? And so the blouse stayed on the hanger.

Sure enough, on the corner taken over by Benetton, that is where Calle Amargura, or Bitterness Street, begins. To get to the Hotel Raquel you have to pass the Benetton shop and walk a few blocks on Bitterness until you reach San Ignacio.

Bitterness Street is under restoration and torn up so badly you have to jump over potholes. "Be careful, please watch your step," I tell my group.

The street is too narrow for our big tour bus. Our suitcases will have to be hand-carried from the plaza by the hotel porters. But the inconvenience, everyone agrees, is worth it when we reach the hotel and see the meticulously restored art nouveau building, its façade brimming with stone flowers, gargoyles, and lion heads. As my friend had predicted, the building had risen from the ruins in six months and looked perfect.

"The building dates from 1908," I announce to my group as we gather at the entrance. "It was once a chamber of commerce for Spanish cloth dealers. Now it's a Jewish-themed hotel. I hear you can get matzah ball soup in the restaurant."

Someone in the group asks, "Why is this street called Calle Amargura?"

"The street, Calle Amargura, is 'bitter' because it was the path of the Holy Week procession in the colonial era. Each corner marked a station of the cross. They started in the Plaza de San Francisco and walked to the church on the other end of the street. It's a weird location for a Jewish-themed hotel, but the oldest Sephardic synagogue in Cuba is on Calle Inquisidor, the Street of the Inquisitor."

When we enter the hotel, I can't help but continue to do my tour leader shtick. "Look," I say, pointing out the mezuzah on the threshold, an amulet that is usually posted at the entrance to Jewish homes and temples.

Inside, no luxury has been spared. Everything that can possibly be done in marble has been done. Thick marble columns sustain the gilded ceilings and the marble floor gleams like an ice-skating rink. At the center is a not-very-Jewish but definitely elegant Italian marble statue of a madonna with a child clinging to her breast.

Light shines into the lobby from a stained glass cupola and through the shuttered windows that are rimmed with stained glass half-circles. The dining room is set off from the rest of the lobby with lush dark wood dividers that are topped with menorahs and Stars of David encrusted into stained glass panels.

Across from the reception desk, there is a bar called "Lejaim," which means "to life" in Hebrew and is the traditional Jewish toast, like "cheers."

At the Garden of Eden restaurant, I learn that not only is matzah ball soup available, but also a mishmash of Jewish dishes, including latkes, knishes, kugel, gefilte fish, Moroccan turkey, Hungarian goulash, hummus, and borscht, all from recipes taken off the Internet.

The gift shop, Bezalel, sells silver Shabbat candle holders handmade in Cuba, as well as Ahava skin-care products from Israel. A *tallit,* or prayer shawl, hangs over the cash register like a canopy and the space is lit by a lamp in the shape of a Star of David, an exact copy of the lamp that hangs in the crumbling Chevet Ahim synagogue.

I don't know what to make of so much seductively marketed Jewishness. It dawns on me that the wide range of American Jewish as well as Latin American Jewish visitors flocking to Cuba—on humanitarian religious missions, art hunts, musical journeys, and volunteer medical trips—have not gone unnoticed by the Cuban government. The Hotel Raquel honors their presence through a romantic and feminized image of Jewishness—a pastel mural of the biblical heroine Raquel with dreamy eyes and a halo of tresses adorns an entire wall—while at the same time tapping into the potentially lucrative Jewish tourist market they represent. But I try not to think too much about all this— I who have spent years searching for a way to return to Cuba as a Jew. I tell myself that the Hotel Raquel is just a hotel and that I should try to enjoy it.

My group, it turns out, is the first group to stay at the Hotel Raquel, and everyone ends up loving it, whether or not they're Jewish, and as the first we are given an excess amount of fawning attention. When it rains, the doormen lend us umbrellas. When I tell the restaurant manager that a member of the group is celebrating her birthday, he provides, on the house, a rum cake decorated with yellow sugar flowers. I try the matzah ball soup and it really isn't bad at all. The small size of the hotel allows the members of our group to occupy all the rooms as if we're sharing our own private mansion. I am congratulated several times for making an excellent hotel choice. The staff, and particularly the Jewish employees, of whom there were eight at the time, treat me affably while also being careful to maintain a respectful distance. I have become a valuable client of the hotel, capable of enticing a group of Americans to book all their rooms.

An intimate hotel with twenty-five rooms, each room is named after a biblical character or biblical place. There are rooms named Abraham, Sarah, Isaac, Rebeca, Leah, Jacob, Ruben, Joseph, Benjamin, Tamar, Miriam, Sefora, Hannah, Samuel, David, Solomon, Elias, Jeremiah, Nejemias, Esther. There is a room named Elizabeth, although she doesn't figure in the Hebrew Bible. Three rooms carry place names: Galilee, Sinai, Jordan. And then there is room 206, the room named Ruth.

I feel strange going in and out of the Ruth room. I have to walk past the Rebeca room (my mother is Rebeca and my paternal grandmother was Rebeca) and the Esther room (my maternal grandmother was Esther)

and the Hannah room (my great-grandmother was Hannah) and the Isaac room (my paternal grandfather was Isaac) and the Abraham room (my great-grandfather was Abraham and the Hebrew name of my father, Alberto, is Abraham). I had a cousin named Solomon and a great-uncle named Jacob. I have a cousin by marriage named Samuel, I have cousins named Miriam and Ruben.

To see the names of family members, living and dead, posted on these hotel rooms in Havana is beyond surreal. I have landed in an uncanny replica of what I'm longing to find, a bizarre Jewish Cuban Diasporaland, where the ultimate experience of displacement is staring me in the face. Is this what's left for people like me, people like Lot's wife, who are always looking back?

My air-conditioned room is so cold that I tremble each night getting into bed. There is no way to adjust the air conditioning and the windows don't open. I put on my only sweater to go to sleep. Who would have thought I'd be freezing in Cuba?

In my room, as in every room at the Hotel Raquel, there is a bedside copy of the King James Bible, rather than the Jewish Old Testament, should I be inspired to read about a few of my ancestors in the middle of the night.

In my room, if I'm ever placed on hold while making a phone call, I can listen to the theme from *Schindler's List*.

Maybe this fate is no worse than Hemingway's, whose room at the Ambos Mundos Hotel, just a few blocks away, is preserved as a museum piece.

But a hotel room in Havana named Ruth wasn't my idea of the home I had hoped to reclaim. What cruel poetic justice! My Jewish ancestors had called the island "Hotel Cuba," thinking of Cuba as a stepping-stone to the golden America that lay ninety miles away. But the course of history led them to stay in Cuba and create a home there, a home they wept for when they left. Now history had led me to return to Cuba to seek that lost home. And what had I found? A hotel. A hotel on Bitterness Street.

.   .   .

One night I had a sad dream in the Ruth room on Bitterness Street.

Somehow it was snowing in Cuba and unbearably cold. I didn't have a coat. I didn't have a roof over my head. Not even all the Jewish ghosts that surrounded me could keep me warm.

Upon awakening I remembered an old photograph from Cuba. I'd lingered over it for years, scrutinized it many times. I'm maybe four months old, resting in the arms of my twenty-year-old rapturously beautiful mother. I'm looking away, but she, with painted ruby lips, presses my head against her cheek, holds me tightly, and looks into the camera with a gaze so intense it seems she, rather than the camera, will freeze that moment in time.

That is the feeling staying in the Ruth room provoked in me: the longing to be a baby again in my mother's arms, cuddled and safe, no destiny or identity yet determined, a newborn on the island of Cuba.

. . .

What place is there in Cuba for a woman named Ruth?

As I know only too well, Ruth is not a common Cuban or Spanish-language name. It is a Jewish name that has always raised eyebrows when I tell people my background. "You're Cuban? But with the name Ruth?" To pronounce the name Ruth in Spanish is impossible. It sounds like "Luz" or "Root." A soap opera that ran on Cuban television a few years ago, featuring twin sisters named Ruth and Raquel, helped to lend popularity to the name. But very few people in Cuba know the biblical story of Ruth.

Ruth, who was a Moabite, is the Bible's best-known convert to Judaism, because after her husband's death she chose to stay with her elderly mother-in-law, Naomi, and the Israelites, rather than return to her own community. Meshing her destiny with that of the Jewish people, her great act of heroism in aiding and comforting Naomi was to imagine that she belonged among strangers.

After my stay in the room named Ruth, I learned that many of the women in Cuba who marry Jewish men and convert to Judaism take the name Ruth as their Hebrew name. I asked the Ruth in Havana, the Ruth in Santa Clara, and the Ruth in Guantánamo why they chose the name Ruth and they all told me because Ruth was the first woman to convert to Judaism. They identified with her, because they too made a choice to be part of the Jewish people and saw Ruth as embodying a vision of Jewishness that embraces those who are not afraid to align themselves with a tribe of wanderers.

I found solace knowing that Ruth isn't just the name of a Havana hotel room, but the name of real women living in Cuba today who are able to call the island home.

. . .

As for me, I hope to keep going back, even if I now know that the purpose of each return journey is to get better at saying goodbye.

It's strange that there isn't a Kaddish a Jew can recite for a lost home. If there were, I'd utter that prayer. Without fear. Finally letting go in order to believe that the only true home is the one we have searched for inconsolably.

HOW THIS BOOK CAME TO BE
A PHOTOJOURNEY

I think it was my obsession with the old black-and-white photographs from Cuba that nurtured in me a love and appreciation for the medium of photography. As a graduate student I studied black-and-white photography and learned to develop and print my own photographs. I adored large-format cameras and lugged them with me on fieldwork trips to Spain and Mexico. But when I got to Cuba I found that I really wasn't a photographer at heart—or maybe I couldn't be a photographer in Cuba. I didn't want to create distance between myself and other Cubans by holding up a camera to my eye. I wanted to look at people and have them look back at me. Even though I eventually made a movie, *Adio Kerida*, about the Sephardic Jews of Cuba, I didn't do the camerawork. It was during the making of the movie that I realized I was more of a writer than a filmmaker because I kept wanting to add voiceovers rather than allow the visual images to tell the story.

While I was visiting my friend Joyce Maio in New York, she showed me some prints by the photographer Humberto Mayol. I was immediately captivated by his black-and-white photographs of everyday Cuban life as well as his photojournalistic work on Afrocuban religious communities. It occurred to me that another way of telling the story of the Jews of Cuba would be in collaboration with a photographer. On a visit to Cuba in 2002, I met with Humberto and asked if he would be interested in working with me. He was intrigued and agreed right away. Over the next few years, between 2002 and 2006, Humberto and I would travel around Cuba together, he with his camera and I with my pen, looking for Jews and looking at Jews.

Humberto isn't Jewish, and he had not known there were Jews living in Cuba, which turned out to be good for our project. Humberto approached his work with the curiosity of someone who had just learned of the existence of an exotic people in his own country—people who were Jewish, but lived just like other Cubans. Our collaboration was unique because both of us were insiders and outsiders in different ways. I was an insider as a Jew while Humberto was an outsider as a non-Jew, but Humberto was an insider as a Cuban who lived on the island, while I was an outsider as a Cuban who lived in the diaspora. What we shared was the same passion for observing people and listening to their stories. Both of us strove to find the poetry that was often hidden right below the surface of what we saw and heard.

As the project progressed, Humberto and I had many discussions about how we would convey visually the mesh of Jewishness and Cubanness. Jews and Cubans are among the most extensively photographed people in the world. But how do you show that a person is a Jew in Cuba? How do you show the Jewish Cubanness of a social space? Coming into contact with a Jewish world that was completely foreign to him, Humberto's first impulse was to take pictures of Jews doing Jewish things: Jews dressed in ritual attire, Jews praying in the synagogues, Jews celebrating bar and bat mitzvahs. But I felt that these pictures only told part of the story, the public story, the heroic story of the Jewish rebirth in Cuba. (They also led viewers to assume that religiosity was the only means through which Cubans expressed pride in a Jewish identity, erasing the presence of Jewish revolutionaries who felt a kinship with José Martí and Che Guevara.) I wanted us to also capture the private story of loss and longing, a subterranean layer of Jewish being. Seeing how Jews in Cuba tenderly held on to old family photographs and Jewish documents that held great power to change their destinies, we hit upon the visual strategy of asking people to hold up these precious things for the camera. Through pictures within pictures, people had the opportunity to interact with the camera, revealing themselves and their sense of history. The photographs that emerged in the course of our journey honored unrehearsed moments of self-awareness and reflection when people seemed to take stock of the flow of time itself.

Before I began writing the book, I lived in the photographic world that

Humberto had created. It was a world that had taken tremendous dedication, skill, and effort to bring forth. Humberto shot all his pictures on black-and-white film, he processed everything using artisanal methods in the kitchen of his apartment, and then scanned all his negatives and painstakingly produced the tones he wanted on an ancient computer. We got along well, but at one point Humberto inadvertently hurt my feelings by suggesting he was the artist and I the documentarian. His photographs, he said, could stand alone, without any commentary from me, and he proved his point by submitting a few pictures to the Havana Bienal and winning first prize. But Humberto stuck with me because he believed in the book, believed in the ideal it represented as a project born from a bridge between a cubana of the diaspora and a cubano of the island.

I felt that Humberto had given me an exciting challenge. Could I write a text that would be on a par artistically with his photographs? I certainly wanted to. I had kept written notes of my encounters with people, and audiotaped and videotaped interviews, but I wanted to offer epiphanies, not explanations. I wanted to uncover those disturbing flashes of insight that had failed to appear in my fieldnotes, but which haunted me long after the encounters had taken place.

But looking to the discipline of anthropology didn't give me much inspiration or guidance for how to use photographs artistically in an ethnography. In fact, I learned that most anthropologists frowned upon the idea of being artistic in their use of photographs. The renowned anthropologist Margaret Mead had high hopes that film, tape recording, and especially the use of still photography would revolutionize anthropology, but only insofar as these media might increase the accuracy of observation and make the discipline more scientific. She was disappointed that "research project after research project fail to include filming and insist on continuing the hopelessly inadequate note-taking of an earlier age, while the behavior that film could have caught and preserved for centuries disappears—disappears right in front of everybody's eyes." Cameras were to be employed to "permit the descendents to repossess their cultural heritage," and give anthropologists "a reliable, reproducible, reanalyzable corpus."[1]

Mead ended up collecting 25,000 photographs with her husband and fellow anthropologist, Gregory Bateson, a few of which became part of their book *Balinese Character*.[2] But since Mead's aim was to be scientific, she and Bateson purposely took bland descriptive photographs that provided information about social behavior, where the subjects were "acting natural" and never looking into the camera. The accompanying text was a dry, literal explanation of what was depicted by the image. Mead wanted word and image to mimic each other. In the end, the documentary impulse proved suffocating. The result was a doomed effort to turn the cathartic experiences of ethnographic fieldwork into a laboratory experiment, rather than exploring how they might be used imaginatively for humanistic storytelling.

It is no wonder anthropologists have shied away from experimenting with storytelling that joins together words and photographs. And yet the taking of photographs in fieldwork is rampant—what anthropologist, indeed what traveler or tourist, doesn't take a camera to the field? Everyone takes pictures but no one knows what to do with them. Anthropology adopted not Mead's optimism about photography's usefulness for the discipline, but Susan Sontag's famed distrust of photographs. As Sontag wrote in her manifesto *On Photography*, "To photograph people is to violate them, by seeing them as they never see themselves, by having knowledge of them they can never have; it turns people into objects that can be symbolically possessed. Just as the camera is a sublimation of the gun, to photograph someone is a sublimated murder—a soft murder, appropriate to a sad, frightened time."[3]

Perhaps, out of fear of causing harm through photographic murder, most anthropologists have stuck to using photographs in what seems an innocent way—as illustrations, rarely ever engaged with, of practices, customs, and behaviors discussed in their books. But I'd like to think we can do more. Contradictory though it may seem, I believe it is possible to combine Mead's undaunted enthusiasm for visual anthropology with Sontag's self-consciousness about the consequences of taking photographs.

I sought to unite these opposed perspectives by creating a dialogue between photography and anthropology. Rather than Humberto's photographs being illustrations for my text, I wrote in response to the photographs that Humberto had taken mostly in situations where he was with me while I spoke to and interacted with people. At times in my writing I wanted to recreate the situation that led to the taking of a photograph. Other times I wanted to produce a parallel text that told the story the photograph couldn't show. I came to feel that Humberto's photographs alone would have been insufficient; my words alone would have been insufficient too. It seemed to me that I knew Cuba as a place where things were left half unsaid, a place where ghosts were in plain sight, a place where I would know only fragments of the truth. My text took form as a patchwork of scenes that, like Humberto's photographs, sought out shimmers of light in the shadows.

Humberto had generously taken hundreds of photographs and told me that I should choose the ones I wanted to tell my story. Looking at them over and over, I reached a point where I knew them all by heart. I treated them as I had the old black-and-white family photographs from Cuba, but, unlike the old photographs that were surrogates for the memories I longed to have, Humberto's elicited true memories—for now I really had memories of Cuba. I had memories of the newly revived Jewish Cuba I had returned to and come to know firsthand. These images became the album of my return to the forbidden home, the place where the hurt of immigration is felt so deeply that if you leave they stamp your passport with the words *salida definitiva*—no return. Just as my family had taken photographs out of Cuba by which to remember the life they were leaving behind, when I sat down to write this book I had Humberto's photographs, my new memoryscape, in my suitcase.

CUBA

Cuando yo te vuelva a ver
No habrá más pena ni olvido

When I see you again
There will be no pain or forgetting

CHRONOLOGY

March 1492 Ferdinand and Isabella of Spain decree that all the Jews of Spain must convert to Christianity or be expelled by the end of July.

Later in 1492 Luís de Torres, a Spanish Jew who had converted to avoid the expulsion, is hired by Christopher Columbus to serve as interpreter for his voyage. Torres, who knows Hebrew, Aramaic, and "a little Arabic" as well as Spanish, is sent into the interior of Cuba on November 2 for a four-day reconnaissance, and therefore is considered the first Jewish visitor to the island. Torres and thirty-nine other crew members are left on Hispaniola when Columbus returns to Spain; when Columbus comes back the following year, the garrison has been destroyed and all the settlers massacred.

1510 After devastating much of the wealth of neighboring Hispaniola, Spanish settlers conquer the island of Cuba.

1514 The city of Santiago is founded by Spanish settlers on the eastern coast of Cuba. It will serve as the capital of Spanish Cuba from 1522 to 1563. Also in 1514, a town named Havana is founded on the southern coast.

1519 Havana is moved to its present location on a large natural bay on the north shore of Cuba, across the narrow island from its first site. The Holy Office of the Inquisition, dedicated to rooting out insincere Jewish converts and their descendents, is established in Cuba.

1563 The Spanish governor moves from Santiago to the growing port city of Havana.

1613 A resident of Havana, Francisco Gómez de León, is tried and executed by the local tribunal of the Inquisition for "Judaizing." His fortune is confiscated.

1762 In a side maneuver of the Seven Years' War between Britain and France, the British capture Havana and hold it for ten months. They later trade it for Florida.

1810–1825 As all of mainland Spanish America moves toward independence, Cuba and Puerto Rico remain the last strongholds of Spain in the Americas. Spanish loyalists flock to Havana, now booming with the sugar trade.

1834 The Spanish Inquisition is abolished by decree from Madrid. Freedom of religion remains elusive in Spain and its colonies, but a handful of Sephardic Jews from the Dutch Caribbean colonies and Ashkenazic Jews from Europe gradually begin to settle in Cuba.

1847 Chinese male migrant workers are brought to Cuba to work on sugar plantations during the crisis of slavery and are exploited even more brutally than African slaves. By 1883, there are 150,000 Chinese workers in Cuba.

1851 Three Jews—Augusto Bondi, Luis Schlessinger, and Janos Blumenthal—join the doomed expedition of Venezuelan-American "filibuster" Narciso López to free Cuba from Spanish rule.

1868 Carlos Manuel de Céspedes, a lawyer and sugar mill owner in Oriente, frees his slaves and invites them to fight with him to liberate Cuba.

1878 Antonio Maceo, a mulato independence leader, refuses to sign the peace treaty with Spain in Baragua, declaring that he will not capitulate until slavery is abolished.

1880 Slavery is abolished in Cuba, but only on paper; in reality, it remains rooted on the island until 1886. Cuba is the next-to-last country to abolish slavery in the Americas. (Brazil does not do so until 1888.)

1881 A change in Spanish law authorizes Jewish immigrants to enter Cuba legally for the first time.

1895–1898 Jews in the tiny Cuban Jewish colony support the Cuban Independence War led by José Martí. In his essay "Nuestra América" (1895), Martí writes, "Whoever rebels with Cuba today, rebels for all time. Since Cuba is our sacred homeland . . . serving it, in so glorious and difficult a time, fills a man with dignity and nobility." Martí is killed fighting for Cuban independence the same year he pens those words.

1897 The rebels struggling for Cuban independence draft a constitution for the new country. One of the articles, which will be retained in the subsequent constitutions of the free island, decrees freedom of religious belief and worship.

1898 The United States intervenes in the Cuban War for Independence and defeats Spain in the Spanish-American War. The United States expeditionary force, which includes a number of Jewish soldiers, remains to occupy Cuba until 1902. Non-Catholic religious services are legalized in Cuba under the occupation.

1901 The United States imposes the Platt amendment on the Cuban constitution, maintaining the right to intervene in Cuba for the preservation of Cuban independence.

1902 The U.S. occupation of Cuba ends. After half a century of struggle, Cubans raise the flag of a free republic.

1903 Cuba leases land in Guantánamo to the United States, where the United States builds a naval base. For the next fifty-seven years, U.S. involvement and investment in Cuba will hasten the modernization of the island. Railroads will be built, hotels erected, baseball will become a national sport, and Cuba will be marketed to Americans as a winter paradise. Protestant churches (Methodists, Presbyterians, Episcopalians, Quakers) from the United States will make inroads in Cuba.

1906 Eleven Jews from the United States, part of a wave of foreign investors and settlers in newly independent Cuba, found the reform United Hebrew Congregation in Havana, the heart of the American Jewish community on the island.

1906–1909 Citing unrest, the United States reoccupies Cuba.

1910 The United Hebrew Congregation consecrates Beth Ha Haim, Cuba's first Jewish cemetery, in Guanabacoa, across the bay from Havana.

1914 At the outset of the First World War, Sephardic emigrants from the Ottoman Empire settle in cities and towns all across Cuba, including Havana, where they form a second Jewish community. They found Chevet Ahim, Cuba's first Sephardic synagogue, in the heart of La Habana Vieja.

1918 A report estimates that there are 100 America Jews and 900 Sephardic Jews, mainly from Istanbul and Thrace, living in Cuba. Jewish immigration from Eastern Europe is still insignificant.

1921–1924 The United States sharply restricts immigration with the passage of the Emergency Quota Act of 1921, revised and codified as the Immigration Act of 1924. Jewish refugees from Eastern Europe begin to settle in Latin America instead of the United States, with Cuba a favored destination. Hundreds of Sephardic families fleeing the Greek occupation of Ottoman Thrace seek refuge in Cuba, where they are attracted by the similarity of language to their native Ladino.

1921–1930 Synagogues are founded in provincial cities all across Cuba: Camagüey (1921), Holguín (1921), Camajuaní (1924), Ciego de Avila (1924), Manzanillo (1924), Santiago (1924), Banes (1926), Matanzas (1928), Guantánamo (1929), Santa Clara (1929), and Artemisa (1930).

1922 The American Jewish Joint Distribution Committee (JDC, or "el Joint," as it is known in Cuba) establishes a branch in Havana and begins charitable activities in Cuba.

1924 Rabbi Guershon Maya, the respected leader of the Sephardic community of Havana (originally from Silivri, Turkey), founds the first Jewish day school in Cuba. Ashkenazic immigrants found the Zionist Union (Unión Sionista) of Cuba, first housed in Chevet Ahim.

1925 With growing immigration from Eastern Europe, an Ashkenazic minyan (prayer group of ten persons), first organized in 1923 by Lithuanian immigrant

Ben Sión Sofer in his Havana apartment, expands into the Adath Israel synagogue, the spiritual center of Cuba's third Jewish community.

Another Ashkenazic synagogue is founded in Camagüey with the help of the U.S.-based Jewish Committee for Cuba, becoming one of the few Ashkenazic organizations in Cuba outside Havana, but after several months it is taken over by anti-religious Bundists and is closed by its American sponsors.

The Centro Israelita is established in Havana, eventually taking under its wing several smaller Jewish schools to become the primary Jewish educational center in Cuba.

Abraham Simjovich (better known as Fabio Grobart, a pseudonym he adopted to avoid arrest) and several other Polish Jews take part in the founding of the Communist Party of Cuba, forming the Yiddish-language Sección Hebrea of the Party.

Reports estimate 100 American Jews, 5,200 Ashkenazic Jews, and 2,700 Sephardic Jews in Havana; perhaps another 2,000 Sephardic Jews live in provincial towns across the island.

1925–1933 Gerardo Machado, elected president of Cuba in 1925, becomes increasingly tyrannical as he confronts economic depression and widespread unrest. At least five Jewish Communists fall as victims of the Machado dictatorship.

1926 The first Jewish high school in Cuba, the Colegio Teodoro Herzl, is founded. On August 13th of this year, Fidel Castro is born on a sugar plantation in eastern Cuba.

1929 A second Ashkenazic synagogue, Knesseth Israel, is founded next door to Adath Israel by the congregation's first rabbi, Zvi Kaplan. The two congregations remain separate for the next twenty years.

1931 Jewish immigration to Cuba comes to a halt in response to the dire political repression under Machado and the economic situation in the country during the Great Depression.

Representatives of Chevet Ahim petition the Spanish Consul in Havana for Spanish passports, arguing that "the Sephardim are united with the Spaniards for ethnic reasons, and spiritually they feel like them." The consul does not reply.

1932 Sender Kaplan (son of Zvi Kaplan) founds the Yiddish newspaper *Habaner Lebn* (*Vida Habanera*). The twice-weekly newspaper is the primary voice of the Ashkenazic Jewish community until Kaplan emigrates to Miami in 1960.

1933 The "Sergeant's Revolt," led by Fulgencio Batista, overthrows Machado. The Law of Nationalization of Labor decrees that 50 percent of all employees in Cuban enterprises must be native-born. As a result, many Jewish refugees from Eastern Europe are fired from the small factories where they used to work and are forced to go into business on their own. Most Sephardic Jews are already self-employed as peddlers and small manufacturers, and so are less affected by the law.

1935 The Jewish charitable organization ORT opens a committee in Cuba to aid Jewish immigrants from Eastern Europe. ORT Cuba will provide crucial services to refugees during World War II, even opening a school for refugee children in 1943, but will cease operations from the early 1960s until its return in 2000.

1939 Increasing numbers of Jewish refugees flee Nazi-dominated Europe after the Kristallnacht pogroms of November 9 and 10, 1938. Cuba takes in more Jewish refugees than any other country relative to its size, but by spring of 1939 the Cuban government is blaming unemployment on the refugee population, and it responds with laws making it nearly impossible for them to enter the country. Unaware of the new laws, 937 Jewish refugees board the S.S. *St. Louis* in Hamburg on May 13, 1939, and set sail for Havana. The ship is refused permission to dock first by the Cuban government and then by the United States, despite spending nearly a month in international waters between Havana and Miami in fruitless negotiations. It finally returns to Europe, where some of the passengers are granted asylum by Belgium, France, the Netherlands, and England; about a third die in the Holocaust.

1940 A large group of Jewish workers in the diamond industry of Antwerp and Amsterdam arrive as refugees in Havana, where they form their own neighborhood in the new middle-class suburb of Vedado just west of central Havana, creating their own synagogue, *mikvah* (ritual bath), school, and a thriving diamond business.

Fulgencio Batista, who has effectively controlled Cuba since 1933 as army chief of staff, is elected to his first term as president (1940–44).

1942 The Sephardic community consecrates a second Jewish cemetery in Guanabacoa.

1943 The B'nai B'rith Maimonides Lodge is founded in Havana.

1944 R. Weinstein founds Moishe Pipik, advertised as "the only American-Jewish kosher restaurant" in Havana.

Post-1945 Many Cuban Jews remain in poverty, like the majority of all Cubans, but a sizeable number begin to prosper in business and the professions. As they do better economically, they move out of Old Havana into the suburbs, especially Vedado. The Jewish population of Cuba reaches a high of between 15,000 and 20,000.

1949 The growing Ashkenazic community in Vedado agree to break away from Adath Israel and found the Patronato de la Casa de la Comunidad Hebrea (Foundation of the Hebrew Community Home), known simply as El Patronato, a large, modern building designed to serve as both a synagogue and a community center. The Ashkenazic congregants who remain in Old Havana reunite the rival congregations of Adath Israel and Knesseth Israel.

1951 The Sephardic community of Havana, which like the Ashkenazic community is growing in the new Vedado suburb, makes plans to build the Centro Hebreo Sefaradí near the Patronato. Construction of the building, the second Sephardic synagogue of Havana, begins in 1957 and is completed after the Revolution in 1960.

Twelve young Jews associated with Hashomer Hatzair leave Cuba for Israel to help found Kibbutz Gaash, twenty miles north of Tel Aviv on the Mediterranean coast. Gaash continues to be a Latin American kibbutz today, with Spanish still spoken there by many residents.

1951–1957 "I Love Lucy" becomes an instant hit on U.S. television and gives Americans a new image of the Cuban male in the character of Ricky Ricardo.

1952 Former president Fulgencio Batista returns to power in a coup. His pro-business policies and the postwar economy of the United States turn Havana into a tourist mecca, with more televisions and telephones per capita than in any city in the Americas. Many Jews prosper in the new business climate and join Cuban high society. But behind the prosperity, Batista's corruption and brutal repression of political opponents gradually turn almost the entire country, including most poor and middle-class Jews, against his regime.

1953 Fidel Castro and a band of supporters launch a failed attack against the Moncada barracks in Santiago de Cuba. While in jail, Castro writes his famous self-defense, *History Will Absolve Me*, in which he declares, "Condemn me, I don't mind, history will absolve me."

1956 After being granted amnesty by Batista, Castro journeys to Mexico, where he meets Che Guevara. Together with Che and other rebels, Castro returns to Cuba on a tiny yacht called the *Granma* to continue the revolutionary struggle. Castro says, "We will be free, or we will be martyrs."

The last of five synagogues, Beth Shalom (popularly known as "*el templo americano*"), is founded in Havana.

The members of Adath Israel begin work on a new, modern synagogue to serve the Jews of Old Havana; it is completed in 1959.

December 31, 1958 Batista flees in disgrace as *los barbudos*, the bearded rebels, advance toward Havana.

January 1, 1959 Cheered on by masses of Havana residents, including Jews disgusted with the corruption of the Batista regime, the rebels enter the city in triumph. On January 8, Fidel Castro assumes control of the government.

1960 In May, Cuba and the Soviet Union establish relations. In June, Cuba nationalizes U.S. petroleum properties. Between August and October, U.S.-owned sugar mills, banks, railroads, hotels, and factories are seized. In October, the United States imposes a trade embargo on Cuba. Along with Cuba's upper and middle classes, Jews start leaving Cuba in large numbers. During the next few years, 90 percent of Cuba's Jews will immigrate to the United States, Puerto Rico, Mexico, and Venezuela.

1961 In January, the United States and Cuba sever diplomatic relations. In April, the Bay of Pigs invasion fails. Castro announces that he is a Marxist-Leninist. Cuba, which had once been included in maps of Florida, is removed from cruise maps of the Caribbean. The CIA and the Catholic Church devise the Peter Pan Operation to assist parents who want to send their children out of Cuba so they won't be indoctrinated into communism. The operation, modeled on the "kindertransports" during the Holocaust, aim to "save" the children by allowing them to reach the United States before their parents attain exit visas. A total of 14,000 unaccompanied minors enter the United States as Peter Pans, including several Jewish children assisted by HIAS (Hebrew Immigrant Aid Society).

October 22–28, 1962 The Cuban missile crisis. The United States institutes a trade embargo against Cuba, declaring it a hostile country under the Trading with the Enemy Act.

1967 Ernesto "Che" Guevara, the asthmatic Argentine doctor who fought for Cuba's revolution and tried to bring revolution to other parts of the world, is killed in Bolivia.

1973 Cuba breaks off diplomatic relations with Israel following the Yom Kippur War.

1974 Cuba invites Yasser Arafat to visit Cuba and offers support to the Palestine Liberation Organization.

The Albert Einstein School in the Havana neighborhood of Santo Suárez ceases to offer optional Jewish subjects as part of its curriculum.

1978 Cuba inaugurates the family reunification program, whereby Cuban exiles are permitted to return to the island for brief family visits. In November, President Castro meets with representatives of the Cuban community in the diaspora, in what becomes known as "The Dialogue." Bernardo Benes, a Cuban Jewish banker living in Miami Beach, negotiates with Castro for the release of 3,000 political prisoners. Benes gains permission to bring back a Torah from the Patronato to the Cuban Hebrew Congregation, a synagogue in Miami Beach founded by Jewish Cuban immigrants.

The Unión Sionista is closed by the Cuban government and its offices are transferred to the delegation of the Palestinian Liberation Organization in Havana.

Dr. José Miller, an oral surgeon, assumes the presidency of the Patronato, becoming the de facto leader of the Jewish community of Cuba.

1979 The synagogue of Santiago de Cuba is closed.

1980 The Mariel exodus of 125,000 Cubans to the United States includes among them a few Jews who settle in Miami.

1981 Facing debt and a shortage of funds to maintain even minimal religious activities, Dr. José Miller and the Jewish community relinquish half of the Patronato building to the Ministry of Culture, which turns it into the Bertolt Brecht Theater.

1984 A Sunday school known as the *escuelita* ("the little school") opens in the Patronato through the combined efforts of Dr. José Miller, Moisés Asis (now in Miami), and Dr. Alberto Mechulam. The school begins to teach the basics of Hebrew, as well as Jewish religion, history, and tradition to the children of inter-married and revolutionary Jews who have abandoned their Jewish identity and faith.

1991 At a meeting of the Fourth Party Congress, it is decreed that Communist Party members can embrace a religious identity if they choose. Catholics, Protestants, and Jews return to their churches and synagogues openly, and Santería practitioners no longer hide their initiations and rituals.

United States Catholic Relief Services begins to deliver medical supplies and equipment to Cuba.

The Lubavitch Chabad movement begins religious and charity missions to Cuba's Jewish community and forms a close bond with the Adath Israel synagogue, which henceforth follows more Orthodox practices.

1992 The Cuban constitution is changed to reflect that the state is now "secular" rather than "atheist."

Dr. Miller and the Comision Coordinadora approach the Joint Distribution Committee requesting support for Cuba's Jews.

A Protestant organization, Pastors for Peace, begins to deliver "friendship-ments" to Cuba, working in conjunction with the Martin Luther King Jr. Memorial Center in Havana and the Cuban Council of Churches.

1993 The U.S. dollar is declared a legal currency in Cuba.

1994 The *balsero* (rafter) crisis: 35,000 Cubans take to the seas in hopes of reaching the United States.

"Operation Cigar," a program that allows Jews in Cuba to resettle in Israel, is initiated, and seventy Cubans leave for Israel. Over the next decade, another six hundred will follow. This operation is kept secret until information is leaked to the press in the late 1990s.

Dr. Rosa Behar, a gastroenterologist, is named president of the Hadassah chapter of Cuba.

The Chabad movement forms an organization, the Canadian Friends of Cuban Jewry, to serve as a permanent liaison with Cuba.

1995 The Foreign Investment Act is passed by the Cuban government to encourage the return of capitalist investors respectful of Cuba's national sovereignty.

The synagogue in Santiago de Cuba is returned to the Jewish community and renovated.

The B'nai B'rith Cuban Jewish Relief Project is founded. Isaac Rousso, an agricultural engineer, is later named the president of B'nai B'rith Maimonides Cuba.

With a declining congregation and its building dangerously dilapidated, the Chevet Ahim synagogue is shut down. Eusebio Leal, the official historian of the city of Havana, has plans to turn the site of the old building on Calle Inquisidor (Inquisitor Street) into a Jewish Museum.

1997 Che Guevara's remains are brought to Cuba and buried ceremonially in Santa Clara.

The *Buena Vista Social Club* album is released and followed in 1999 by Wim Wenders's documentary about Ry Cooder's "discovery" of the Cuban musicians.

1998 Pope John Paul II visits Cuba and meets with representatives of different religious faiths, including Jewish leaders.

Castro visits the Patronato on the last day of Hanukkah, where he speaks to the assembled Jewish community about Jewish religious traditions being a source of revolutionary inspiration.

A new synagogue is built in Camagüey.

1999–2000 American programs to Cuba become hugely popular. Marazul Tours, a travel agency in New Jersey that organizes licensed American visits to Cuba, lists 300 programs to take place throughout the year, including an Architects Conference, a Chinese Diaspora Conference, a Cuba-American Jewish Mission, and an Oral Hygiene Congress.

2000 Renovations are completed on the Patronato synagogue in Havana. Returning to Cuba after four decades, the charitable organization ORT sponsors the opening of the Ana and Ben Dizik Technological Center for computer and technology training in the Patronato building.

2002 Hollywood filmmaker Steven Spielberg visits Havana during a festival screening of his films and asks to meet with the Jewish community. He also meets with Fidel Castro for eight hours. In the same year, the U.S. Holocaust Memorial Museum in Washington, D.C., gives Miriam Saul, a Cuban Jew living in Atlanta, two cobblestones from the Warsaw ghetto to take to Cuba. One of the stones becomes part of the Holocaust memorial in the Jewish cemetery of Santa Clara.

2003 The Hotel Raquel, a boutique hotel catering to Jewish tourists, opens on Calle Amargura (Bitterness Street) in La Habana Vieja.

2004 Writer Jaime Sarusky wins the National Prize for Literature.

2005 The *mikvah* at the Adath Israel synagogue is restored after falling into disrepair during the 1990s.

February 2006 Death of Dr. José Miller. In March, Adela Dworin, the former vice president and librarian of the Patronato, becomes the new president, and William Miller, a grandson of José Miller living in Canada, returns to Cuba and becomes the vice president.

July 31, 2006 Fidel Castro, severely ill from a mysterious intestinal disorder, passes the baton to his brother Raúl Castro.

November–December 2006 Celebration of the "Centennial of the Jewish Community of Cuba" at the Patronato.

January 2007 Departure of a group of Jewish Cubans to Israel.

NOTES

Running Away from Home to Run toward Home

1. Jaime Sarusky, *Los fantasmas de Omaja* (Havana: Girón, 1986).
2. Robert M. Levine, *Tropical Diaspora: The Jewish Experience in Cuba* (Gainesville: University Press of Florida, 1993), 33.
3. Hugh Thomas, *Cuba: The Pursuit of Freedom* (New York: Harper and Row, 1971), 577.
4. Robert M. Levine and Mark D. Szuchman, *Hotel Cuba: A Historical Diary of the Pre-Castro Jewish Experience* (videotape distributed by University of Illinois Film Service, 1985).
5. Levine, *Tropical Diaspora*, 33.
6. About Zayde, see Ruth Behar, "Juban América," in *King David's Harp: Autobiographical Essays by Jewish Latin American Writers*, edited by Stephen A. Sadow (Albuquerque: University of New Mexico Press, 1999), 201–223; and Behar, *The Vulnerable Observer: Anthropology That Breaks Your Heart* (Boston: Beacon Press, 1996).
7. Pinkhes Berniker, "Jesús," in *Yiddish South of the Border: An Anthology of Latin American Yiddish Writing*, edited by Alan Astro, with an introduction by Ilan Stavans (Albuquerque: University of New Mexico Press, 2003), 137–148.
8. Judith Elkin, *The Jews of Latin America*, rev. ed. (New York: Holmes and Meier, 1998), 89.
9. Margalit Bejarano, "The Deproletarianization of Cuban Jewry," *Judaica Latino-americana: Estudios históricos-sociales*, ed. AMILAT (Jerusalem: Editorial Universitario Magnes, Universidad Hebrea, 1988), 57–67.
10. Accounts of the pre-revolutionary Jewish community in Cuba can be found in Levine, *Tropical Diaspora*; Margalit Bejarano, *La comunidad hebrea de Cuba: La memoria y la historia* (Jerusalem: Avraham Harman Institute of Contemporary Jewry, Hebrew University, 1996); Richard Pava, *Les juifs de Cuba, 1492–2001: Essai* (Nantes: Éditions du Petit Véhicule, 2001); and Jay

Levinson, *Jewish Community of Cuba: The Golden Years, 1906–1958* (Nashville: Westview Publishing, 2006).

11. "'Son propios del fascismo el odio y el prejuicio racial,' declara Dr. Fidel Castro." In S. M. Kaplan and A. J. Dubelman, *Vida Habanera: Almanaque Hebreo*, vol. 18 (Havana: October 1960), 74.

12. Ruth Behar, ed., *Bridges to Cuba/Puentes a Cuba* (Ann Arbor: University of Michigan Press, 1995).

13. Ana María Dopico, "Picturing Havana: History, Vision, and the Scramble for Cuba," *Nepantla: Views from South* 3, 3 (2002): 451–493; José Quiroga, *Cuban Palimpsests* (Minneapolis: University of Minnesota Press, 2005). Some examples of photography books about Cuba: Tony Mendoza, *Cuba—Going Back* (Austin: University of Texas Press, 1997); Tim B. Wride, with an essay by Cristina Vives, *Cuban Photography after the Revolution* (Los Angeles County Museum of Art and Merrel Publishers, 2001); Xavier Zimbardo, with a foreword by Cristina García, *Cuba: Mi Amor* (New York: Rizzoli, 2002); Terry McCoy, ed., *Cuba on the Verge: An Island in Transition* (Boston: Bullfinch Press, 2003).

14. Rosa Lowinger and Ofelia Fox, *Tropicana Nights: The Life and Times of the Legendary Cuban Nightclub* (New York: Harcourt, 2005).

15. Andrei Codrescu, *Ay, Cuba! A Socio-Erotic Journey* (New York: Picador USA, 1999).

16. John J. Putman, "Cuba: Evolution in the Revolution," *National Geographic* (June 1999): 2–45.

17. Pico Iyer, "Holguín, Santiago, Havana, and the Beach: 1987–1992," in *The Reader's Companion to Cuba*, edited by Alan Ryan (New York: Harcourt Brace, 1997), 383.

18. Anne Rueter, "Ann Arbor's Cuba Craze," *Ann Arbor News*, April 6, 2003, E1–E2.

19. Dana Evan Kaplan, "The Jews of Cuba since the Castro Revolution," in *American Jewish Yearbook 2001*, vol. 101, edited by David Singer and Lawrence Grossman (New York: American Jewish Committee, 2001), 21–87.

20. Edward Bruner, *Culture on Tour: Ethnographies of Travel* (Chicago: University of Chicago Press, 2005), 7.

21. Hasia Diner, *The Jews of the United States, 1654 to 2000* (Berkeley: University of California Press, 2004), 305.

22. Deborah Dash Moore and S. Ilan Troen, *Divergent Jewish Cultures: Israel and America* (New Haven: Yale University Press, 2001), 22.

23. Larry Tye, *Homelands: Portraits of the New Jewish Diaspora* (New York: Henry Holt, 2001), 12.

24. Caryn Aviv and David Shneer, *New Jews: The End of the Jewish Diaspora* (New York: New York University Press, 2005), 71.

25. James R. Ross, *Fragile Branches: Travels Through the Jewish Diaspora* (New York: Riverhead Books, 2000); Ken Blady, *Jewish Communities in Exotic Places* (Northvale, N.J.: Jason Aronson, 2000).

26. Kerri P. Steinberg, "Contesting Identities in Jewish Philanthropy," in *Diasporas and Exiles: Varieties of Jewish Identity*, edited by Howard Wettstein (Berkeley: University of California Press, 2002), 253–278.

27. Stanley Falkenstein, "Carta abierta," *Fragmentos* (June 2005).

28. Jaime Suchlicki, quoted in Dana Evan Kaplan, "Fidel and the Jews," *Moment* (August 2004): 92.

29. Maritza Corrales, *The Chosen Island: Jews in Cuba* (Chicago: Salsedo Press, 2005).

30. Caroline Bettinger-López, *Cuban-Jewish Journeys: Searching for Identity, Home, and History in Miami*, with a foreword by Ruth Behar (Knoxville: University of Tennessee Press, 2000).

31. Dana Evan Kaplan, "The Future of Religious Life in Communist Cuba," *CCAR (Central Conference of American Rabbis) Journal: A Reform Jewish Quarterly* (Summer 2001): 38–46.

32. Arturo López Levy, "The Jewish Community in Cuba in the 1990s," in *Religion, Culture, and Society: The Case of Cuba*, edited by Margaret Crahan (Washington, D.C.: Woodrow Wilson International Center for Scholars, 2003), 79–89.

33. Levine and Szuchman, *Hotel Cuba*.

34. Judith Laiken Elkin and Gilbert W. Merkx, eds., *The Jewish Presence in Latin America* (Boston: Allen and Unwin, 1987).

35. Errol Daniels, *Cuba: A Jewish Journey* (Rochester, N.Y.: Errol Daniels Photography, 2003); James Colbert, "Letter from Santiago: Breaking through the Wall," *Hadassah Magazine* (January 2004): 13–15; Ben G. Frank, "The Jewish Traveler: Havana," *Hadassah Magazine* (January 2005): 52–57. Films include Laura Paull and Evan Garelle, *Havana Nagila: The Jews in Cuba* (videotape distributed by Schnitzki and Stone Video Journalism, 1995); and

Ruth Behar, *Adio Kerida/Goodbye Dear Love: A Cuban Sephardic Journey* (videotape distributed by Women Make Movies, 2002).

36. Caren Osten Gerszberg, "In Cuba, Finding a Tiny Corner of Jewish Life," *New York Times*, February 4, 2007, Travel section 5, 3.

37. Roberto Juan Rodríguez, *El Danzón de Moisés* (New York: Tzadik, 2002).

38. Alina Fernández, *Castro's Daughter: An Exile's Memoir of Cuba* (New York: St. Martin's Press, 1998), 1; Tom Miller, *Trading with the Enemy: A Yankee Travels through Castro's Cuba* (New York: Atheneum, 1992), 69.

39. Román de la Campa, *Cuba on My Mind: Journeys to a Severed Nation* (New York: Verso, 2000), 16.

40. Rafael Campo, "Jews of the Caribbean," in *Landscape with Human Figure* (Durham, N.C.: Duke University Press, 2002).

How This Book Came to Be a Photojourney

1. Margaret Mead, "Visual Anthropology in a Discipline of Words," in *Principles of Visual Anthropology,* ed. Paul Hockings (The Hague: Mouton, 1995), 4–5.

2. Gregory Bateson and Margaret Mead, *Balinese Character: A Photographic Analysis* (New York: New York Academy of Sciences, 1942).

3. Susan Sontag, *On Photography* (New York: Farrar, Straus, and Giroux 1977), 14.

BIBLIOGRAPHY

Printed Sources

Aviv, Caryn, and David Shneer. *New Jews: The End of the Jewish Diaspora.* New York: New York University Press, 2005.

Bateson, Gregory, and Margaret Mead. *Balinese Character: A Photographic Analysis.* New York: New York Academy of Sciences, 1942.

Behar, Ruth. "Juban América." In *King David's Harp: Autobiographical Essays by Jewish Latin American Writers,* edited by Stephen A. Sadow, 201–223. Albuquerque: University of New Mexico Press, 1999.

———. *The Vulnerable Observer: Anthropology That Breaks Your Heart.* Boston: Beacon Press, 1996.

———, ed. *Bridges to Cuba/Puentes a Cuba.* Ann Arbor: University of Michigan Press, 1995.

Bejarano, Margalit. *La comunidad hebrea de Cuba: La memoria y la historia.* Jerusalem: Avraham Harman Institute of Contemporary Jewry, Hebrew University, 1996.

———. "The Deproletarianization of Cuban Jewry." In *Judaica Latino-americana: Estudios históricos-sociales,* edited by AMILAT, 57–67. Jerusalem: Magnes Press, 1988.

———. "Sephardic Jews in Cuba (From All Their Habitations)." *Judaism: A Quarterly Journal of Jewish Life and Thought* 51, no. 1 (Winter 2002): 96-108.

Berniker, Pinkhes. "Jesús." In *Yiddish South of the Border: An Anthology of Latin American Yiddish Writing,* edited by Alan Astro, 137–148. Albuquerque: University of New Mexico Press, 2003.

Bettinger-López, Caroline. *Cuban-Jewish Journeys: Searching for Identity, Home, and History in Miami.* Foreword by Ruth Behar. Knoxville: University of Tennessee Press, 2000.

Biblioteca de la Casa de la Comunidad Hebrea. Invitation to "Banquete de Gala:

Quinto Aniversario de su Fundación" in the Gran Salón Casa Comunidad Hebrea, Havana, November 12, 1960.

Blady, Ken. *Jewish Communities in Exotic Places.* Northvale, N.J.: Jason Aronson, 2000.

Blanco, Richard. *Directions to the Beach of the Dead.* Tucson: University of Arizona Press, 2005.

Brenner, Frédéric. *Diaspora: Homelands in Exile.* New York: HarperCollins, 2003.

Bruner, Edward M. *Culture on Tour: Ethnographies of Travel.* Chicago: University of Chicago Press, 2005.

Campo, Rafael. *Landscape with Human Figure.* Durham, N.C.: Duke University Press, 2002.

Codrescu, Andrei. *Ay, Cuba! A Socio-Erotic Journey.* New York: Picador USA, 1999.

Colbert, James. "Letter from Santiago: Breaking through the Wall." *Hadassah Magazine* (January 2004): 13–15.

Corrales, Maritza. *The Chosen Island: Jews in Cuba.* Translated by Debra Evenson. Chicago: Salsedo Press, 2005.

Daniels, Errol. *Cuba: A Jewish Journey.* Rochester, N.Y.: Errol Daniels Photography, 2003.

de la Campa, Román. *Cuba on My Mind: Journeys to a Severed Nation.* New York: Verso, 2000.

Diner, Hasia. *The Jews of the United States, 1654 to 2000.* Berkeley: University of California Press, 2004.

Dopico, Ana María. "Picturing Havana: History, Vision, and the Scramble for Cuba." *Nepantla: Views from South* 3, 3 (2002): 451–493.

Elkin, Judith Laiken. *The Jews of Latin America.* Revised edition. New York: Holmes and Meier, 1998.

Elkin, Judith Laiken, and Gilbert W. Merkx, eds. *The Jewish Presence in Latin America.* Boston: Allen and Unwin, 1987.

Farín Levy, Eugenia. *El judaísmo en Cuba.* Santiago de Cuba: Comunidad Hebrea de Santiago de Cuba, 2004.

———. *Sinagoga de Santiago de Cuba.* Santiago de Cuba: Comunidad Hebrea de Santiago de Cuba, 1997.

Fernández, Alina. *Castro's Daughter: An Exile's Memoir of Cuba.* New York: St. Martin's Press, 1998.

Frank, Ben G. "The Jewish Traveler: Havana." *Hadassah Magazine* (January 2005): 52–57.

Galeano, Eduardo. *El libro de los abrazos*. Madrid: Siglo Veintiuno, 1989.

Gerszberg, Caren Osten. "In Cuba, Finding a Tiny Corner of Jewish Life." *New York Times*, February 4, 2007, Travel section 5, 3.

Iyer, Pico. "Holguín, Santiago, Havana, and the Beach: 1987–1992." In *The Reader's Companion to Cuba*, edited by Alan Ryan, 373–389. New York: Harcourt Brace, 1997.

Kaplan, Dana Evan. "Fidel and the Jews." *Moment* (August 2004): 36–45, 83–93.

———. "The Future of Religious Life in Communist Cuba." *CCAR (Central Conference of American Rabbis) Journal: A Reform Jewish Quarterly* (Summer 2001): 38–46.

———. "The Jews of Cuba since the Castro Revolution." In *American Jewish Yearbook 2001*, vol. 101, edited by David Singer and Lawrence Grossman, 21–87. New York: American Jewish Committee, 2001.

Kaplan, S. M., and A. J. Dubelman, eds. *Vida Habanera: Almanaque Hebreo, tomo 18 / Havaner Lebn, Almanakh 5721*. Havana, October 1960.

Kozer, José. *Bajo este cien y otras poemas*. Barcelona: El Pardo, 2002.

Levine, Robert M. *Tropical Diaspora: The Jewish Experience in Cuba*. Gainesville: University Press of Florida, 1993.

Levinson, Jay. *Jewish Community of Cuba: The Golden Years, 1906–1958*. Nashville: Westview Publishing, 2006.

López Levy, Arturo. "The Jewish Community in Cuba in the 1990s." In *Religion, Culture and Society: The Case of Cuba*, edited by Margaret E. Crahan, 79–89. Washington, D.C.: Woodrow Wilson International Center for Scholars, 2003.

Lowinger, Rosa, and Ofelia Fox. *Tropicana Nights: The Life and Times of the Legendary Cuban Nightclub*. New York: Harcourt, 2005.

McCoy, Terry, ed. *Cuba on the Verge: An Island in Transition*. Boston: Bullfinch Press, 2003.

Mead, Margaret. "Visual Anthropology in a Discipline of Words." In *Principles of Visual Anthropology*, edited by Paul Hockings, 3–10. The Hague: Mouton, 1975.

Mendoza, Tony. *Cuba—Going Back*. Austin: University of Texas Press, 1997.

Miller, Tom. *Trading with the Enemy: A Yankee Travels through Castro's Cuba*. New York: Atheneum, 1992.

Moore, Deborah Dash, and S. Ilan Troen, eds. *Divergent Jewish Cultures: Israel and America*. New Haven: Yale University Press, 2001.

Pava, Richard. *Les juifs de Cuba, 1492–2001: Essai*. Nantes: Éditions du Petit Véhicule, 2001.

Putman, John J. "Cuba: Evolution in the Revolution." *National Geographic* (June 1999): 2–45.

Quiroga, José. *Cuban Palimpsests*. Minneapolis: University of Minnesota Press, 2005.

Ross, James R. *Fragile Branches: Travels Through the Jewish Diaspora*. New York: Riverhead Books, 2000.

Rueter, Anne. "Ann Arbor's Cuba Craze." *Ann Arbor News*, April 6, 2003, E1–E2.

Sarusky, Jaime. *Los fantasmas de Omaja*. Havana: Girón, 1986.

Sontag, Susan. *On Photography*. New York: Farrar, Straus and Giroux, 1977.

Steinberg, Kerri P. "Contesting Identities in Jewish Philanthropy." In *Diasporas and Exiles: Varieties of Jewish Identity*, edited by Howard Wettstein, 253–278. Berkeley and Los Angeles: University of California Press, 2002.

Thomas, Hugh. *Cuba: The Pursuit of Freedom*. New York: Harper and Row, 1971.

Tye, Larry. *Homelands: Portraits of the New Jewish Diaspora*: New York: Henry Holt, 2001.

Vainstein, Abraham Z. *Mitn Pnim Tsu Der Zun / "De cara al sol": Homenaje a Martí en yiddish en el centenario de su natalicio*. Havana: Ediciones de la Agrupación Cultural Hebreo-Cubana, Colección "Martí Visto por Hebreos," 1954.

Wieseltier, Leon. *Kaddish*. New York: Knopf, 1998.

Wride, Tim B., with an essay by Cristina Vives. *Cuban Photography after the Revolution*. Los Angeles County Museum of Art and Merrel Publishers, 2001.

Zimbardo, Xavier, with a foreword by Cristina García. *Cuba: Mi Amor*. New York: Rizzoli, 2002.

Films

Behar, Ruth. *Adio Kerida/Goodbye Dear Love: A Cuban Sephardic Journey*. Distributed by Women Make Movies, 2002 (82 minutes).

Levine, Robert M., and Mark D. Szuchman. *Hotel Cuba: A Historical Diary of the Pre-Castro Jewish Experience.* Distributed by University of Illinois Film Service, 1985 (48 minutes).

Paull, Laura, and Evan Garelle. *Havana Nagila: The Jews in Cuba.* Distributed by Schnitzki and Stone Video Journalism, 1995 (56 minutes).

Sound Recordings

Rodríguez, Roberto Juan. *El Danzón de Moisés.* New York: Tzadik, 2002.

Web Sites

Adath Israel, Havana. http://www.adathcuba.com/index.html.

American Jewish Joint Distribution Committee. http://www.jdc.org/p_amer_cuba_current.html.

Cuba-American Jewish Mission. http://www.thecajm.org.

Jewish Cuba Connection. http://www.jewban.org.

Jews of Cuba. http://www.jewishcuba.org.

Patronato synagogue. "Comunidad Hebrea de Cuba." http://www.chcuba.org.

ACKNOWLEDGMENTS

I could not have written this book without the trust of the Jewish community in Cuba. I am grateful to all those who participated in my journey and gave me the gift of a Jewish community to return to in Cuba. I want to offer an especially warm thanks to José Levy, Maritza Corrales Capestany, Eugenia Farin Levy, and Adela Dworin for generously helping me in my research in countless ways over the years.

Although this book focuses on experiences from 2002 to 2006, it was in the making for fifteen years, beginning in December of 1991, when I started traveling regularly to Cuba and teaching and writing about my research. I began my work with the support of a MacArthur Foundation Fellows Award. Over time, other support followed, including a John Simon Guggenheim Memorial Foundation Award; an American Council of Learned Societies/ Social Science Research Council International Postdoctoral Fellowship; a Rockefeller Residence Fellowship in the Humanities at the Cuban Research Institute of Florida International University; a Creative Artist Grant from the Michigan Council for Arts and Cultural Affairs; and an International Institute and Office of the Vice President for Research Faculty Travel Grant, as well as an Institute for the Humanities Hunting Family Faculty Fellowship, both from the University of Michigan. I would like to thank all these institutions for their encouragement of my work. In addition, I wish to thank the Office of the Vice President for Research at the University of Michigan and the Lucius N. Littauer Foundation for providing generous publication subventions that made it possible to include so many photographs in this book.

I was lucky to meet Adi Hovav in the early stages of my work. From the first moment, I knew she was the right editor for this book. Her patience and thoughtful advice nurtured me throughout the process of writing. I also wish to express deep thanks to everyone at Rutgers University Press, especially

Marilyn Campbell and Jeremy Wang-Iverson, for believing in my book. Through the press, I met Shira Dicker, my publicist, who has been a joy to work with.

Two readers, Deborah Dash Moore and María de los Angeles Torres, read the proposal I submitted to Rutgers University Press and offered insightful comments, for which I am very grateful.

I was blessed to meet Humberto Mayol, a photographer with the soul of a poet and the compassionate eye of a gentle anthropologist. Without his photographs, I couldn't have and wouldn't have written this book. I am so glad our paths crossed. My thanks to Joyce Maio for showing me Humberto's work and planting the first seed for this project.

In the final stages of writing, I came to understand the importance of being part of a community of writers. Beloved writer-friends from the Macondo Writers Workshop were there for me just at the moment when I was done with a draft of the manuscript and wondering how to make it better. The first to respond was Sandra Cisneros, founder of the Macondo Writers Workshop, who called me in the middle of the night a day after receiving the manuscript and helped me to understand the dramatic tension around giving and receiving that is at the center of my story. As the writing evolved, she continued to offer sensitive comments and then gave me a special gift with her suggestion of the title for the book. Vicente Lozano, a fellow Macondista, gave me twenty pages of subtle and detailed commentary, raising questions that forced me to go deeper into issues I had been afraid to write about. Richard Blanco, a Macondista and a fellow seeker of a lost home in Cuba, read my manuscript like the poet he is, word by word, showing me when my words sang and when they fell flat, and read it also like the engineer of bridges that he is, helping me build the structure to support my stories. Afterward, more friends came to the rescue when I most needed their assistance. A huge thanks to my old friend Rosa Lowinger, my new friend Yael Flusberg, and my "hermanita" Lucía Suárez for their wisdom. And more thanks to Erasmo Guerra, a fellow Macondista, who offered very helpful practical advice about organization during the last stage of revision.

It is also a pleasure to thank Ricardo Ortiz, who gave me Rafael Campo's poem, "Jews of the Caribbean," whose opening lines became the epigraph for my book with, of course, the kind permission of Rafael Campo.

And my warmest thanks to my favorite rabbi, Greg Epstein, my cousin, who has shared his knowledge about secular Jewish humanism with me.

My husband, David Frye, has been by my side throughout this project, reading the stories as they emerged, and helping me to organize the photographs and to prepare the chronology. His love saw me through the final stretch when I was writing day and night.

My son, Gabriel, traveled with me to Cuba and met many of the people I have written about. He has a truly profound understanding of photography and film and gave me wonderful advice about which pictures spoke most powerfully with my story. He is the best and most beautiful son a mother could ask for. This book is his, with my love.

LIST OF PHOTOGRAPHS

Note: All photographs are by Humberto Mayol, except where indicated otherwise.

List of Photographs